AF324667

LIMITS TO DEMOCRATIC CONSTITUTIONALISM IN CENTRAL AND EASTERN EUROPE

Limits to Democratic Constitutionalism in Central and Eastern Europe

BOGUSIA PUCHALSKA
University of Central Lancashire, UK

ASHGATE

Published by
Ashgate Publishing Limited
Wey Court East
Union Road
Farnham
Surrey, GU9 7PT
England

Ashgate Publishing Company
Suite 420
101 Cherry Street
Burlington
VT 05401-4405
USA

www.ashgate.com

British Library Cataloguing in Publication Data
Puchalska, Bogusia.
   Limits to democratic constitutionalism in Central and Eastern Europe.
   1. Constituent power–Europe, Central–History. 2. Constituent power–Europe, Eastern–History. 3. Poland–Politics and government–1989– 4. Constitutional history–Poland. 5. Constitutional law– Poland. 6. Democratization–Poland.
   I. Title
   320.9'438-dc22

Library of Congress Cataloging-in-Publication Data
Puchalska, Bogusia.
   Limits to democratic constitutionalism in Central and Eastern Europe / by Bogusia Puchalska.
     p. cm.
   Includes bibliographical references and index.
   ISBN 978-1-4094-1983-9 (hardback : alk. paper) – ISBN 978-1-4094-1984-6 (ebook)
   1. Europe, Central–Politics and government–1989– 2. Europe, Eastern–Politics and government–1989- 3. Constitutional history–Europe, Central. 4. Constitutional history–Europe, Eastern. I. Title.
   JN96.A58P83 2011
   320.943–dc22

                                                                      2011007386

ISBN 9781409419839 (hbk)
ISBN 9781409419846 (ebk)

Printed and bound in Great Britain by the
MPG Books Group, UK

Contents

Abbreviations

CBOS	Centrum Badania Opinii Społecznej [Centre for Public Opinion Research]
CCRP	Commissioner for Citizens' Rights Protection
CEE	Central and Eastern Europe
CIS	Confederation of Independent States
CT	Constitutional Tribunal
EBRD	European Bank for Reconstruction and Development
ECHR	European Convention of Human Rights
ECtHR	European Court of Human Rights
HFHR	Helsinki Foundation for Human Rights
HR	Human Rights
IMF	International Monetary Fund
KOR	Komitet Obrony Robotników [Committee for the Protection of Workers]
NATO	North Atlantic Treaty Organisation
NDB	New Democracies Barometer
NGO	Non-governmental organisation
OECD	Organisation for Economic Coordination and Development
OSCE	Organisation for Security and Co-operation in Europe
PAP	Polska Agencja Prasowa [Polish Press Agency]
PHARE	Poland & Hungary Aid for Restructuring Economy
PUWP	see PZPR
PZPR	Polska Zjednoczona Partia Robotnicza [Polish United Worker's Party]
RTT	Round Table Talks
SLD	Social-Liberal Democratic Party
TACIS	Technical Assistance for the CIS
TEC	Treaty of European Community
TEU	Treaty of European Union
WB	World Bank
WTO	World Trade Organisation

Acknowledgements

I would like to thank my employer, University of Central Lancashire, for granting me sabbatical leave which allowed me to do preliminary research for this book.

I thank my husband, Pieter Kahrel, the first reader of my drafts for all his work on the text, and my daughter Kasia for her comments. I would also like to thank the publisher's reviewers for their helpful suggestions.

Introduction

The fall of one party-states in the (Central and Eastern Europe) CEE countries was precipitated by events that mobilised the people of these countries into political action on an unprecedented scale. There were mass demonstrations in Prague, East Berlin, Budapest and other places, as well as earlier, more organised forms of channelling popular opposition, such as Charter 77 in Czechoslovakia and Solidarność in Poland, which at the height of its popularity reached 10 million members. In Budapest, the mass rallies on the National Day of 15 March 1989 were the most likely prompts that brought the two sides of the political divide to the Round Table.

Yet, this mass of civil and social energy dissipated with the start of the negotiations between the incumbents and the political oppositions, and was not revived again during the constitutional milestones that were the laying of new political and economic foundations of the CEE countries. The Round Table Agreements, packages of systemic reforms and constitutional re-drafting that took place across CEE, were the result of elite agreements between the political opposition and the incumbent communists leadership. 'They were not intended to be expression of the "will", values, or demands of the masses who in varying degrees participated in the process resulting in the collapse of Communist rule' (Sajó and Losonci 1993: 328). Yet, despite this exclusion of the people – the sovereign power – from the political process of constitutional decision-taking and the making of new constitutions, neither the policies of the first years of systemic reforms across CEE nor the new constitutions promulgated across the region have been seriously contested. This might mean that the legitimacy of CEE constitutions and constitutional law-making have been largely decoupled from the authorship and related questions of democratic participation in those events.

The idea of democratic constitutionalism offers a way of analysing the process of legitimisation of the new systemic arrangements across CEE countries in the context of weak popular participation in putting those arrangements in place, and assessing the potential consequences of such legitimisation for the democratic development of these countries. This is mainly because democratic constitutionalism focuses on democratic participation in constitutional politics in constitutional moments (Ackerman 1992), or in 'constitutional' as opposed to 'normal' law-making (Ackerman 1993). When applied to the reformed systems of the CEE countries, this focus on democratic politics at watershed moments of a state's history offers an insight into the type of governance that has been instituted in CEE and the political processes that led to such arrangements. This approach also makes possible a more general question: Does denying the masses an influence on the shape of fundamental aspects of the organisation of their states in constitutional moments that occurred after 1989 have a lasting bearing on the quality of future development of democracy and constitutionalism in CEE?

Such inquiry goes beyond the narrow institutionalist perspective of constitutionalism and democracy, and focuses on the reality and dynamics of the political process behind constitutional developments in the specific context of post-communist transitions. The need for such an approach relates to the particular circumstances of the CEE countries after 1989, since, as suggested by Alexander, institutions in new democracies are less stable and less capable of providing a predictable framework for everyday politics. Instead, these tend be vulnerable to changes of rules and practices, which in turn follow the actual rules of such politics (Alexander 2001, Wołek 2004). Hence, the rules and practices of everyday politics, both formal and informal, should be seen as more important for understanding democracy and constitutionalism in CEE transition countries than the political institutions themselves.

Constitutionalism and Democracy

Constitutions are politically constructed (Hirschl 2005: 291). Legitimising and protecting a status quo by introducing fundamental rules limiting the power of government and keeping in check the might of popular sovereign power have always been some of the of the core objectives that constitutions were designed to secure. Constitutions seem ideally suited for such tasks due to their entrenched nature,[1] the strong legitimating power of constitutional referenda and the use of constitutional discourse that links constitutional texts with the core matters of sovereignty and national identity; a perfect marriage of security and the rule of law, an expression of popular will in a constitutional referendum with powerful symbolic appeal. The lasting success of this union has been apparent in almost universal recognition of constitutionalism as the preferred model for the organisation of modern states.

The renewed interest in constitutionalism occurred in the aftermath of the World War II, and was driven by the widely acknowledged need for more effective protection of human rights. A number of African countries regaining independence in the 1950s and 1960s adopted constitutions soon after breaking away from the direct colonial dependency: 'even rulers who are not inclined to submit themselves to legal norms feel compelled at least to pretend to be exercising their power within the constitutional framework [...]. After 225 years constitutionalism seems now to have reached the peak of its development' (Grimm 2010: 3). However, this rise of constitutionalism has hardly been matched by improvements in the quality of democratic politics, despite the clear inseparability of the two. Transition countries of CEE are one of the clearest examples, as they struggle with fundamental problems

---

1   The unwritten UK Constitution is an exception to this rule, despite the entrenched nature of some of its parts, for instance, the European Communities Act 1972.

in trying to consolidate democratic governance and to develop democratically inclined citizenship, despite successfully promulgating new Constitutions. The European Union, boasting a degree of constitutionalised order, still suffers form the infamous democratic deficit. Many other regimes around the world that successfully adopted constitutions can hardly be called democratic.[2]

In response to this rise of undemocratic constitutionalism Mandel developed a rather extreme argument which, nevertheless, is not entirely without merit: 'new constitutionalism was intended to operate and it does operate as an *antidote* to democracy' (1998: 252, emphasis in the original). Given the persistence of this inherent, and unresolvable tension between law and politics in any constitution, might it be the case that the success of modern constitutionalism occurred at the expense of weakening democratic politics? Or, has the balance between constitutionalism and democracy (Tully 2002: 206) been skewed too much towards the former?

Constitution and constitutionalism need democratic politics, albeit of a type that stays within the confines of constitutional rules. This dependence is, or at least should be, mutually reinforcing and sustaining. Yet, both the historic and more recent experiences show that the weakness of the democratic political process leading to promulgation of constitutions, save for constitutional referenda, is rarely – if ever – the reason for denying constitutions their legitimacy. This means that there is a perceptible lack of concern with the quality of the political process leading to the creation of constitutions. This contrasts with the great deal of attention and resources devoted to constitutional referenda, which do not give the electorate any real power to influence the content of constitutions, but only to vote on the final text. The reasons for this oversight lie in political practices, but its justification has been provided by modern constitutional theory.[3]

One of this theory's main concerns is to curb the potential tyranny of the majority which should be prevented from shaping the text of the constitution to its own advantage. The insistence on allowing only constituted power – that is, constituent power that is already constrained by an agreed set of rules – to act as constitution-makers is one way of achieving this. Constituted power can only act as constitution makers through the constitutional conventions or national assemblies charged with the task of constitution drafting. Under such arrangements the effective popular participation depends on the degree of the representativeness of those gatherings, the way they communicate and respond to public input, and the level of popular interests in the process. The evidence from across CEE shows these conditions to be only weakly satisfied. The other way of creating a perception of popular participation in constitution-making is to allow the

---

2   The state of democracy in the First World countries is not entirely sound either; the dominance of political lobbying in the US, the weakness of the UK electoral system and the role of the privately owned media, whose political influence is widely acknowledged but not transparent, are just some of the examples of systemic weaknesses of democracy.

3   I use the term 'modern' to denote the dominating model of liberal constitutional theory.

electorate to vote in a constitutional referendum. Since a referendum legitimises the text without allowing it to be changed, it is a more attractive option of securing popular legitimacy: the effectiveness of the process and the results are clear cut and easy to evaluate. This is in contrast with the insistence on democratic input through public debate and deliberations under the first option: time- and resource-consuming and tricky to conduct, its effectiveness is much more uncertain, both as a way of ensuring a popular input into the constitution-making and as a way of curbing the power of the majority.

A more general risk posed by the theoretical imperative to curb the majoritarian power is that it may be detracting from the damage to democratic process in constitution-making. This is particulary the case when referenda are chosen as the only mechanism of effective democratic input and verification which bestow the seal of popular legitimacy on constitutions. Such arrangements largely amount to a fiction of democratic politics in constitution-making. Such fiction plays an important role in elevating constitutions to symbols of national unity and stability based on achieved settlements and compromises. However, might it be the case that at least occasionally, constitutions force the legitimisation of political practice that relies on democratic myth rather than democratic practice? The evidence from CEE seems to confirm such a possibility, since the objective of securing legitimacy may have been prioritised over the actual effort to heed the democratic process. The use of the democratic myth at constitutional moments therefore implies that poor democratic practices are overlooked, and, consequently also legitimised. As noted by Cólon-Ríos: 'it would be astonishing that constitutional traditions which originated in an attempt to protect certain institutions from the passions of the disorganized multitudes would not be wanting, even a bit, from the point of view of democracy' (2010: 26).

From the Past to the Present

The problematic relationship between democratic politics and constitution-making started in the early modern era with the promulgation of the first written constitutions in North America and France. These documents were claimed to be grounded in a democratic process in their drafting and enactment. But this was an obvious fiction, as any other claim of this type that was made before the spread of universal political rights would be. The eighteenth-century constitutions might have been legitimate in the legal sense, since their drafting usually followed a set of agreed rules, but lacked the political legitimacy that required the democratic process to underpin their drafting and promulgation. And that is because the concept of a 'democratic process' cannot be reasonably applied to the constitutional politics of early modernity where the majority of people did not have political rights.

The tradition of Polish constitutionalism and that of other states in continental Europe is different in that constitutions were 'a specific privilege granted by rules rather that social contracts' (Osiatyński 1993: 313), hence the fiction of democratic origins of constitutions was not necessary for constitutional legitimacy. Only the fall of one-party-state regimes signalled the possibility of restoring the democratic process in constitution-making, hence it seems important to ask: have the people of CEE been democratically empowered to influence the constitutional arrangements under which they are living? Such an enquiry implies the need to re-examine the nature and potential implications of the legal and political nexus of constitutions and constitutionalism in the changed conditions of twenty first century, and in the specific circumstances of systemic transitions. Not for some time has the tension between the legal and political dimensions of constitutions and constitutionalism been made so apparent. Some of the main lines of these tensions can be demarcated along the following contrasting phenomena: mass protests which led to the change of a political system, but which did not translate into popular involvement in taking fundamental decision on the future shape of transforming states; the doubtful politics of constitution drafting, allowing behind-the scenes influences and the exclusion of the electorate from the process; National Assemblies dominated by partisan interests and power politics of the day.

There is sufficient evidence to suggest that the legitimacy of CEE constitution-making and law-making in constitutional moments has been decoupled from public debate and deliberation. Yet, both historical[4] and contemporary developments[5] confirm that such decoupling has not been seen as problematic; its legitimacy has not been questioned effectively, neither in the 'old' democracies, nor in any of the newly constitutionalised states of CEE.[6] Since this fundamental weakness of constitutionalism did not erode the positive reception of the new constitutions in the past and in the 1990s across CEE, is there a lesson that can be learned by going beyond the fact of popular acceptance and analysing the politics and practices behind constitution- and constitutional-law-making? Should we see as problematic the type of constitutionalism that avoids, by design, public debate and deliberation, that is, one whose political legitimacy is weak?

The limited attempts at public debate on constitutional issues often revolved around the symbolic meaning of constitutions, and were conducted in celebratory mode rather than in a matter-of-fact manner. Popular participation in constitution-making across CEE has been limited to a vote in the constitutional referenda and was not grounded in the active shaping of constitutional provisions, not even in matters which were likely to have direct impact on people's lives, such as moral

---

4   The most frequently discussed constitutions – the American (1787) and the French (1791) ones – which clearly were elite projects, enjoyed a high level of popular support and legitimacy.

5   Popular support for the 1997 Polish Constitution stands at more than half of respondents satisfied (CBOS 2002b). That is despite the result of the constitutional referendum described as 'tragic' by Gonenc (2002: 133), at 30 per cent of total electorate.

6   Initially, there were the short-lived and inconsequential protests of, for instance, Solidarność and the Catholic Church in Poland against the 1997 Constitution.

values, individual rights and freedoms. Despite this exclusion, the referenda were, on the whole, successful across the CEE.[7] Moreover, poor knowledge of the constitutional text did not stop people in Poland, for instance, from claiming that the constitution plays a very important role in their lives (CBOS 1994a). These apparent paradoxes indicate a formal/legal legitimacy of the constitutions, close to a Weberian 'charismatic' type, rather than a democratic/republican one based on informed judgement and civic engagement. Taken together, this type of popular support stays well within the parameters of accepted standards of modern constitutional theory, but falls short of basic criteria of democratic politics.

Keeping society at arms' length from political bargaining surrounding constitution-making in many countries in CEE can be described as manipulative and ritualistic. This is particularly so, since intense political battles were taking place in the National Assemblies. Both, limiting of popular involvement in shaping the constitutions and the political process accompanying their drafting and promulgation that focused on issues of national unity and moral values, were more likely to have facilitated formal, symbolic and mainly ritualistic type of constitutional culture. The dominance of the politics of rituals and symbols has resulted in constitutions that are not likely to inspire a sense of empowerment of the electorate as the constituent power, not as the primary beneficiaries of constitutional protection, nor as political actors capable of shaping their own constitutional destiny. In other words, the promise to forge a new sense of citizenship in transition countries within the process of constitutionalisation have largely failed.

In a broader context, the lack of attention to the democratic process in those watershed moments of the CEE countries' recent history has, in all likelihood, influenced the emerging systems of political governance in CEE in a deep and lasting manner. It has facilitated and legitimised a certain type of constitutionalism: elitist, lacking in transparency, dominated by party and other sectarian interests and politically alienating – that is, largely removed from the influence and control of the electorate. This type of legitimisation took place in the context of not only the systemic transformation that the CEE countries have been undergoing: its occurrence should also be seen as linked to the historical experience of democratic and constitutional systems, which is either weak or absent in CEE.

> […] it is a rule, both in the communist systems (which comes as no surprise) and also in a "young democracy", that the leading political forces do not intend to involve masses of interested citizens in the discussion on the shape of the system and individual institutional solutions. Currently, this may be attributable to the manifest trend of parties dominating the political life. (Popławska 2008: 279)

---

7   See n. 5.

Central and Eastern European Constitutionalism and Constitutional Theory

It was a certain historic necessity to adopt the Western liberal democratic political and economic model in CEE. The fundamental choices underpinning this model, now enshrined in CEE constitutions, were taken from the shelf, or 'fell from the sky',[8] but have not been 'brought down to Earth and worked out politically, by trial and error, by consultation and debate' (Holmes and Sunstein 1995: 281), which, at least in theory, is needed to secure popular support. The fact that this support was secured despite rather than due to such processes means two things: the type of support is of doubtful democratic quality, as discussed above, but this also signals the possibility that the type of constitutionalism which was instrumental in securing such legitimacy may be impeding democratic development in the specific conditions of CEE. In contrast to this suggestion, the state of democracy and constitutionalism in CEE is assessed generally positively in Western academic literature.

The external legitimisation that was first bestowed by the international money-lending institutions – the World Bank and IMF, and later the EU, which admitted the CEE states into its fold – can also be taken as a positive verification of those developments. I suggest that the contrast between these positive perceptions and the confirmed weaknesses of democratic constitutionalism in CEE might be explained, at least in some measure, by some of the myths that liberal constitutional theory successfully deploys. I believe that the following myths have played a particularly crucial role in shaping the perception of constitutionalism in CEE as democratic and legitimate:

- a particular definition of constitutional moments which confines such moments to constitution-making only. This means that the fundamental decisions on the re-shaping of the order of the state taken on other than constitution-making occasions – such as the Round Table Talks (RTT) – could escape public scrutiny and not require electoral acquiescence;
- the concept of constituent power, which must be first constituted by agreed rules to prevent it from turning into the tyranny of the majority. This particular concept allowed to define the people of CEE countries as an 'unorganised multitude' which must acquire organisational form before they can be allowed to have a say on a new constitutional order under which they are going to live, despite successfully coordinating the democratic movement that brought down previous regimes and acting in compliance with the quasi-constitutional rules that developed during decades of political struggle;

---

8   It needs to be acknowledged that the most important reforms took place under domestic pressure, since the CEE elites embraced Western European matrixes and modelled their own systems accordingly (Sadurski 2006: 29).

- the fiction of the popular legitimacy of the new constitutions and the involvement of sovereign popular power of the people in constitution-making. In practice, this has been limited to acceptance of the ready text in referenda.

Those fictions have been used to great effect not just recently in CEE transition countries, but, with obvious modifications, also during the more than two hundred years of modern constitutional history. However, how transplantable and sustainable are those fictions in the twentieth and twenty-first centuries, particularly from a perspective that accepts political agency and a degree of political organisation of the *constituent* power in modern democracies, respecting constitutional and quasi-constitutional rules, and, hence, amounting to a *constituted* one?

The Distinction Between Constituted and Constituent Power – Still Valid?

Identified as one of the greatest paradoxes of constitutional theory, the circular conundrum of constituent power, which needs to be first *constituted* (Loughlin and Walker 2007: 3), may be due for revision. To deny this need would equal a denial of the political development and social learning that took place, at least in the countries of Europe, over the last 230 years or so since the promulgation of the first written constitutions in France, the British colonies in north America and in Poland. It is not the aim of this book to trace this evolution. Suffice it to focus on one of the most crucial differences between constituent power at the end of eighteenth century and the present – when most people in Europe enjoy political rights granted by their national governments alongside a variety of fundamental and other rights contained in International Treaties. The observance of rights on the national level is monitored by international and regional organisations, as well as the international media and NGOs. The point is that even if practical observance of individual rights in twenty-first-century Europe does not always live up to a desired ideal, the position of most individuals in the contemporary political reality differs from that of the comparable numbers living in the eighteenth, nineteenth and even the first half of the twentieth centuries. After the second World War in Europe, probably the most significant proliferation of political and human rights took place. These were conceived as primarily, aiming to control and limit political power of the state, a process that can be described as constitutionalisation of domestic and international/regional political governance. The United Nations, the Council of Europe, the Organisation of Security and Cooperation in Europe and the European Union, were some of the most active fora behind these developments. This unprecedented scale of recognition of political power and agency of individuals, and the conferral of democratic rights needed to exercise it must be seen as one of the core qualities setting apart constituent power of the twentieth and twenty-first century from its early modern predecessor.

Following the above argument asserting the existence of constituent power in modern democratic states, I suggest that a constitutional theory fit for the contemporary conditions should refocus from prioritising the need to control the potential tyranny of constituent power, to the acceptance of this power constituted, or constitutionalised quality, at least under some circumstances, such as those that occurred in CEE transition countries. Shedding the fear of the democratic majority, that is of constituent power running wild, might shift attention to the political leaders, who – under the protective umbrella of constitutional legitimacy – often usurp the cloak of constitutional power, to cover the promotion of the elites' interests and to the entrenchment of their power, but pay little attention to forging links or allegiances beyond the narrow circle of their immediate political base. The recent experience of Poland and other CEE countries shows that the lack of attention to the quality of democratic process during constitutional transformations often results in secretive, *statist* type of political systems which may be formally constitutionalised, but whose standards of democratisation seem to be set at the level where the people are unlikely to become 'the truly reliable guard of the revolutionary achievements and their preservation in the future' (Preuss 2007: 221).[9]

Aims of This Book

This books aims to make a case for recognising that inclusiveness and popular involvement in constitution-making and in constitutional law-making in constitutional moments matters for democratic consolidation in post-communist societies. This approach sets it apart from the majority of constitutional scholarship which focuses on the legitimacy of the constitution and the soundness of constitutional democracy, in the sense of rule of law. In contrast to such approaches I will base my analysis on the idea of *democratic constitutionalism*, which needs to be distinguished from constitutional democracy, a much more common term in modern constitutional theory. The crucial difference between the two is that the latter refers to democratic government limited by the constitutional regime of legal controls/checks and balances, which is supported by judicial review, and which amounts to the rule of law state. The focal point of democratic constitutionalism,

---

9   Compare with the following comment that appeared in *The Economist*: 'Much of the recovery [in the post-communist countries of Eastern Europe] is thanks to swingeing cuts and tax hikes, often imposed at the behest of outsiders such, as the IMF and sometimes with scant regard for legality and democratic niceties. East European politicians, perhaps because of their history, are use to obeying tough instructions from outside, and imposing them brusquely. Their voters do not object much. Whereas West Europeans riot when squeezed, their eastern counterparts just glumly emigrate. […] There is a worrying trend in Eastern Europe towards what, with only some exaggeration, might be called "Putinisation": a noxious cocktail of cronyism and authoritarianism exemplified by Russia's strongman prime minister, Vladimir Putin. Political and economic power fuse, undermining independent institutions and silencing criticism' (2010).

on the other hand, is the quality of political processes behind constitutional law-making and constitution-making and the insistence that 'the laws must always be open to criticism, negotiation, and modification of those who are the subjects of them as they follow them' (Tully 2007: 334). That implies, at the very least, democratic participation, debate and the power to shape the most fundamental policies of a reforming state. Hence, democratic constitutionalism could be used to ask what happens when the criteria listed by Tully are not satisfied and if such neglect might impair the long-term prospects of democratic development. One possibility or hypothesis that this book suggests is that legitimisation of constitutional arrangements which lack democratic foundations might result in limiting the domestic dynamics of democratic growth and solidifying a state of permanent democratic underdevelopment. This danger appears particularly strong when such arrangements are validated by external authorities, such as the European Union and international organisations.

Testing such a hypothesis is particularly important in relation to CEE countries – which two decades ago went through a profound political and economic change – as there are reasons to suggest that the lack of inclusiveness and popular involvement in moments of social mobilisation associated with constitutional moments which these countries experienced, partly contributed to the annihilation of social involvement in the political process and reinforced the alienation of the political elite from the electorate (Skąpska 1999; Osiatyński 2000). Could it be the case that the elite-led, top-down nature of the process of fundamental policy-changes have undermined the popular democratic instinct that was in evidence during the struggle against the party-state regimes? The evidence from across CEE certainly points that way: most countries suffer a high degree of political apathy, negligible civil society, political parties alienated from the electorate, political capture of the media, and weak or non-existent trade unions. In contrast, governing institutions and power elites seem well settled in a system of self-contained, and largely self-sustaining structure of multiparty *nomenklatura*, supported by a network of business and, in some countries – Catholic Church relations – and are largely isolated from the electorate, its views and preferences.

Structure of This Book

The first chapter aims to define the concept of democratic constitutionalism and to turn it into a workable framework for discussing the politics of constitutional law-making and constitution-making in Poland. To achieve this, the two concepts of constitutional moment and constituent power will be discussed and their meaning clarified so that it will be possible to establish if the events that took place in the 1990s in CEE can be considered constitutional moments and if the presence of constituent power can be confirmed or denied.

Such an approach must be distinguished from the prevailing approaches of liberal constitutional theory that focus on constitutionalism as a rule of law and the separation of powers, judicial review and bills of rights – that is, institutional and procedural aspects – and pay less attention to the realities of the politics underlying and shaping constitutional decision-taking and law-making at extraordinary junctures of states' history. This analysis will focus on the prospects of democratic constitutionalism in CEE, which seems particularly appropriate since the connection between constitutionalism and democracy was firmly established in the late 1980s and early1990s; democratic movements lead to the constitutional transformations across CEE. This approach will be based on the theories of political constitutionalism of Bellamy (2007), democratic constitutionalism of Loewenstein (1965) and also on the writings of Sajó, Sen, Tully, Raz, Habermas, and others.

In the second chapter I will use the concepts of constitutional moment and constituent power developed in Chapter 1 to discuss the main watersheds in Poland's recent political history. The selection of events classed as constitutional moments will go beyond the constitution-drafting and include those political and legislative milestones at which issues of fundamental importance were at stake which amounted to the constitutional transformation of Poland. Before mapping out developments leading to events of 1989 and the formation of constituent power in Poland under the banner of Solidarność, I will briefly outline the early historical evidence and tradition of Polish constitutionalism. The substantive discussion of this chapter will be traced through the key events: the RTT, the introduction of the systemic reforms, the re-drafting of the constitution and accession to the EU. The analysis and discussion of democratic politics at these crucial junctures of Poland's political history in this chapter should help to answer this book's main question: Is the democratic legitimacy of constitutional politics relevant, and if so in what way, to the democratic development in CEE?

Chapter 3 will discuss the impact of international and European pressures and conditionality on Polish democratic and constitutional development. In particular, I will examine the claim that the external pressure from international organisations such as the IMF, the World Bank, the Council of Europe and the EU have been overwhelmingly beneficial for the democratic consolidation of Poland and other CEE countries. I base my discussion on Whitehead's classic work on the international dimension of democratisation: contagion, control and consent (1996: 4) and theories and perspectives on Europeanisation (Schimmelfenning and Sedelmeier 2005a; Schimmelfenning 2007; Featherstone and Radaelli 2003) and on EU conditionality (Kochenov 2007; Grabbe 2006). In contrast to the prevailing approaches, I will focus on the dynamics of the processes through which the external policies directed to Poland and other CEE countries have been created and carried out, and less on the substance of these policies. I will be asking what the impact was of external policies aimed at achieving democratic change, given that the creation and delivery of those policies did not always follow democratic and constitutional standards.

In the final, fourth chapter, I will analyse the contribution of the Polish Constitutional Tribunal (CT) to achieving the constitutionalism-democracy balance. The reason for such a focus comes from liberal constitutional theory that places Constitutional Tribunals at the centre of constitutional democracy. Among the many tasks that these Courts perform, guarding the constitution against the tyranny of a parliamentary majority and defining – by interpreting and enforcing – individual rights are the most fundamental. These two broad powers also link the uneasy nexus of the constitutional imperative to limit political power with the democratic one which gives a voice to citizens and protects their constitutional rights. Striking a balance between the two has been considered as fundamental in preventing constitutionalism from stifling the corrective force of democratic politics that should, in principle, underlie it (Mandel 1998; Tully 2002; Hirschl 2004; Colón-Ríos 2010).

Although I will provide an account of the CT activities within the broad context of Polish politics, I will limit my inquiry to just one aspect of the CT's jurisdiction: constitutional rights of individuals related to moral values: abortion and religious freedom in the context of religious education. Such a limitation is dictated by two reasons – this area of the CT's jurisdiction is proving most controversial across the CEE region, yet it denotes an aspects of democratic constitutionalism that matters particularly for individuals whose life-styles and ethical choices put them in position of minorities within certain cultural settings. I will also examine the possibility that the system of appointments to the CT and the influence of organised religion partially explains the politicisation of the Polish CT's judgements in cases related to abortion and freedom of religion.

Chapter 1
Democratic Constitutionalism in Context of Transitional Politics

Successful transitions need empowered citizens (Dahrendorf)

Introduction

This chapter will aim to define the concept of *democratic constitutionalism*[1] and turn it into a workable framework for discussing the politics of constitutional law-making and constitution-making in Poland. To achieve this, the two concepts of constitutional moments and constituent power will be discussed and their meaning clarified so that it will be possible to establish if the events that took place in the 1990s in CEE can be considered constitutional moments and if the presence of constituent power can be confirmed or denied. This will be done by a limited analysis of existing theories of constitutionalism with an aim to identify those aspects which directly relate to democratic participation in constitutional politics in 'constitutional moments' (Ackerman 1992), or in 'constitutional' as opposed to 'normal' law-making (Ackerman 1993).[2]

Such an approach differs from, and is much narrower than, the prevailing accounts, which focus on constitutionalism as a rule of law and the separation of powers, judicial review and bills of rights – that is institutional and procedural aspects – and pay less attention to the realities of the politics underlying and shaping constitutional decision-taking and legislation at extraordinary junctures of the states' history. Consequently, concentrating on constitutional politics, or on the political aspects of constitutionalism, should allow us to fill this relative gap with a more sustained analysis that could help to understand the current state of democracy and constitutionalism in Poland and in other CEE countries. In some way, this analysis will follow Skąpska's call to 'reach "beyond the heads of lawyers" into the political process' (1999: 154) to debate the state and the prospects of grass-root, or democratic constitutionalism in CEE. The rationale for linking

---

1   For an elaboration, see e.g. Loewenstein (1965); Tully (2002, 2007).

2   I will not fully engage in discussing the famous paradox of constitutional theory, the antagonism between the constituent power and constitutional form (Loughlin and Walker 2007), for reasons that will be explained later.

democratic expectations and constitutional politics[3] seems particularly appropriate in the case of CEE since this connection has been firmly established in the 1990s:[4] CEE constitutionalism simply cannot be separated from its ultimate origins – democratic movements that lead to the systemic changes across the CEE.[5]

The main questions that I will be asking are whether constitution-making and taking decisions in constitutional matters should be politically – i.e. democratically, not just legally – legitimate,[6] and whether such legitimacy matters for the long-term prospects of democratic development. In other words, is the democratic robustness of constitutional politics relevant for the overall condition of democracy in CEE, and also, possibly, elsewhere?

Such a focus cannot be entirely separated from the umbrella term 'constitutional democracy' – in the sense of control of power by democratic means which, in turn, are limited by constitutional rules – but will be kept apart from these main concerns of constitutional theory, as far as it is reasonable without jeopardising the clarity of discussion. I will attempt to develop an approach which captures the specific conditions of the CEE countries, yet that stays within recognised strand of constitutional scholarship. This approach will be based on the theories of political constitutionalism of Bellamy (2007), democratic constitutionalism of Loewenstein (1965) and also on writings of Sajó, Sen, Tully, Raz, Habermas, and others. I will first identify the basic parameters of democratic constitutionalism required in political systems that want to be called *democratic* and *constitutional*. Next, the concepts of constitutional moments and constituent power will be analysed and developed in relation to the political reality of Poland over the past two decades. This should lead to a workable framework which will be applied to assess if these

---

3   I am aware that such a link is considered highly controversial in constitutional theory. Democracy is usually challenged on the grounds of posing a threat of the tyranny of majority, which is a priority target for constitutional control. I suggest that in case of Poland, the nascent constitutionalisation which developed from ca. the 1970s can be considered as sufficient guard against the tyranny of majority. See chapter 2 for a full discussion.

4   Some scholars point out that the masses were absent in the events leading to the systemic reforms in Poland, for instance, whereas in Germany and Czechoslovakia people took to the streets only after the authorities had abdicated (Poznański 1999: 327). It is undeniable, however, that the events in 1989 had their roots in Solidarność strikes in the summer 1980, a mass democratic protest. The street demonstrations in 1989 and 1990 cannot be so easily dismissed as non-significant either, even, if, as Poznański suggests, the power has already been passed to democratic opposition parties in most CEE countries.

5   Historically, all 'constitutional moments' result from revolutions or other dramatic events. I believe that events occurring in a pre-democratic era, where vast majorities did not have political rights, should be distinguished from those occurring in a democratic mass society which took root in the early/mid twentieth century with the arrival of universal political rights.

6   Compare with de Raadt (2009), who argued that the process of constitution-making is not directly relevant to their legitimacy.

concepts of constitutional theory can be used to explain the weaknesses in the democratic development of Poland and other CEE countries.[7]

What is Democratic Constitutionalism and Why Could it Be More Relevant in Central and Eastern Europe After 1989?

Scholarship on constitutional theory has not yet managed to produce a conceptual framework able to capture and make sense of the politics behind the constitutional changes which swept the CEE in the 1990s and assess their impact on the prospects of democratic consolidation and constitutionalism. Few theorists venture into the dangerous territory of relating the political process behind constitution-making with the legitimacy of the constitution. Those few who link it with the overall condition of democracy do so in an indirect manner (Skąpska 1999, Sajó 2005). Most accounts, particularly those associated with the 'transitology' approach, focus on the construction and functioning of institutional order and constitutional architecture.[8] Although such approaches are undoubtedly valuable and much needed, they leave unexplained the nature of the political process that leads to the enacting of the constitution, in particular shying away from trying to evaluate the democratic quality of this process. This is not surprising, given the diffused nature of politics on which constitution-making is based, and the difficulties in reconciling the official, publicly available and the 'behind the scenes' accounts of constitutional bargaining. In the case of Polish constitution making, for instance, the official communications from the National Assembly were often limited to reports summarising the work of constitutional convention, and to the summaries of submitted drafts (Chruściak and Osiatyński 2001). These and other similar experiences with drafting constitutions in the CEE confirm that all too often the main concern was the legitimacy of the constitution related 'vote-centric' (Kymlicka 2001: 290) concept of political participation – which usually coincides with the outcomes of constitutional referendums – and not to the politics leading to the drafting of the constitutional document.

Democratic constitutionalism, on the other hand, might offer some insight – even if not comprehensive – into the nature of constitutional political processes by providing a conceptual framework for assessing whether constitutional politics was/

---

7   There is no agreement of this point. The majority of 'transition' literature, focused on institutional aspects, considers the CEE countries as democratically consolidated. A number of native accounts, on the other hand, stress the weaknesses of democratic consolidation, related, in particular, to the poor levels of civic activity and weak political culture. Opinion polls seem to confirm this second approach. For instance: in 1990, 83 per cent of Poles discussed politics often, in 1997 this fell to only 18 per cent. (Klingeman et al. 2006: 221). Across the CEE countries, levels of trust and civic engagement remain considerably low (Poland scored zero per cent in civic engagement) (Klingemann et al. 2006: 48).

8   See for instance: Sanford (2002), Volten (1992), Pridham, and Vanhanen (1994).

is open, inclusive, accountable and responsive – in other words, whether it satisfies the basic democratic criteria. This approach can be justified if we accept that the roots of current constitutionalism in CEE lie in the democratic upheavals of the late 1980s and early 1990s.[9] We should, then, want to ask whether the democratic energy and mobilisation, apparent in the mass protests that swept CEE, continues and finds reflection in the quality of the democratic process in constitution-making and at other extraordinary junctures, or 'constitutional law making' in the CEE states' recent history: the Round Table Talks, and accession to the European Union. The prevailing evidence, which suggests that democratic consolidation in CEE is still weak – particularly those aspects which relate to participation, interest representation and civil society – raises the interesting question of whether the mass protests were just one-off events of democratic mobilisation in otherwise democracy-averse societies, or if these were true constitutional manifestations of democratic will that has been allowed to disappear instead of being channelled into a more sustained process of grass-root democratisation.

The term 'democratic constitutionalism' occurs only infrequently in the vast body of literature on constitutional theory, unlike the concept of constitutional democracy, which is much more widely used.[10] Even though it might be argued that the former snugly fits in the broad meaning of the latter, I believe that focusing on the former in its own right – bearing in mind that the two approaches cannot and should not be entirely separated – offers a unique inroad into the state of constitutionalism and democratic politics in CEE transition countries and, possibly, elsewhere. In the constitutional democracy literature there is agreement on the prerequisite basic fundamentals necessary in any constitutional order worthy of such description: rule of law, checks and balances, separation of powers, judicial review and bills of rights. This relative consensus ends when it comes to detailed elaborations of how desired outcomes of constitutional democracies are to be achieved, what reasons and rationales should inform them, and what should be the ultimate objectives of constitutionalism.[11]

Given the scope and complexity of the field of constitutional theory, it is remarkable that the two-sided principle of constitutional democracy consisting of substantive limits to political power – that is, bills of rights and procedural–democratic control – has been accepted as a legitimising platform of constitutionalism by vast majority of scholars. Less surprising, even within this broad consensus, are some serious disparities, sometimes overlaps and arguments which are often taken into unexpected directions. Within this complex field, one of the clearest dividing

---

9   Sajó recalled that a certain democratic interpretation of popular sovereignty, namely, that all power comes from the people and with their collaboration, was nevertheless linked to the idea of constitutionalism (1999: 53).

10   For a recent overview of the literature on both concepts, see for instance Murkens (2009).

11   For the most recent comprehensive account of constitutional justice and critique of Rawls classic theory, see Sen (2009).

lines runs between rights-based or legal constitutionalism, which puts the judicial review and constitutional adjudication at the helm of policing the constitutional boundaries[12] and political constitutionalism, which places democratic politics in this role (Bellamy 2007; Tully 2002). The latter remains close to the republican tradition of democratic participation and it should be distinguished in this sense from the liberal approach, for which the values enshrined in a constitution carry more viable legitimising force (Allan 1993; Raz 1977).[13] This suggests that in the search for a paradigm of democratic constitutionalism, republican approaches offer a better starting point. Even though their main concern is with the constitutional limits to political power rooted in democratic system, they also strongly support the idea of popular participation in the actual constitution-making as a necessary legitimising factor of constitutional politics.[14] Such participation can take the form of 'democratic practices of deliberations [that] are themselves rule governed (to be constitutionally legitimate)' (Tully 2002: 205).

The idea of democratic constitutionalism illustrates that there is more overlap between republican and most liberal approaches than there are real differences. One clear difference is that the latter is more emphatic in its insistence that a balance should be achieved between constitutionalism (understood as the rule of law) and democracy, and in recognising the necessity of an on-going democratic policing of constitutional boundaries within the confines of constitutional rules. As argued by Tully, a legitimate constitutional system should be not just democratic, in the Rawlsian sense (the sovereign people 'impose' the constitutional system on themselves), but must also provide a balance between constitutionalism and democracy: 'a political association is legitimate if and only if it is equally constitutional and democratic: that is, the combination of *constitutional* democracy and *democratic* constitutionalism' (2002: 206). It is clear that such a balance is an ideal and an aspiration or a 'background critical principle of judgement that orient participants in their critical discussion and contestation of the legitimacy or illegitimacy of the practice of governance'.

The more practical explanation of the idea democratic constitutionalism takes it close to Bellamy's theory of political constitutionalism, particularly when the freedom to participate in a constitutional system (in accordance with the rules and procedures of that system) includes stepping back, dissenting and calling into question the principles, rules and procedures by which one is governed and entering into deliberations over them (Tully 2002: 206). The 'stepping back' and the power to dissent, even if they are exercised in accordance with the existing

---

12   For a critical overview of legal constitutionalism, see Bellamy (2007), particularly chapters 1 and 2.

13   Otherwise there is not much to separate the republican and liberal traditions of constitutional thinking. See for instance Bellamy (2007: 154–6).

14   Sources that repeat the mantra that people should be bound only by laws which they impose on themselves are too numerous to list, as most constitutional theorists agree on this point.

constitutional rules, clearly disturb the balance towards democratic checks and balanced, and, therefore, democratic constitutionalism. In that sense, Tully's concept seems close to the more radical meaning of constitutionalism offered by Bellamy and his idea of political constitutionalism. This basically shatters the possibility of balance to be achieved between constitutionalism and democracy and suggests that democratic politics should take priority over law-making in the sense of the 'thick' constitutional process (2007: 155–6). The process by which the democratic process should operate might be linked to the recently revived by Sen's idea of 'government by discussion' (2009: 324–7).[15] Sen used this concept in his polemic against Rawls's institutionalism, and it seems that this is an approach that supports Bellamy's political constitutionalism, taking it closer to the strand of constitutional theory that places the democratic process at the centre of contemporary constitutionalism. Sen's idea clearly echoes Habermas's (1995, 1996) deliberative democracy. An important advantage offered by the notion of 'government by discussion' is that it does away with the myth of general will, focussing on everybody's right to participate in discussions:

> The source of legitimacy is not the predetermined will of the individuals, but more a process of change: deliberation and discussion. The legitimate decision does not represent everybody's will, but it is the result of everyone's discussions, where all citizens are entitled to participate. [...] The principle of deliberation is individualist and democratic at the same time. (Manin 1987: 351)

What emerges, then, is a suggestion that for constitution-making and constitutional law-making to be legitimate, they must be grounded in a process of democratic discussion and deliberation by the people in their capacity as the sovereign power. The main function of constitutional deliberations is to arrive at agreements and compromises on issues causing disagreements. Such processes must be protected from the 'tyranny of the majority'. A deliberative democracy grounded in constitutional rules that would provide a clear procedure for conducting the deliberations might offer such protection by 'attempting to create institutions that will ensure reflection and reason-giving' (Sunstein 2001: 239). Hence:

> Constitutional institutions, such as a system of checks and balances, are best understood not as a way of reducing accountability to the public but as a guarantee of deliberation. Deliberative democracies do not respond mechanically to what a majority currently thinks. They do not take snapshots of public opinion. A deliberative democracy requires the exercise of governmental power, and the distribution of benefits and burdens, to be justified not by the fact that majority is in favour of it but on the basis of reason that can be seen, by all or almost all citizens, as public-regarding. (Sunstein 2001: 239)

---

15   This is clearly one of the 'talk-centric' approaches to democracy (Kymlicka 2001: 290), such as Habermasian's deliberative democracy. See also Elster (1998).

Is Political Constitutionalism Democratic Constitutionalism?

Bellamy's radical idea of equating democracy with the constitution – 'democratic process *is* the constitution' (2007: 5) – is in a sense close to the traditional notion of a system of limits and controls over political power, which he claims might be more viable when exercised through democratic politics than that of rights-based judicial reviews. Tully's approach, although developed from the angle of the intercultural dialogue, comes to a similar conclusion:

> Perhaps the great constitutional struggles and failures around the world today are groping towards the third way of constitutional change, symbolised by the ability of the members of the canoe to discuss and reform their constitutional arrangements in response to the demands for recognition as they paddle. [...] a constitution can be both the foundation of democracy and, at the same time, subject to democratic discussion and change in practice. (1995: 29)

There is clearly lots of potential in these suggestions, since it is obvious that over-relying on the alternative – a right-based legal constitutionalism – raises many difficult questions: decisions in individual cases provide a doubtful basis for forging public policy, the judges are rarely politically neutral agents, so that matters of public policy might be tainted by their views (Garlicki 2008: 356).[16] Equally, the democratic process is not free from its own particular challenges, mainly related to its function as a source of constitutional order and an effective mechanism to control and constrain the exercise of governmental power. Although it would be difficult for a democratic constitutionalist to disagree in principle with Bellamy's point that the democratic process is more legitimate and effective than the judicial process at resolving disagreements about the direction of public policy (2007: 4), the demands that democratic politics must comply with before the claim of such superiority can be made are almost impossible to satisfy.[17] Universal suffrage and 'one person one vote' under majority rule probably is one of the very few unproblematic features of the 'vote-centred' political system. All other elements, however, raise many questions even in mature democracies such as the UK: party competition and parliamentary politics, including the whip system, which institutionalises the balance of power; the 'first-past-the-post' electoral system,

---

16   See also Landes and Posner (2009). I note, but do not engage in, other types of argument questioning judges' role as policy makers – since their role should be limited to applying the law; or their status as appointed, not elected, officials versus their influence on public policy.

17   A similar argument has been made by Colón-Ríos, who argued that popular participation in the production of constitutional norms should be limited to *episodes of constitutional change* (my emphasis), since such participation is impossible in large and complex societies at the level of daily governance (2010: 25). Compare also with Arato (1992–1993).

which creates doubtful results from the point of view of representativeness;[18] the provision of 'safe seats', which precludes any alternative party from challenging the position of the two major parties that have dominated British politics for decades; the PM's power to appoint peers to the House of Lords; and the controversial role of the media – the conundrum of commercial interest of privately owned media and their public role.[19]

Compared to the UK, the state of democratic politics is much more problematic in the CEE countries. In Poland, for example, the system of political representation has not been established in any viable sense: parties function as a rent-seeking and political patronage conglomerates best described as 'multiparty nomenklatura' (Gwiazda 2008); the civil society is largely confined to religious, sport and hobby pursuits types of activity and therefore remains 'inconsequential in political terms' (Regulska 1998).[20] The more recent Polish data confirms these findings (Baczko and Ogrocka 2008) (CBOS: January 2009).[21] The influence of some other, traditional, participants in democratic politics such as the trade unions remains weak[22] and the media are increasingly subordinated to party interests under conditions of political capitalism (Godzic 2009: 233). Commercial imperative and reliance on advertising revenue puts their role as the 'fourth estate' in serious doubt.[23] Problems with political representation apply to most countries

---

18   For instance, Labour gained 55 per cent of seats in 2005 on an overall share of 35.5 per cent of the votes. *The Guardian*, 2 December 2009.

19   See 'The Sun and Labour support: how newspaper readers have voted in UK general elections?' *The Guardian*, 5 October 2009, on how Murdoch's media empire decided the outcome of the UK elections in the past three decades.

20   Despite the overall positive assessment of the local government in facilitating the political revival of local communities, Regulska identified structural weaknesses such as the negligible influence of the citizens on the decision-making process and the absence of local representatives at national level. The entrenchment of these weaknesses has been confirmed in Gliński, Lewenstein and Siciński (2002). In addition, this study has identified some problems in the functioning of self-government structures on local level and in the NGOs which probably have their roots in the weaknesses identified by Regulska, which by now have become deeply entrenched in the local structures of self-government. Despite the high number of NGOs in Poland (ca. 20,000) they are considered to have a negligible impact on the shape of central and local politics.

21   Only every ninth Pole was a member of a society or organisation, and only 7 per cent actively worked for such an organisation.

22   The unions have been much reduced in size and lost much of their bargaining power (Urbański 1994). On low unionisations in Poland, see for instance Gardawski (1999), Gardawski et al. (2001), Ostrowski (2009). See also '20 lat rządow korporacji, 20 lat fałszywej demokracji' [20 years of corporation rule, 20 years of false democracy] available at: http://www.ozzip.pl/dokumenty/oswiadczenia/719-20-lat-rzadow-korporacji-20-lat-falszywej-demokracji.

23   This is felt particularly acutely at the level of city or borough council, where the threat of a loss of advertising revenue from local businesses influences the way politics is reported there.

in the region and relate as much to everyday political processes as they do to the constitutional decisions such as the RTT, accession to the EU or the constitution-drafting itself. Yet, more than a decade after the Polish constitution came into force and more than two decades after the Hungarian, Czech and Slovak ones, there are few signs of constitutional revolt. In Poland, the majority are satisfied with the constitution, and the overwhelming majority would not contemplate the need for a new constitution (4 per cent).[24] Should this be taken as evidence that the idea of democratic control of constitutional politics in CEE is either impossible to achieve or not needed for securing the constitution's legitimacy? On the other hand, even if we accept that the legitimacy of the constitution is not affected by weaknesses of democratic process in its making, will this be likely to damage the prospect of democratic consolidation?

A Tentative Definition

Serious weaknesses of democratic politics in the CEE countries, but also in the mature democracy of the UK, heavily qualify Bellamy's idea of political constitutionalism. Equating the democratic process with the constitution is likely to work only in a perfect system of political democracy, and prospects for such a system seem remote both in the UK and in CEE. Bellamy's rejection of constitutional moments, based on the alleged 'populist constitutional politics' characteristic of such moments for the sake of 'genuinely constitutional and constitutive qualities of normal politics'[25] (2007: 8) thus looks unconvincing. Yet, the core of the idea of political constitutionalism remains valid: constitutional law-making should be controlled by democratic politics. To break with the risks posed by the deficiencies of everyday democratic politics, I suggest that political constitutionalism should be limited to law-making in constitutional moments or moments where social mobilisation is more likely to occur.

> What is true is that constitutional politics, due to its extraordinary nature, has the potential to promote the public participation of individuals otherwise dedicated to private happiness, and whose political involvement is inevitably a shifting one. (Arato 1992–93: 670)

On such occasions the issues under discussion will be those which most people would recognise as affecting their lives as members of a polity in some important sense.[26] As stated by one of the oldest conventions of constitutionalism: what

---

24   See CBOS BS/69/2002.

25   The growing indifference and alienation of people from politics which seems to affect both Western and Eastern Europe also put a question mark over Bellamy's idea. See for instance Kymlicka (2001: 293).

26   Recent examples of constitutional issues are Gordon Brown's plan to hold a referendum on electoral reform, indicating that this is a constitutional matter. Reported in *The Guardian*, 2 December 2009. In addition, decisions to go to war by a country might

touches all should be agreed by all (Tully 1995: 75). Hence, in such moments, open, inclusive, debates or deliberations seem the least that sovereign people could expect. It seems that political constitutionalism can be equated with democratic constitutionalism but should be limited to broadly understood constitutional moments. In order for this suggestion to hold, the concept 'constitutional moment' should be developed and clarified. What follows is an attempt to do that.

Constitutional Moments

Most accounts of constitutional theory agree that the problem of choosing the constitutional foundations of a state or other organisation occurs only on rare occasions when some 'funding event', or 'extraordinary moments of constitutional politics takes place' (Ackerman 1991: 191–5).[27] Bellamy, on the other hand, argues that it is hard to accord any special weight to constitutional politics as it is 'remarkably similar to normal politics [...] since most of the agreements reached will simply reflect the concerns and beliefs of people at a given time and these can be expected to change' (2007: 133). The constitution binds people to a vision of democracy that they rejected even at the time when they were negotiating the shape of the constitutional agreement (2007: 134). This sustains one of Bellamy's main theses – that democratic, everyday politics *is* the constitution.

The main points of disagreement between the two theoreticians are the possibility or denial of social mobilisation when public interest and fundamental principles are at stake. Under such conditions, the factional politics may be put aside for the sake of reaching general consensus on matters of fundamental importance, goes the argument of Ackermann. Bellamy rejects this possibility, based on evidence from constitutional conventions which reveals that political division and promoting group/party interests was in evidence during most of the constitutional deliberations (2007: 133). Experiences in Poland and in other CEE countries strongly confirm Bellamy's observation (Chruściak and Osiatyński 2001). In the face of this evidence, Ackerman's insistence that the constitutional conventions have the ability to raise above the political squabbles of everyday politics seems unconvincing. However, neither Bellamy or Ackerman distinguish between the constitutional convention and the societies who, as illustrated by the events in CEE, often were the ultimate authors of the upheavals leading to

---

seem to be making the constitutional mark. Sir Jeremy Greenstock stated, 'I regard our participation in the military action in Iraq in March 2003 *as legal but of questionable legitimacy* in that it did not have the democratically observable backing of the great majority of [UN] member states, or even perhaps of the majority of people inside the UK'. *The Guardian*, 27 November 2009 [emphasis added].

27   Two historical events in particular are used by most sources to illustrate this point, namely, the American and French revolutions. See also Habermas, for whom constitutional moments are the opportunity to 'reignite the radical democratic embers of the original position' (1995: 128).

constitutional moments, and who might still be in the grip of the 'psychological and valuative unification of social souls and minds' (Skąpska 1999: 153), or of 'heightened political consciousness' (Ackerman 1988: 163); in other words, a state that might be defined as a constitutional moment.

The evidence from CEE on capturing such defined constitutional moments is patchy: Hungary, for instance, passed its constitution under such heightened social emotions, whereas Poland seems to have missed it, not only as far as constitution-making goes, but also in other instances of decision-making of fundamental nature. This refers to the three-layered types of reform in which the CEE countries were engaged alongside changing the constitutional order (Elster 1993: 170). Elster suggested that the constitutional reforms have influenced and have been influenced by all three tasks related to fundamental re-shaping of their political and economic orders. Most existing accounts of constitutional theory shy away from recognising these events as 'constitutional moments'. Elster refers to RRTs in several CEE countries as 'pre-constitutional or quasi-constitutional stage' (1993: 169). Skąpska is one of the few who explicitly classifies the introduction of economic market reforms and fundamental reshaping of the political system at RTT as a 'constitutional moment' (1999). She went even further and claimed that the 'Gdańsk Agreement of 1981' could be considered a 'social constitution' (1999: 156, 171). I agree with Skąpska and suggest that these events, which were to lay the foundations of economic, political and social orders, have all the defining qualities of 'constitutional moments'.

That the political mobilisation at the early stages of economic and political reforms in the 1990s (constitutional moment), did indeed take place can de inferred from the 'exceptionally high social support for the economic reforms, especially, since they were not favourable to the majority of Poles' (Skąpska 1999: 164; Kideckel 1994: 143). The RTT were also confirmed by most Poles as more of a defining moment in Poland's recent history than the later drafting of the constitution: 46 per cent against 26 per cent (CBOS 1999). In addition, the turn-out at the first semi-free elections has been, so far, the highest of any elections after 1989 in Poland. The very high support for the idea of democracy, at 60 to 80 per cent of the CEE population might also be interpreted as reflecting an unusual optimism and hope for the future in countries where a functioning democracy was a big unknown (Miller, White and Heywood 1998: 143). Krzemiński and Śpiewak arrived at similar results in relation to Poland (2001: 69). Since the early 1990s, however, most indicators of democratic development either remain low or have deteriorated. This, I think, suggests that the failure to capitalise on the political mobilisation which did occur in the early 1990s amounts to squandering of constitutional democratic momentum by ignoring the voice of the people who, at that particular moment, were more ready to engage in shaping their political destiny than in any other time in the following decades. Or, as another interpretation suggests, the constitutional moment of 1989 has not been turned into the permanent 'power of the people' (Preuss 2007: 218).

Whose Constitutional Moments: Elite's or Society's?

The constitutional moments[28] that were gripping the CEE societies were hardly in evidence in the working of governments and parliaments. Even the Constitutional Assemblies became forums for political bargaining and competing party interests, instead of acting in the spirit of the constitutional moment, by putting to one side 'factional divisions' as would have been expected in light of the experience of common struggle for independence and the need to consolidate the resulting polity (Hamilton et al. 1992: 260). This different political mood of the society and elites entrenched the gap between them that became apparent during the earlier turning points in the systemic transformation journey such as the Round Table Talks of 1989.

A peculiarity of the elite–society gap found its expression in the way that the elites misread the public mood on a number of issues of constitutional importance. Another aspect of this was the relative neglect of individual rights and freedoms by the elites: instead, much attention has been lavished on the perceived need to protect Poland's sovereignty.[29] This neglect was already apparent when the Polish Small Constitution was adopted in the Autumn of 1992, where provisions related to individual rights and freedoms remained, in principle, unchanged – in other words, the same as in the old 1952 Constitution. The squabbles over the Charter of Rights and Fundamental Freedoms after the enactment of the Small Constitution and its subsequent fate are, probably, the clearest example of a fundamental constitutional issue falling a victim to ideological confrontations and party interests – in other words, elite in-fights.[30] As a result, during the first eight years of the post-communist era the fundamental rights of the Poles were not protected in any constitutional sense. This might seem a serious constitutional blunder.[31] Certainly the prospects of introducing a liberal constitution might have been undermined, as this required the creation of a culture in which individual rights would be fundamental to political and legal order (Zuzowski 1998). That

---

28   In Poland, these constitutional moments were the spell shortly after the first semi-democratic elections in 1989 (Skąpska 1999: 164) followed the first, unsuccessful, attempt to enact the new constitution on 3 May 1991. The eight years that it took to enact the 1997 constitution cannot really be considered as a 'moment'.

29   Such was the case with the perceived need to defend Polish sovereignty in the face of the EU supremacy clause – the Poles are not very concerned with this (60 per cent of Poles support political integration with the EU according to Eurobarometer, Autumn 2006) yet, the judgement of the Polish Constitutional Tribunal K 18/40 of 11 May 2005, and the Constitutional provision in art. 90 and 91 of the Polish Constitution of 2 April 1997 contain a strong guarantee of sovereignty under international law. For a different view see Albi (2005: 78–80).

30   See Chruściak and Osiatyński (2001: chapter 7) for an account of the debates over the Charter.

31   For a different view of the lack of fundamental rights protection, see Brzeziński (2000: 108–10).

this might have been the case is confirmed by a surprising 74 per cent of the Poles who declare that the Constitution – despite the stalemate on the rights issue – has a big significance in the daily lives of the inhabitants of the country. It is first of all the source of rights and individual freedoms, and it is a legal act of the highest rank (CBOS 1994).

These paradoxes of the elite's disdain and lack of social sensitivity to issues of individual rights can be best explained by looking into political and societal culture. The most relevant explanatory traits relate to the importance of historic memory, relevance of symbols, and the attitude to rights. In Poland, as in other CEE countries, symbolic meaning is often more relevant to shaping attitudes and behaviour than the pragmatic/experiential aspects of certain phenomena. That would explain the enthusiasm of the Poles for Constitutional arrangements which hardly afforded them enforceable rights. Given the widespread ignorance of the text of the Constitution, such overwhelming support might also mean that Polish society is highly patriotic, seeing the Constitution more as a symbol of independent Poland than as a source of individual rights, and deferential to the political elites who drafted and enacted the Constitution.

The above evidence leads me to suggest that neither Ackerman's nor Bellamy's concepts of constitutional moments can be fully related to the CEE countries. Ackerman does not sufficiently account for the politics (dominated by party interests) carried from the parliaments into the constitutional assemblies, from which societies, in the grip of their own constitutional moments, have been largely excluded. This exclusion was particularly poignant when the individual rights and freedoms provisions were under discussion. Bellamy, on the other hand, does not fully appreciate that in certain types of society, in which political culture revolves around historic memories and symbolic meanings,[32] constitutions and constitutional moments have a great mobilising potential, as is the case in Poland and probably in other CEE countries.[33] Neither of the two constitutionalists account for the different meaning of the constitutional moments for the political elites and the societies: for Ackerman, constitutional politics is much more about factional/party interests than common good; for Bellamy, the symbolic weight of this particular constitutional moment and patriotic elation might have blinded the constituent power to the unsatisfactory realities of their share of constitutional bargain, and reinforced the deferential relation between the society and the elites.

Despite the doubtful outcome of the Polish 1989/90 and 1993 constitutional moments, such events should be recognised as indispensable for mobilising society around common policy goals and as providing a signpost of its political

---

32   This phenomenon was aptly summed up by Walicki: 'Poland is a country where everything has a historical dimension' (1990: 21). See also '70 years after WW2 erupted, a new battle for history rages', *The Guardian*, 12 November 2009.

33   Compare with Kideckel, who described the post-revolutionary enthusiasm and unity for effective change as 'essentially the only developmental capital possessed by the post-socialist states' (1994: 143).

identity.[34] Supporting this argument is Ackerman's idea of constitutional moment, useful despite not allowing for the possibility that the constitutional assembly and the society might react and behave differently under such conditions. Bellamy, on the other hand, in his political-constitutionalism thesis, offers an attractive tool which allows us, potentially, to understand the need to capitalise on constitutional moments by turning the social surge of political energy into a lesson in democratic politics and active participation.[35] Hence, my own understanding of constitutional moments steers a middle-course between Bellamy's political constitutionalism and Ackermann's constitutional moments. I am reluctant fully to accept Bellamy's thesis, as I do not think that democratic politics can ever achieve the robustness and relevance required for such conceived constitutionalism to work. On the other hand, I think it is acceptable to extend Ackermann's constitutional moments to events – such as the RTT, introduction of systemic reforms and accession to the EU – because of their potential impact on the economic, political and legal situation of the whole society. This would also chime with Bellamy's suggestion that it is useful to distinguish fundamental constitutional moments from 'periodic' ones (Bellamy 2007: 135), which occur when a singular matter of constitutional importance is considered. I accept that these events might not be universally recognised as 'constitutional' in a very narrow understanding of constitutional moment, one that is limited to constitution-making only.

Constituent Power in Constitutional Theory

Modern constitutional theory assumes that a polity comes into being as a result of some founding act (or constitutional moment) which creates a framework for government in the sense of institutions and procedures, and which defines the collective identity of the people (Loughlin and Walker 2007: 3). Who should be legitimately empowered – and on what authority – to constitute or create the constitutive power are the usual basic questions that are asked next.

The ideas offered by the classic social-contract approaches of Rousseau and Hobbes lost some of their appeal since they rest on a fiction that is difficult to sustain or even to relate to the current social and political reality.[36] Likewise, some of the more modern approaches seem unable to escape other clearly fictional

---

34   The failed attempt to enact the new constitution on the bicentenary of the 3 May 1791 one was lamented as a real lost chance to create a new symbol of national revival and unity.

35   Compare with Loughlin's and Walker's thesis of constitutional moment stretching beyond the founding event into 'continuous deliberations' through which 'the constitution acquires its mature meaning' (2006: 3), which, in some ways, seems close to Bellamy's political constitutionalism.

36   'Social contract' and 'general will' are such fictional concepts. Compare Dyzenhaus's (2007) discussion of Hobbes and Rousseau.

assumptions, most of which are employed to capture and explain the tricky moment of metamorphosis of the politically disorganised 'multitude' into constituent power, politically organised and capable of creating and imposing the law and constitutional rules on themselves. In times when direct democracy is simply not possible in the majority of places,[37] law makers and constitution writers are elected and appointed to perform such tasks. Despite this, some theoretical accounts still insist on the myth of people who deliberate over the text of the constitution or whose authority and approval is often needed to legitimise constitutional text in a referendum. Even though the role of the people in constitution-making was, in most known cases, rather passive and limited, high standards of civic virtue and personal attributes were ascribed to them. They should be seen as empirically informed, politically organised and active, rational or at least reasonable individuals (Loughlin and Walker 2007: 3). This set of characteristics, described as 'question-begging abstraction' flies in the face of any known social reality, and it also stands in stark conflict with the latest findings on how the human 'social' brain works.[38] More crucially, these tensions prompt the question of whether the 18th-century myth is still in some way useful in helping to understand the concept and the role of the people in post-communist constitutionalism. They also expose the unclear nature of the process by virtue of which the transformation from the disorganised, politically unaware, multitude to constituent power takes place.[39]

A useful starting point in seeking the origins of constituent power might be Preuss's suggestion that the 'empowering condition can be found in the role which active political minorities play in the downfall of the previous political order' (2007: 215). For this suggestion to work, however, we should first abandon the unsustainable 18th-century myths of the sovereignty of the people. In the classic examples of the English, French and American revolutions, the manner in which the people are conceptualised as the constituent power not only reinforces the abstract quality of such constructs, but their patently fictional nature renders them useless, even as theoretical devices – in twenty-first-century constitutional theory. Such is the case where references are made to 'popular sovereignty' in seventeenth-century England (Loughlin and Walker 2007: 33–5), when political rights where limited to men of property, which amounted to anything between 7–15 per cent of the population in most countries in Europe. Or, when the American Constitutional Convention is said to be elected by the people, and on that bases the legitimacy the American Constitution is, supposedly, confirmed. The lack of mention of the native and black population, as well as propertyless whites and women in a theoretical construction of constituent power and as a source of normative legitimacy, makes

---

37　Switzerland is the obvious exception, but even there some issues are not subjected to referendums.

38　See the RSA 'Social Brain' Project: http://www.thersa.org/projects/pro-social-behaviour/social-brain.

39　Compare with Kant's famous idea of a master or legislator necessary to act in the name of the people, without their consent until the people are 'civilized'.

such claims misguided.[40] Only the arrival of universal suffrage in the beginning of twentieth century could provide a more sustaining context for the possibility of 'popular sovereignty' and the existence of 'the people'.[41]

Many theorists admit that the fiction of constituent power might have been widely employed to cover the promotion of the elites' interests and to entrench their power (Loughlin and Walker 2007: 3). Interestingly, such a cover-up of the elite-nature of constitution-making did not visibly diminish the popular support and, hence, the claimed legitimacy of the American, French, and the unwritten British constitutions. Drafted in the 1990s, the constitutions of the CEE countries also confirm the uncertain importance of constituent power: most were drafted by political elites with minimum involvement of the people, yet they seem to be considered authoritative and legitimate. Could it be that the authority and sovereignty of the constituent power of the people should remain a fiction since its exercise seems not to matter for the legal and political legitimacy of constitutions? I think not because, as this work is trying to argue, much more than legitimacy of constitutions (already secured) might be at stake – namely, prospects of democratic consolidation.

An Alternative (Contemporary) Approach to Constituent Power: Constituent Power in CEE Before 1989

The fiction of constitutive power in constitutional theory might be hiding a much more fundamental problem, namely, that of the fear of democracy, which is presented as a threat of majoritarian politics to constitutional order. This fear, which is often expressed in the paradox of constitutional power and form (Loughlin and Walker 2007) might in turn be obscuring some crucial aspects of constitutional politics at constitutional moments such as those that occurred in the CEE countries in the 1990s. One way of trying to clear this obstruction is to distinguish the socio-political context of these recent events from the classic eighteenth- and nineteenth-centuries ones, which are most commonly used in constitutional theory. For one thing, it should be recognised that the socially constructed concepts of 'the people' (Preuss 2007: 216) and 'the constituent power imposing constitutional rules of themselves' (Tully 2007: 334) have a different meaning in the era of universal franchise than in times when only a fraction of the inhabitants of any given territory had political rights.

---

40   Compare with Mandel, who observed that American constitution has been drafted by the fifty-five of its richest men aiming to protect their property, including ownership of slaves (1998: 271).

41   Compare with Tully's discussion of the fight of the Aboriginal and Indigenous people for recognition 'in international law and in the constitutions of modern societies that have been imposed on them during the last five hundred years of European expansion and imperialism' (1995: 3).

Another crucial distinguishing factor is the establishment of international and supranational organisations such as the United Nations, the Council of Europe and the European Union, which made a striking difference to the political and legal empowerment of people after the second World War. It is fair to say that in the second half of the twentieth century the masses were recognised as bearers of political rights to a incomparably greater and more substantial degree than ever before. However, the political rights of CEE societies suffered under oppressive political regimes since the communist takeover in the late 1940s until 1989/90, hence the question arises whether these societies should be considered as possessing sufficient political agency to count as constituent power at that time of political breakthrough of 1989. Tully suggests that constituent powers of the people are constituted by the two classes of constitutional forms (state and suprastate) into two main political formations: 'constitutional democracy' and suprastate constitutional form (2007: 321). Suprastate constitutionalism is not always democratic, and mostly non-representative, but no longer can it be dismissed as entirely ineffectual in driving democratisation and the lifting of political oppression, necessary for the people to regain their political identity. If we were to apply Tully's construction to the CEE countries, would it be possible to argue that the politically suppressed people of CEE could be considered as, partially at least, constituted in their constitutive power by the suprastate constitutionalism? It is clear that the evolution of the CEE states and societies have taken place in the post-second World War era in response to external factors. Not only did it lead to the strengthening of 'social pluralism' (Sanford 2002: 39) in Poland, but it also limited the party's capacity to control society and amounted, alongside the political reforms of the early 1980s, to 'a primitive form of the rule of law […] as a precursor to democracy' (Sokolewicz 1990: 13).[42]

It seems, then, that the Polish authoritarian state can be seen as the second constituting form in the reverse (so to speak), not only by playing the role of the political adversary against which the political opposition shaped their identity, but also in reacting and evolving towards limited forms of constitutionalism. More generally, such creeping constitutionalism should be seen against the background of society on the whole being aware of political manipulation through political propaganda, ideology and censorship – as these means became, with time, less effective, or less functionally successful. The ranks of 'true believers' in socialist ideology have been shrinking throughout the 1970s and 1980s, even among the members of the top echelons of the party elite (Przeworski 1991: 6). All in all, the political awareness of society which main modus operandi was to question most of state's action and policies, is, surely, greater than a society which believes itself to be democratic, hence accepts more readily actions and policies of its democratically elected government. All of which leads me to suggest that the

---

42   Similarly, Sanford argued that 'the necessary groundwork including the bases for a constitutional Rechtsstaat had emerged during 1980s' (1994: 190). For a elaboration of this point see chapter 3.

pre-1989 CEE societies were already sufficiently politically mature to classify as a constituent power not only in absolute terms, but also compared with their Western counterparts. Of course, such defined constituent power can only exist as a nucleus, a potentiality which can only act when the political suppression is lifted completely.

Constituent Power in the Early 1990s in Poland
The question whether or not constituent power existed in Poland and the other CEE countries at the beginning of the transition is a complex one and far from settled. As argued earlier, a dormant form of such power can certainly be said to have existed. Since the importance of constituent power for the emancipation and energisation of the polity is well recognised (Loughlin and Walker 2007: 8), it may be claimed that had conditions at the beginning of the revolutions of 1989 been more favourable, what was only a promise of such power being exercised in the CEE societies would have become a reality. However, the scholarship on CEE constitutionalism shies away from providing a clear suggestion of such potentiality, which may be due to the lack of clear rules 'of recognition of the people as constituent power' (Preuss 2007: 212).

Some accounts bypass this issue altogether; others, such as Elgie and Zielonka, use the concept of *demos* in relation to CEE societies as a given that denotes the existence of constituent power (2001: 28). Sanford, for example, provides a stronger and more grounded endorsement of the existence of the *demos* thesis by locating the source of constitutional sovereignty in the Polish nation.[43] According to him the Polish notion of citizenship is rooted in 'democratic civil republicanism marked by native linguistic–cultural characteristic' (2002: 74–5). If describing the Poles as democratic republicans with civic inclinations seems too rosy a picture,[44] it may still be closer to the mark than Preuss's thesis that the people of CEE, including the Poles, before 1990s should be defined as *ethnos* rather than *demos* since they appear to be bound mainly by ethnic ties such as language, religion and culture (2007: 226–8). According to Sanford 'the systemic revolutions created an empty space [...] where hardly any pre-constitutional force [...] remained'. He states in relation to Poland that the collapse of communism not only destroyed the political regime, but the polity itself. Hardly any pre-constitutional cohesive forces – such as a common political will to live together, a shared national history, or at least history of statehood – remained and which could provide a sustainable sense of commonality of fellow citizenship to serve as the basis of the constituent power (2007: 224).

---

43   Compare also with Chalmers: 'nation has emerged as a central form of constituent power [...] because it embodies three filaments of the political – freedom, equality, and authenticity' (2007: 292).

44   What best describes the prevailing orientations of the Poles is the 'collective individualism' (Szacki 1994: 104–6).

Such suggestions fail to acknowledge the persistence of the Polish nation and culture throughout modern era, despite the loss of statehood through the 123 years of partitions.[45] Such survival was possible due to resistance against the occupiers, which clearly had a strong political element – the aim was to regain sovereignty – and this aim drove two national uprisings against the occupiers in 1830 and 1864. So, even if the main strategy of survival aimed at cultivating the language and culture, it was also, ultimately, a political struggle for independence that might be said to be rooted in strong ties and a will to live together, but which also, surely, strengthened those ties and this will (Walicki 1990). The post-war and post-1948 political reality created a society politically more aware than many others; most aspects of people's lives were politicised by the state. Hence, for the best part of its modern history, Polish society was kept together not just by ethnic and cultural ties, but also by a political identity forged in decades of living under, first, the partitions, and more recently, under the post-war 'system' of authoritarian, party-state polity. Even if the majority of people withdrew from public life into the private sphere, ever-present political oppression and manipulation sharpened social sensitivity to all things political. Such political identity has not been limited to a 'purely negative resentment against the old regime' (Preuss 2007: 224), but took the shape of dissident groups, clubs and organisations, most of which had a clear political agenda.[46] The realisation that the political opposition movement cannot rely on the heroism of individuals and requires institutionalisation existed from the early days (Michnik 1984: 25). KOR (Committee for the Protection of Workers) was the first such attempt on a national scale, Solidarność followed later. The added context of 'social pluralism' strengthens the argument that those organisational forms clearly amounted to more than 'resentment against the old regime'. Gonenc noted 'the unity of Polish civil society was one of the most important factors in its success in challenging the communist authorities' (2002: 126). I also contest the view that those groupings were erased by the revolutions to create a political vacuum – rather, the reason was their deliberate destruction by the authoritarian in style, secretive, elite-led process that started with the Round Table Talks, and developed into the undemocratic constitutionalism that is now in evidence in Poland and other CEE countries.

I therefore suggest that the concept of potentiality of constitutional power in CEE countries needs to be distinguished from the 'unformed constitutional power' and the concept of 'multitude' used in constitutional theory to denote the constituent power that existed prior to its actual constitutional form that can only bring 'their form of constitutional organization into being in some founding moment' (Tully 2007: 320). According to Preuss, the pre-1990 CEE societies amounted to such an unorganised multitude, essentially suffering from the absence

---

45   See for instance Norman Davis (1981).

46   These were probably more viable 'civil society' organisations then, in the sense of engagement and agendas, than many of the contemporary ones parachuted into Poland and financed by international bodies which failed to put more permanent roots in Polish society.

of 'pre-constitutional cohesive forces' (Preuss 2007: 224). I do not think that this vision is helpful, as I argued earlier in this chapter.

Preuss's suggestion is based on two assumptions which are at least partly problematic. First, he argues that the CEE revolutions were 'systemic' and not 'political'; secondly, I believe that he ascribes too much weight and significance to ethnic and national aspects of social mobilisations (2007: 222–8).[47] The key of the 'political' versus 'systemic' distinction is the difference between the German, French and Russian revolutions in the early twentieth century and the CEE ones. In the latter, his argument goes, there was 'the absence of actors who represented socio-economic interests which could identify with the interest of the society at large without being rejected as particularistic and purely class-based' (2007: 223). Solidarność in Poland clearly gave voice to ten million Poles who manifested their support for its political, social and economic programme in 1980 – hardly a particularistic interest. The difficulty was, however, that in the face of such mass mobilisation another actor – the party nomenklatura, or at least the 'reformers' within its ranks – also raised their game.

The old elites' interests could probably be classed as *particularistic*, even if only from a narrow point of view. For instance, the legislation that was introduced in 1980[48] and whose main aim was to assist primarily the nomenklatura in setting up first private companies with foreign capital, surely also benefited the whole society. Things became even more complicated when the two sides reached an agreement: the opposition and the old elites during the Round Table Talks, which legitimised the transfer of state property – already well under way in the early 1980s – into the hands of party nomenklatura, as this made it even less obvious if the competing interests were particularistic or general. As is often the case with peaceful settlements, no party was a decisive winner: a compromise had been reached which ensured the peaceful transfer of political power (a clear gain for society), but which left the old elites empowered economically.

---

47   Comparatively speaking, ethnic politics are highly visible in many countries of Western Europe: suffice it to mention the Basques, Walloons, or the Scots and Welsh. Yet the societies that contain these minorities are considered as demos rather than ethnos. If a crisis of the scale of the 1989 were to occur in these countries, there is a good chance that the separatist movements would have become stronger. Would this mean that they would revert to the state of ethnos?

48   Ustawa z dnia 25 września 1981r. o przedsiębiorstwach państwowych [State Enterprises Act of 25 September] Dziennik Ustaw z 2002 r. Nr 112 poz. 981; Ustawa z dnia 6 lipca 1982 r. o zasadach prowadzenia na terytorium Polskiej Rzeczypospolitej Ludowej działalności gospodarczej w zakresie drobnej wytwórczości przez zagraniczne osoby prawne i fizyczne [Act regulating economic activity of small enterprises run by physical and legal foreign entities] (Dz. U. z 1989 r. Nr 27, poz. 148 i Nr 74, poz. 442).

Evolution of Constituent Power After 1989

'Systemic' or 'Political' Revolutions?

As argued above, Preuss based his argument about the absence of *demos* in the CEE countries on a doubtful claim that the revolutions that took place in CEE countries were 'systemic', not 'political'. According to this logic, the driving force behind the 'systemic revolution' is said to acquire the quality of being politically organised only after the new institutions and laws have been in place to facilitate such organisation. Hence, the systemic events lack the politically organised force of constituent power as the events themselves lead to its establishment. The political change, on the other hand, is 'launched by the agents who represent more or less established collective "transformative" interests which [...] will immediately gain from the change of the political regime' (Preuss 2007: 223).

The real picture might be somewhat more complicated. On the face of it, the events unfolded as Preuss and others[49] saw them: the old system was dismantled and the middle-classes and other potential actors who could take advantage of the new freedoms to own private property or use contracts to develop/organise their economic relations were visibly absent. However, the political system which looked as if it was being dismantled, might in fact have been 'adjusted to the requirements of the socio-economic system' (Preuss 2007: 223), a process which started in the early 1980s and which led to the enfranchisement of the nomenklatura and transfer of state property into the hands of the old elites. The society (and economy) benefited as well: for the first time in post-war history people were allowed some limited freedom to set up private companies and develop links with foreign capital. So the conditions of political change have been satisfied, but in a sense different from those suggested by Preuss. And that is because the old elites were the more effectual driver behind the change, since from the early 1980s they started laying the groundwork for the free-market reforms.

The moment of 'launching', or the ignition, was helped by the unstable social situation and pressure from the political opposition. The state's weakness became apparent and so did the realisation that the cost of holding on to the status quo would be enormous. The governing elites saw their control weakening. Gorbachev's renouncement of the Brezniev Doctrine took away one of the crucial safeguards of party-state hold on power. The loyalty of the military and police could also no longer be taken for granted. From this point of view, the Solidarność-led upheavals taking place throughout the 1980s have been only indirectly implicated in the revolutions of the 1990s, more as a catalyst than as a main force driving the change. The main driving force had been the party reformers who, 'recognizing that the regime was facing economic collapse, responded as political entrepreneurs

---

49   See for instance Ash (1990) and Elster (1998).

[by] bringing about a resolution [...] in the hope of securing nation's economic fate and, thus ensuring their own power in the new order' (Hayden 2006: 7).[50]

This interpretation chimes with those scholars who dispute the 'revolutionary' – i.e. grass-root origins – of the revolutions. According to those accounts, the change has been driven partly by the network of power holders under the old system who wanted to legitimise the changed ownership structure of the economy, or their new position as the new capitalists and property owners or *entrepreneurchiks* (Poznański 1999: 329; Łoś and Zybertowicz 2000). Their hope of retaining political power had been dashed by the unexpected turn of events during the first semi-free elections in June 1989. As a result, as argued by Przeworski, 'the agreed transition to democracy might have been an outcome only of misinformed or miscalculating actors' strategies' (1991: 62).

Following the 'political capitalism' thesis (Staniszkis 1991), one of the ways in which the power of the Party could have been retained under the conditions of social unrest and political disintegration was to change the foundations on which it rested: from political to economic. This was necessary in order to transform the extensive use-rights[51] enjoyed by the nomenklatura into full ownership rights. Changing the rights of use into proprietary rights was one of the important triggers that started the economic transformation – the privatisation of state property, which has began already in the 1980s, at first secretly (Bauman 1993; Łoś and Zybertowicz 2000: 223) and after the Round Table Talks openly.

To summarise, the change of ownership structure, or the beginning of 'political capitalism'[52] in Poland, has been taking place since the early-1980s reforms with the introduction of the new packet of legislation on state enterprises and private companies with foreign capital, providing a legal basis for the transfer of state property into private hands. This process accelerated, reaching its peak in the 1990s, but it is still in evidence today:

> One can compare this process [the transformation of the state-owned into private property] to the earlier epoch of colonialism, when the conquistadors, pirates and simple crooks participated in the primary accumulation of capital in order to legalize it, and later become prestigious, law-abiding entrepreneurs. [...] In the conditions of post-communist states, the object of a quasi colonial conquest [...] was – and still is – the state-owned, or national property, and the tools of

---

50   Compare with Zuzowski, who suggested 'the sudden fall of communism in Eastern Europe and the Soviet Union had much more to do with the Soviet leaders' loss of faith in communism as a superior system to capitalism than their countries' poor performance in economics, science and the arms race' (1998: 24). Also Poznański suggested that the revolutions of 1989 were engineered by the the Party (1999: 225).

51   Mączak (1984) compared such rights to the feudal interests in property.

52   Staniszkis (1999). This is also known as the 'nomenklatura privatisation' thesis, which has been rejected by, for instance, Sanford (2002). I think that the explanatory potential of this thesis is underappreciated in mainstream 'transitology'.

> conquest often became the law, perceived as the instrument for the protection of
> strong interests. (Skąpska 2009: 285)

So the nature of the peaceful revolution in Poland was partly the outcome of the legislative reforms allowing the establishment of limited private companies and political activities such as the rapprochement between the Party and Solidarność.[53] It is then possible to argue that what took place in Poland (and similarly in other CEE countries) was, mostly, a political revolution, which, through the privatisation taking place since the 1980s, subordinated important aspects of the 1990s reforms to the short- and long-term interests of the old elites (Łoś and Zybertowicz 2000: 154). Hence, the forces that were instrumental in bringing the system down – 'helped' by the Solidarność-led mass-protest movement – were the ones who benefited most from the changes in the sense of property acquisition. Their political power, seriously weakened, was reinstated in the 1993 elections, which saw the re-branded post-communist SLD (the Social-Liberal Democratic Party) form the government.

Hence, in contrast to Preuss, I argue that the revolutions in Poland and some other CEE countries were driven by the need to secure political and economic rights of the old elite (representing particular interest), who started the changes as early as in the 1980s. They were 'helped' and 'prompted' to legitimise their gains by the visible success of opposition movement (representing interest of society at large), which agreed to continue and extend the programme of privatisation at the RTT. In an added twist, the interest of both the old elites and the political opposition gained from the change of political regime. In some sense, then, the change should be considered 'political' rather than 'systemic', although the transfer of political power (in social interest) in fact, indicates a 'mixed' case scenario. This, in turn, leads to the question if the idea of the 'interest of the society at large' can serve as a conceptual basis for the distinction between the systemic and political change.

My own analysis below will further develop the thesis that in the case of Poland, the 'political' or mixed revolution should be accepted as basis of the 'constituent power'. This will further strengthen my challenge to Preuss's conclusion that pre-1989 CEE societies are best understood as *ethnos*, pre-political communities, not possessing the qualities of constituent power (2007: 227) and allow for a better understanding of the evolution of Polish society as a 'constituent power' after 1989.

Constituent Power in Poland: A Challenge to Constitutional Theory

Countering existing accounts grounded in mainstream constitutional theory, I argued that Polish society should be considered as constituent power at the

---

53   Some scholars stress that it was a price that the political opposition considered as worth paying for the sake of avoiding full-on confrontation (Łoś and Zybertowicz 2000: 223–4).

watershed moment in its recent history – the 1989 change of the political and economic system. Not only were the Poles politically aware and to some extent organised but also the threat of the tyranny of the majority has been kept in check by strapping the democratic energy of the Poles to the mast[54] of a type of constitutionalism that developed more as a political practice than as institutional reforms.[55] Democratic mobilisation under the banner of Solidarność in 1980 and 1981 and the enthusiasm for the economic and political reforms clearly demonstrated after the RTT[56] are a testimony to the readiness of the Poles to take part in shaping their political future.

The real constituent power of the Poles in 1989 should be distinguished from the almost entirely fictional construction that was the constituent power of the American and French people at the end of the eighteenth century. Applying this thinking to the times of political disfranchisement of prevailing social majorities it must be concluded that the oppositional political constitution of the CEE populations, helped by the suprastate form in their construction, describes them as a more viable constituent power than early modern societies. Or, to put it another way, the fiction of the CEE societies as formed constituent power is more convincing than that applied to the early modern societies.

The new constitutional paradox, then, is less between the constituent power and its form, and more between the real existence of such power and the fiction that substituted this power in constitutional law-making and constitution-making at the key junctures of recent Polish history. It was precisely this fiction that created a veneer of constitutional (legal) legitimacy over the exclusion of the Polish society from participating in constitutional moments and constitution drafting. Political legitimacy of such process, however, could not have been sustained, in line with the democratic constitutionalism thesis. As it turned out, this exclusion of the Poles did not matter for the popular support for the constitution, but it had, very likely, impaired the social learning of democracy by extinguishing the grass-root democratic constitutionalism at source, and, therefore, it had weakened those aspects of political and constitutional culture that are necessary for democracy to consolidate.

Conclusions

I have arrived at the understanding of democratic constitutionalism that fuses Bellamy's idea of political constitutionalism with Sen's concepts of 'government

---

54   Reference to Elster's famous Ulysses metaphor (1993: 5).

55   Although the establishment in 1985 of the Constitutional Tribunal, the Commissioner for Citizen's Rights Protection (CCPR) in 1987 and the High Administrative Court were important institutional developments.

56   42 per cent of Poles supported Balcerowicz plan in January 1990 and only 9 per cent were against it (Wyborcza 1990).

by discussion' and Tully's 'democratic practices of deliberations'. Sunstein demonstrated how deliberative democracies keep majoritarian and populist politics in check with the help of constitutional parameters within which the process of such deliberations takes place. Such forms of constitutionalism should be practised at all moments of constitution-making and constitutional law-making. This meaning of constitutional moments widens the classic Ackermann idea, but it restricts Bellamy's notion to only those legislative events when issues of fundamental importance are at stake which are likely to affect people as members of a particular polity in some crucial sense.

I have also argued that the people in CEE countries could be considered as fully formed constituent powers since the revolutions that took place are better understood as political rather than systemic events, contrary to Preuss's elaboration of this topic. As to the existing constitutional theory, I suggested that it might be time to abandon the fiction of the constituent power that most of the classic eighteenth- and nineteenth-century accounts are based on, since the link between such fictions and the legitimacy of the constitutions based on them is at best uncertain. In addition, the seeming paradox between constitutional power and form might – in conditions where the constituent power is already constrained by nascent, if unorthodox constitutional and legal forms – obscure more pressing issues such as the quality of the democratic process leading to constitution-making or constitutional law-making. Yet, it might be the case that the weakness of the democratic process at such moments might weaken the processes of democratic consolidation of countries in which the re-constitution of their political, legal and economic orders is rooted in mass democratic movements. Bellamy and Castilgione summed this last point as follows:

> The identification of the peoples with the new regimes can only be secured if constitutionalism is integrated with forms of democratic politics that give them say in the forming and maintaining of the legal order governing their lives. (1996: 124)

Chapter 2

Constitutional Moments and Constituent Power in Poland's Recent Political History

Introduction

In this chapter I use the concepts of constitutional moments and constituent power developed in Chapter 1 to discuss the main watersheds in Poland's recent political history from the Round Table Talks (RTT) onwards. The selection of events classed as constitutional moments goes beyond constitution drafting and reforms, to encompass those political and legislative milestones at which issues of fundamental importance are at stake that are likely to affect people as members of a particular polity in some crucial sense. The analysis and discussion of democratic politics at these crucial junctures of Poland's political history should help to answer one of this book's main questions: Is the democratic legitimacy of constitutional politics relevant, and if so in what way, for the democratic development in CEE?

The chapter will proceed as follows: first, I will briefly outline the early historical evidence and tradition of Polish constitutionalism. This will be followed by a mapping out of developments before 1989 and the formation of constituent power in Poland under the banner of Solidarność. The further discussion will centre around the two main themes developed in Chapter 1 – constituent power and constitutional moments – and will be traced through the key post-1989 events: the Round Table Talks, introduction of the systemic reforms, the re-drafting of the constitution and accession to the EU.

Constitutionalism in Poland Before 1989

Brief History

Poland's historical tradition of constitutionalism can be described as rich and inspiring, although not always glorious.[1] There is no need to outline it here, as this has been done by a number of scholars,[2] but it might be useful to focus on

---

1   Compare with Gralczyk, who controversially concluded that Poland does not have any constitutional traditions (1997: 36).

2   A number of sources cover the historical development of Polish constitutionalism. One of the most comprehensive is Brzeziński (2000), but see also Davis (2001) and Sanford (2002).

those of its aspects that are still relevant and continue to influence constitutional developments in today's Poland.

The first evidence of constitutionalism in Poland is usually located in the thirteenth-century successful struggle of the gentry to limit the power of the King. The protection of personal liberty and property granted by Władysław Jagiełło in the 1430 acts of Jedlnia and known as the *neminen captivabimus nisi iure victum* – essentially the same as Habeas Corpus, or right to due process – is one of the most striking examples of control of royal power secured by the gentry, as is the *Nihil Novi Constitution* of 1505, in which the king guaranteed that nothing new could be enacted without the consent of the nobility. In 1573 a rather peculiar form of democratic government was established – an elected monarchy in which the position of the king was comparable to that of a president elected for life (Wagner 1970: 99; Cole 1999). The gradual broadening of the electoral franchise later on, even to landless noblemen, meant that Poland had the greatest proportion of the population that enjoyed political rights at that time in the whole of Europe (Łukowski 1991: 10).

Since the political rights of lesser nobles were also a shield against the more powerful landlords and the crown, what looked like a growth of a pre-modern form of constitutionalism, in practice did not amount to much. It rarely protected the propertyless nobles from falling into serfhood, but it did mean that they kept their legal and political rights even in such circumstances. The symbolic appeal of this formal legal and political entitlements, or 'beautiful fiction' in the words of Davis (1981), was crucial to the consolidation of the 'noble nation' around the ideas of equality in law and limited government. Part of this particular instance of national identity was also a powerful sense of individual entitlement combined with the neglect of the interest of the monarchy (the state), and weak sense of civic responsibility (Davis 1981: 241–5).

Osiatyński concluded that these historic developments amounted to 'constitutionalism as a contract between the nominal power [of the king] and the real power in the society' and pointed out the striking resemblance of this part of the historical constitutional tradition to the Round Table Agreement (1991: 127), where the Polish United Workers' Party (PZPR) was the 'nominal power holder' and Solidarność represented the real power, that is Polish society. The two traditions also share powerful symbolic appeal – RTT are still considered by the majority of Poles as more of a defining moment in Poland's recent history than the later drafting of the constitution (CBOS 1999).

The Constitution of the 3 May 1791
Firmly based in the above tradition is the 3 May 1791 Constitution; probably the best known and most cherished by the Poles, and the most enduring symbol of national survival (Zahorski 1991). Its anniversary used to be celebrated in secret and under the threat of prosecution during the socialist era: in the early days of the 'new Poland' of the 1990s it was announced as the first new public holiday, restoring the 1918 decision which established 3 May Constitution Day as

the most important date in official calendar. It is obvious that to Poles, the 1791 constitution is an important symbol of independence and sovereignty enduring from generation to generation. Such glorifications, however, contrast sharply with the negligible practical impact of the 3 May Constitution, and its failure to stem the disappearance of Poland as an independent state. The Constitution was defeated after just one year, and followed by the two final partitions in 1793 and 1795 which erased Poland as an independent state from the map. This early demise of the Constitution – a result of a political challenge by the opposition, the Targowica Confederation, assisted by Catherine the Great and her Russian army, only one year after its promulgation, probably bolstered the appeal of this document as a symbol of Polish martyrdom. 'Targowica' entered the Polish language as the term denoting high treason. These developments help to explain why even the unconstitutional manner of the enactment of the Constitution failed to dent the reverence surrounding it. There was no debate on its final version, and the vote was taken in absence of the opposition – misinformed as to the date and time of the crucial vote, hence prevented from attending.

Constitutionalism Leading to 1989

The end of the First World War marks the rebirth of Poland as an independent state, and a new chapter in its constitutional history. The mixed fortunes of the inter-war period[3] have been followed by – what amounted to – a denial of constitutionalism by the post-war communist government, despite the adoption of the 1952 Constitution and the democratic proclamations contained in it. In the words of Brzeziński, 'During the most of forty years of communist rule it was not the constitution but Party structure which provided the key to understanding politics and state policy-making' (2000: 1).

One of first signs of the *actual* post-war Polish constitutionalism can be traced to efforts to create a more palatable image of Poland in the early 1970s,[4] which were aimed, in particular, at Western money-lending institutions[5] and which developed into a more sustained constitutionalisation or 'creeping legalism' (Grudzińska-Gross 1997).[6] Not only the state, but also the dissidents increasingly used the

---

3   For a most recent account of this period in Poland's legal and constitutional history, see for instance Fijałkowski (2010), especially chapter 2.

4   Efforts before the 1970s, such as the 1952 Constitution, have been described as meaningless in constitutional terms (Brzeziński 2000: 1), hence cannot be considered as instances of constitutionalism.

5   Edward Gierek's regime borrowed heavily from the West to boost the supply of life-style goods. Some shops in bigger cities famously sold French carrots. This seemed a bad joke in the prevailing conditions of permanent shortages of basic consumer goods.

6   Compare with Sanford, who argued that 'much of the necessary groundwork, including the bases for a constitutional Rechtsstaat had emerged [in Poland] during the

idea of constitutionalism by framing many of their political objectives in the language of rights, and by accepting clear rules of procedure in mutual dealings, particularly in the 1970s and 1980s.[7] These tendencies were significantly boosted by the signing of the 1975 Helsinki Final Act of the Conference on Security and Co-operation in Europe (OSCE).

Apart from paving the way for the political opposition to acquire institutional form, the Helsinki Final Act also provided a legal frame of reference and a language that both sides could use as a mechanism of containment, facilitating in this way a smoother transition later on. Public statements by the dissidents, the so-called democratic opposition, already in the 1970s testified to the deep attachment to the notion of democracy and the rule of law. In the Summer of 1980, both Solidarność and the government demonstrated their will to uphold those constitutional principles of self-restraint. Solidarność struggled for democracy using democratic means (Jasiewicz 1992: 181), and both sides agreed to honour a number of pledges, such as non-violence, constraint in political demands and listening to the other side during the Solidarność-driven mass protests. Even though none of these agreements made it into the actual text of the Constitution, it was recognised that the government accepted limits to its power and the opposition agreed to obey the constitutional rules in their bargaining with the government (Garlicki 2008: 15, 17).[8] Those self-imposed rules of conduct should be seen as a fundamental turn in constitutional thinking by the main political powers in Poland at that time (Garlicki 2008: 15).

Accepting the limited constitutional rules as constrains of behaviour by both sides of the political divide can be seen as a minimum condition for the emergence of a grass-root democratic movement of any consequence: Solidarność could not have reached its 10 million membership if the authorities had used force against it in the early days of August 1980. These constitutional restraints, that re-emerged in dealings between Solidarność and the Party at the RTT, had their roots in the August 1980 agreements, and in earlier developments after the signing of Helsinki Final Act. Even though the imposition of Martial Law on 13 December 1981 changed this picture dramatically, this should be best seen as a temporary crisis – particularly in the face of threat of Russian intervention – rather than a permanent derailment of the nascent constitutionalism. Then, however, the stand-off between the two parties divided the country and plunged it into a political turmoil. The continuous

---

1980s' (1994: 190).

7   Solidarność is probably the best known example of a political movement which placed fundamental rights demands on its banners. Kurczewski, for instance, suggested that civility and political rights and human rights have always been part of the struggle against the communist regime (1993).

8   Davis commented, 'Solidarność saw itself as a 'self-limiting revolution' from the start, fully responsive to the constraints of Poland's political situation' (2001: 50). This was the case despite Wałęsa stating during the shipyard strike and the Round Table Talks in 1989 that the Polish Constitution (of 1952) was for him 'just a piece of paper' (Osiatyński 1993: 45).

economic crisis, to some degree an inherent feature in the command economy, worsened in 1980s, particularly during the aftermath of the Martial Law. With time, two things became obvious: without reforms the economy might shift from a state of crisis to total collapse, and secondly, without social support, which could be secured only by Solidarność, no reforms could be undertaken without risking an repeat of the August 1980 strikes. Since at least 1987, both Solidarność and the PUWP started preparing the ground for potential future talks. The third pilgrimage of the Pope, and Mazowiecki's visits to Vatican clarified the core framework for such talks (Bartoszewski 2010). The Summer of 1988 saw a wave of strikes and the re-emergence from political exile of Wałęsa, who was called to talk to the workers. In a parallel move, Jaruzelski was trying to persuade the Party hardliners that there was no other option but to talk to Solidarność. Initially, Jaruzelski hoped that official recognition of Solidarność could be avoided, but it soon became obvious that this was one of the non-negotiable pre-conditions. Before the first RTT meeting on 6 February 1989[9] took place, both sides continued their behind-the-scenes manoeuvrings seeking to agree on a set of demands allowing for a compromise solution to the stalemate.[10] The key issue was the reinstatement of Solidarność's legal status, in exchange for its support for economic reforms (Elster 1996: 5; Brzeziński 2000: 83). Securing badly needed Western financial help also depended on this condition. Consequently, seeking the West' assistance facilitated indirectly the internal development of constitutionalism already underway.

Institutional developments such as the establishment of High Administrative Court, the Tribunal of State and, perhaps most significantly, the Ombudsman – otherwise known as the Commissioner for Citizens' Rights Protection (CCRP) in the late 1980s – were part of the quest to present to the outside world Polish system of government as politically and legally legitimate. Of the new institutions, the Ombudsman exceeded most expectations by proving to be reasonably effective in challenging the state authorities, hence, it could not have been dismissed as yet another exercise in 'socialist legality'. The CCRP earned public respect, particularly during the 'reign' of its first incumbent, Ewa Łętowska (Elcock 1996). It was clear that the government did not anticipate the impact of the Ombudsman[11] on the state institutions whose powers were subjected to its control, and, most importantly, on the Poles, who turned to the Ombudsman in great numbers.[12]

---

9   There are numerous accounts covering the events leading to the RTT and the RTT proper; see e.g. Davis (2001); Sanford (2002); Brzeziński (2000).

10   For an overview of theories explaining the communist collapse of 1989, see Sanford (2002: 51–2).

11   'The office was meant to be powerless, and mainly for this reason a woman, the law Professor, Ewa Łętowska, was appointed as the first Polish Ombudsman. Yet, despite the intentions of the Polish government, Prof. Łętowska had great success in the role, and the Polish Ombudsman significantly contributed to the country's transition to democracy' (Finkel 1994: 9).

12   See Łętowska (1992) for a full account of the Ombudsman's first years in office.

Even if the practical outcomes of the Ombudsman's decisions affected comparatively small number of claimants, the symbolic significance of this institution should not be underestimated. The actual control over the state through the Ombudsman was limited in scope and accessibility, but the fact of the availability of a mechanism through which it was possible to challenge certain classes of decisions of public bodies boosted the popular sense of empowerment.[13] All in all, the institutional reforms which were initially undertaken to improve the international image of Poland, and were, in some measure, designed to remain more fictional than real, in fact boosted Polish constitutionalism and forced the state authorities to accept its rise.

Organising the Multitude: Solidarność and Constituent Power

The appearance of Solidarność on the political scene channelled the bi-polar structure of Polish society, the 'us' and 'them', into the first truly popular, organised form. Its rapid growth and mass appeal were rooted in the three sources of its power: political, economic and symbolic, which reflected the perception of the movement as a symbol of democracy, economic prosperity, Catholic values and a ticket to the Western World (Reykowski 1992: 219). The story of Solidarność's rise and demise from a mass organisation to its almost complete disappearance from political scene, and its limited presence in the trade union sector after 1990, are not of direct relevance here. Hence this will be referred to only briefly later on, and only to an extent that it is necessary to explain the role of Solidarność in organising the first authentic grass-root social/political movement in CEE and in leading this movement through the upheavals of early transition, and its transformation into a constituent power during the 1980s.

Solidarność grew from a rather fragmented strike actions of August 1980 into an organised social or civic movement with clear political ambitions. This metamorphosis occurred when the decision was taken by the Strike Committee to redefine its demands from mainly economic to political. The most important of those demands, which were included in the Gdańsk Agreements of 31 August 1980, and called by some scholars a 'social constitution' (Skąpska 1999: 156, 171), were the right to establish free trade unions, the right to strike and limits to censorship (Katka 2005). The development of Solidarność's political and social agenda was in some ways inevitable under the conditions existing then in Poland. The party-state not only held total political power, but it was also the main employer (Kurczewski 1993: 195–6), hence, 'conflict with management became per force conflicts with the state' (Bielasiak 1992: 207). However, the shift towards political objectives targeting the party-state rule rather than its employment and

---

13   This was helped by the publicity that the Ombudsman's work received. Rzeczpospolita, one of Poland's most popular newspapers, published the Ombudsman's weekly column.

social policies took place at the expense of the trade union interests that 'were to be postponed or relegated to a minor position' (Kurczewski 1993: 196).

In a sense, allowing values such as 'living in truth' (Přibáň 2007), dignity and respect for honour to take priority over economic demands was a continuation of the noble Polish traditions of 'golden freedom' and *liberum veto*, harking back to the electoral monarchy of the late sixteenth century and the cherished Constitution of 3 May 1791 (Szacki 1994: 103). However, even if this mixed economic and political agenda initially secured Solidarność a mass following, it later proved unsustainable and most likely contributed to Solidarność's disintegration and its loss of standing within the working class (Ost 2005), leaving one quarter of Polish society who were once its members without political representation. 'Solidarność brought communism in Poland to its end. But with the end of communism comes the end of Solidarność' (Jasiewicz 1992: 181). The question that I would like to ask is whether, and if that's the case, in what shape constituent power has survived the disintegration of Solidarność. The next section will attempt to answer these questions in the context of the Round Table Talks (RTT) and the introduction of systemic reforms in 1990. First of all, I will make a case for recognising those two events as constitutional moments.

Constitutional Moments of the Round Table Talks and the Introduction of Systemic Reforms

The concept of constitutional moments developed in Chapter 1 differs from the one offered by mainstream constitutional theory, where only constitution-making is thus defined. I argued that such a narrow understanding of constitutional moments is unsustainable as it fails to encompass other than constitution-making momentous events where choices are made of fundamental importance for the future of state and society. These are occurrences which most people would recognise as affecting their lives as members of a polity in some important and lasting sense.[14] Such events not always coincide with drafting the constitution of a state, which occurs only on rare occasions when some 'founding event', or 'extraordinary moments of constitutional politics takes place' (Ackerman 1991: 191–5).[15]

The necessity to recognise the upheavals in CEE in 1989 and early 1990s as constitutional moments relates to both of the above attributes: the gravity of the events and a particular type of social mobilisation occurring at such events, which Skąpska described as 'psychological and valuative unification of social souls and minds' (1999: 153). Sajó commented

---

14   See chapter 1.

15   Two historical events in particular are used by most sources to illustrate this point, namely, the American and French revolutions. See also Habermas, for whom constitutional moments are an opportunity to 'reignite the radical democratic embers of the original position' (1995: 128).

> The concept of 'constitutional moment' is distinguished by lasting constitutional
> arrangements that result from specific, emotionally shared responses to shared
> political experiences. (2005: 243)

The RTT and the introduction of reforms, which were to lay the foundations of economic, political and social orders of the CEE states, have all the defining qualities of 'constitutional moments'. The crumbling down of the party-state systems were those political experiences to which the people of CEE responded in visibly emotional manner. The restructuring of the state orders at the RTTs created firm bases to systemic arrangements that were later enshrined in many of the CEE countries' constitutions. Scholars such as Elster lend support to the above thesis by referring to RTTs in several CEE countries as 'pre-constitutional or quasi-constitutional stage' (1993: 169). Skąpska echoes this by explicitly classifying the economic market reforms and fundamental reshaping of the political system as a 'constitutional moment' (1999). This particular reasoning is analogous to that of Ackerman's, who suggested that the 'New Deal' represented a constitutional moment in the U.S. history (1992).

The Round Table talks were nothing short of the beginning of fundamental reshaping of Poland's political system. An opinion poll conducted in 1999 identified the RTT as the main event of the last decade of Polish history. Forty-six per cent of the respondents selected the RTT as such an event. In comparison, the promulgation of the Constitution took third place with only 26 per cent considering it important (CBOS 1999). Popławska was right to stress that

> the reforms of state institutions and foundations of systemic principles agreed at
> the Round Table were decisive for the systemic transformation and continue to
> be constant elements of the Constitution in force. (2008: 282)

The agreement that was reached at the RTT initiated the two core processes that were to define the future shape of the Polish state: the establishment of a free-market economy and laying the democratic groundwork of the political system. Despite such foundational significance, from the beginning, the RTT took the shape of a clandestine deal between the old and the emerging power brokers: the PUWP and Solidarność. The main concessions secured by Solidarność, as part of a bargain allowing the Party to remain in power, were as follows; re-legalisation of Solidarność not only as a trade union, but also as a political movement; re-instatement of the office of the President and the second chamber of the Parliament or Senat [*Senate*]; and the semi-free elections to be held on 4 June 1989, where 35 per cent of the votes were allocated to Solidarność in the lower chamber and an open contest was declared for seats in the Senat. Solidarność's winning all but one of Senat's seats not only defeated all expectations (Bartoszewski 2010); it could also be construed as an act of condemnation by the electorate – which had been excluded from negotiating this bargain – of the pact of Solidarność with the Party. This act demonstrated the electorate's commitments to democracy and political rights that was to prove a strong and lasting legacy of the quasi-constitutionalism of the 1980s: it grew during mass protests in 1989 and was not extinguished by the undemocratic and exclusionary politics of the RTT.

Round Table Talks – Social Contract or Secret Bargain?

In line with Tully's dictum 'what touches all should be agreed by all' (1995: 75), the constitutional moment that was the RTT should have laid the foundations of democracy within the confines of Poland's nascent constitutionalism. Yet the evidence suggests that even though constitutionalism, in the sense of following the rules which limited and controlled the power of the negotiating parties, has been largely observed, the basic criteria of the democratic process were mostly absent. The RTT were neither transparent nor representative of the interests of the rank and file of Solidarność or the wider society, nor were the decision-makers accountable – many of Solidarność leaders traded in their mandates for political positions in the power structures being established in place of the Party apparatus.

Most sources described the RTT agreement between the PUWP and Solidarność as a 'contract' (Gebethner 1992: 238) or a 'social contract', others use the phrase 'trade' or 'deal' (Skąpska 2009: 299). The key question that these suggestions pose is: What was the position and bargaining power of the sovereign Poles? Or, who and to what effect represented their interests at the negotiating table? Elster argued that the Solidarność delegation at the RTT 'was in no way representative of the population' (1996: 4). In contrast, I suggest that Solidarność emerging from the eight years of illegal existence, at least *held* the mandate to represent the overwhelming majority of Poles: the landslide victory in the 4 June 1989 elections clearly confirmed the mass support of the Poles.[16] There was also no alternative: even if defective, Solidarność was the only political platform that gave the Poles at least some hope of being represented. How effectively this mandate was used is a different story. It is obvious that the assumption of the existence of such a mandate relays on a fiction of Solidarność's representativeness, just like some other fundamental concepts of constitutional and democratic theory. However, I suggest that this particular fictitiousness is closer to reality than many other fictions successfully employed by constitutional theory which often creates a façade constituent power out of a politically disempowered, unaware and often repressed multitude to justify the 'social contract' bases of constitutional settlements (see Chapter 1). The Poles were indeed disempowered, but probably ready to embrace the dawning era of political freedom. The 1980s were a unique lesson in political awareness affecting anybody who simply happened to live in Poland at the time of the first strikes of Solidarność, the tense period of Martial Law and Gorbachev's perestroika.

---

16   Solidarność's approval ratings in March 1989 stood at 75 per cent, see Mason (1992: 160), for a discussion.

So, even though no specific political or economic programme was agreed between Polish society and Solidarność, the basic core demands that can be assumed as supported by most were: democracy, the rule of law, and respect for human rights. These aspirations constituted the most fundamental set of political demands included in the August 1980 agreements, and were present on the banners/declarations used by Solidarność throughout its legal and illegal existence. These demands were also reflected in the statement published by the group of political oppositionists led by Geremek. This statement amounted to a general outline of the political programme of the opposition and contained, among others: the right to live in truth, democracy; equality and respect for law (Skórzyński 2006). The other parties at the RTT also supported these objectives (Sadurski 2006: 200), which leads to the conclusion that the vast majority of Poles considered these demands to be the agreed core agenda of the RTT.

Accepting this premise allows us to posit the legitimacy of the RTT's agreement as a 'social contract', based on the sufficient degree of representation and consent of the society. Fuller assessment, however, requires us to ask how, or to what ends, the mandate held by Solidarność had been used and if the process of negotiations was inclusive, deliberative and transparent. The majority of sources concluded that none of these criteria have been satisfied, as the informal and secretive manner developed during the pre-RTT negotiations continued to be the dominant mode of the negotiations during the RTT proper. Skąpska commented that 'Some of the important proceedings were not public at all, and these were not subjected to sustained, public critical evaluation' (1999: 162). Others talked about the elite nature of the RTT and the 'horse trading' (Sanford 2002: 53). The lack of consultation and public debate mattered not only from the procedural point of view, that is, Solidarność not complying with its mandate, but it also meant that the third party – society – had not been given a say over substantive policies, yet, the cost of implementing those policies was going to be borne mainly by the society (Skąpska 1999: 163). Solidarność, in its two guises – as a trade union and as a political block – emerged as double winner by securing important gains, the official recognition and a participation in the political institutions of the country: the government and the Sejm. The workers and other pro-Solidarność sections of society were told to adjust to the new reality, the shape of which was decided behind their backs in a process that clearly lacked democratic legitimacy.

Skąpska made a similar point, but termed it 'negative ethical evaluation' (instead of 'weak political legitimacy') expressed by the 'third party' (the society) affected by the outcomes of the RTT bargain. Such negative evaluation is likely where the bargaining parties represent power that may affect the third party adversely, that is, where the costs of the bargain will have to be borne by the third party (1999: 162–3). The anticipation of the backlash against difficult economic reforms led to the exclusion of democratic society (the third party) from the RTT agreement, despite an impressive political maturity that the Poles demonstrated in giving priority to political freedom over economic hardship. The consistency with which the Poles and other CEE nationals identified political factors as decisive in shaping their opinions and views on public matters contradicted many early analyses and expectations which predicted that economic factors will take priority in CEE (Harper 2000: 1197; Kozarzewski 2007: 54). The high popular identification with constitutional and democratic values has become the most consistent and stable explanatory variables that determined voting intentions of the Poles for years to come (Harper 2000: 1221). These findings, which were confirmed by a number of studies that also extended it to most other countries in CEE (Harper 2000: 1197; Kozarzewski 2007: 54), provide a strong rebuttal to those responsible for excluding the electorate from participation in decision-taking at constitutional moments of early transition, since such exclusion was justified by the anticipated populist threat to the unavoidable reforms (Przeworski 1986).[17] Both the high degree of social acquiescence to the programme of reforms and the decisive role of political, rather than economic, factors in shaping the CEE societies' standpoint on the process of transition proved erroneousness of such anticipations. The political, long-term cost of such an error looks serious – the negative evaluation of the RTT bargain by the society deepened the gap between the governing elites and the people, and was behind the growing disillusionment and disengagement from politics.

In conclusion, the RTT process satisfies the idea of social contract only partially: Solidarność, despite its falling popularity, held the social mandate for pushing for respect of human rights, democratisation and the rule of law. Yet the secrecy of the RTT and the way in which its terms were agreed – including the promise of Solidarność's support for economic reforms in exchange for Solidarność-only centred concessions – suggest that 'deal' or 'bargain' would be more accurate terms. One of the crucial side-effects of the RTT bargain was the avoidance of a potentially violent confrontation between the PUWP and Solidarność. This success, however, must be pitched against laying the roots for potential future conflicts by legitimising the unlawful takeover of state property by communist elites that was well under way around this time (Popławska 2008: 282).

Despite these difficulties in capturing the true nature of the RTT agreement, its constitutional, or legal legitimacy could be asserted with some confidence. Both sides observed constitutional constraints during the negotiations, respecting the confines of nascent Polish constitutionalism (Osiatyński 1996: 32; Skąpska 1999: 152) even if some of the provisions of the 1952 Constitution, still binding at the time, had been breached. Political legitimacy, however, is much more problematic, since the basic standards of democratic process were missing from the RTT: transparency, open debate, accountability. Chruściak and Osiatyński supply one more explanation of the democratic weakness of the RTT that stays in line with the above thesis – the main objective behind the new political system whose foundations had been laid at the RTT was not to build a democratic state, but to limit its authoritarian tendencies (2001: 123). Such a choice indicates that constitutionalism was to be the preferred means to temper the

---

17   Compare with Gardawski (1996).

threat of authoritarianism and not democratic politics. However, the cementing and legitimising of the emerging structures of power – the new status quo – which included the old nomenklatura and its new status as a business class, can hardly be seen as a success in taming authoritarianism of Polish politics: the position of the new ruling classes was strengthened, while the corrective force of democracy was undermined. If we accept that was a part of the core agenda of the RTT, than the relegation of Polish society – the constituent power – to the position of a third party, or 'silent actor' (Skąpska 1999: 155) should be seen as deliberate in order to protect the new status quo from the vagaries of democratic politics. The successful execution of this strategy reduced the Poles to the role of passive recipients of decisions that were to bring dramatic, often adverse changes into their lives, in contradiction to the basic principle of democratic constitutionalism. Hence, it should come as no surprise that the democratic energy and social mobilisation that occurred under the banner of Solidarność during the events leading to the RTT began to dissipate once the leadership of Solidarność started pursuing their own agenda under the deal negotiated at the RTT (Ost 2005).

The Introduction of Systemic Reforms: The Process

Solidarność's acquiescence to support Balcerowicz's plan or 'shock therapy' at the RTT was crucial for creating the *perception* of political legitimacy of the proposed economic and political reforms, contrary to the actual, serious weaknesses of the democratic standards within this process. On 6 October 1989 the Polish people were presented with the most profound package of economic and political reforms in generations, and in December, a packet of 11 acts was passed by the Sejm. During the next two years further numerous new laws were passed which altogether amounted to a truly systemic change. The reforms were introduced in a top-down, authoritarian manner – there was no public debate or engagement in deciding the shape of reforms. Despite this, and despite the draconian measures that were part of the reforms package, spelling hardship and uncertainty ahead, 42 per cent of Poles supported the programme, 40 per cent were undecided, and only 9 per cent opposed it (Wyborcza 1990: 1).

The explanation for this high acceptance of reforms must, at least partly, relate to a state of heightened social mobilisation which occurs in moments of dramatic systemic change, which, according to the theory developed in Chapter 1, amount to constitutional moments. Most theorists agree that in such moments, particularly when the direction of the change leads away from a repressive regime, rejected by the majority, the receptiveness to replacement of such a regime is higher than at other times.[18] The level of trust that is bestowed on the new leaders is also usually very high. Taken together, the two factors amount to a repository of social and political capital vital for securing a conciliatory social response to difficult policies and for setting firm foundations for grass-root political activity and representative,

---

18   Compare with Ackerman's concept of 'jurisgenerative force' of such events (1996).

accountable political system. That means that not only the policy choices but also the nature of political process at such a time of unprecedented revival of social activity is bound to have a long-term impact on both democratisation and constitutionalism.

> During the first decade of transition, little emphasis was given to broader issues of popular control and government accountability outside of the electoral process. This relative neglect has been costly for those countries and deserves greater emphasis as the transition proceeds. The costs are not primarily economic. Rather, there is an increased risk of popular disengagement from political life based on disillusionment and distrust of the state and its officials. (Rose-Ackerman 2007: 32)

If this explanation is accepted as applying to post-RTT Poland in the 1990s, then we can suggest that the social mobilisation that occurred at that time in Poland might have been eroded by a lack of attention to the political legitimacy of the RTT and to the process leading to an agreement on the package of reforms in the Sejm. Following this logic, it can be inferred that the initial overwhelming support for the reforms might have occurred *despite*, rather than be credited to, the perceived success of the RTT.

Hausner offered a similar argument. According to him, the elites scored a relative success in gaining social approval for the programme of reforms but not for the methods or institutions directing the process of change (Hausner 1992). This might explain the rapidly diminishing support for reforms that followed their initial acceptance. Consequently, it can be argued that the RTT and its aftermath failed to convert the social/political capital expressed in the early support for reforms into a foundation of sustainable democratic and constitutional order in Poland. Detrimental to this was the descent of the politics at that time into an elite-bargain and pandering to political interests of the political parties and the Church. This suggestion echoes Skąpska's (1999) negative assessment of the chances of 'grass-root' constitutionalism at the RTT and in the early 1990s. Such interpretations also stay in line with Ost's argument that it was the lack of representation of economic interests by Solidarność that left the workers disowned, disempowered and alienated from the political process (2005: 4–5). A similar path of political alienation could be observed in relation to the whole of Polish society, since the wider mechanisms of representation of interests was weakened by the fragmentation of the political scene, the estrangement of political parties from society and the suppression of pluralistic debate, a phenomenon summarily described as 'a syndrome of abandoned society' (Gardawski 2001; Hausner 2003).

In the next section of this chapter I further develop the argument that some of the fundamental political and economic choices and strategies of their implementation decided at the RTT and at the early days of systemic reforms, as outlined above, had contributed to the long-term weaknesses of democratic constitutionalism in Poland.

The Reforms of the Early 1990s

The necessity to re-organise most aspects of the state simultaneously after the semi-free elections of 4 June 1989 was probably the main logistic challenge of this period (Elster 1993, 1996). It should then not surprise that the matrix for reforms was taken 'off the shelf' (Osiatyński 2003): a Western model of successful capitalism, which at that time was based on the 'Washington consensus' or neo-liberal market doctrine. I will not engage in the lively and still on-going debate assessing this model.[19] However, in my quest to shed light on the possible reasons for neglecting the democratic politics in this phase of systemic change, at least two aspects of such a choice must be given closer consideration: a conviction that successful economic reforms will facilitate political and cultural democratic change, and that economic reforms should not be the subject of democratic or constitutional politics (Gavison 2002; Van der Pijl 2006). The first of these core commitments of the neo-liberal model of reforms was partly based on the belief that economic factors are more important for sustaining democracy and constitutionalism than social and political ones (Kurz and Barnes 2002). This, combined with the necessity to prioritise certain aspects of reform in the conditions of 'rebuilding the ship at sea' (Elster 1993: 170) might have contributed to pushing the democratic and social concerns off the early reforms agenda.

The second tenet of the neo-liberal doctrine contains the claim that democratic participation often obstructs economic change (Bellamy and Castiglione 1996: 115; Przeworski 1986: 62). It also defines economies as private spheres, hence excluding the possibility of constitutional regulations.[20] The use of neoliberal doctrine combined with the need for efficiency create a convincing argument justifying the barring of democratic participation – those who would be on the receiving end of the painful economic reforms would not support such reforms (Ost 2005: 17, 109). Trying to obtain a social consensus would take too long, and the outcome is too uncertain. Yet, the initial reaction of the Poles to the reforms package does not confirm such thinking. The Poles were willing to bear the brunt of the 'shock therapy' since it was the way out of the party-state system towards freedom and prosperity. Ost (2005: 51–2) commented on the zealous attitudes of workers who were keen, and uncritical supporters of the markets reforms. This initial support survived the undemocratic process at the RTT, but eroded in the early 1990s. Part of the reason was the economic hardship, but this is not the whole answer. At least as important must have been the inability of the elites to sustain

---

19　Such an assessment of a specially the long-term impact of this model on CEE countries will be particularly problematic, since, as suggested by Ganev (2005: 371), 'the East Europeans were willing to take neoliberal money and run with it in nonneoliberal directions'.

20　Compare with Anderson (2005) who argued that economic power exercised by private actors and the policy framework within which they operate is constitutional in nature. See also Hirschl (2004), who developed a similar argument.

those positive attitudes by developing a sense of ownership and identification with the new economic regime through giving people a say in how this regime is to operate (Bellamy and Castiglione 1996: 124). Failure to do so might have led to the erosion of those societies' democratic instincts.

Democracy and the Regulation of the Economy in the Early 1990s
In a sense then, the deficit of democratic constitutionalism has been, inherent in the programme of reforms itself. Evidence from across CEE confirm this (Klingemann et al. 2006; Pogany 1993). The need to attract investors, hence to introduce stable economic regulation as quickly and efficiently as possible, was bound to create tension with the democratic imperative (Kolarska-Bobińska 1993: 302). The politically controversial choice of settling on the most extreme version of free-market doctrine might have deepened this tension even further. According to Gray, Poland has adopted the Anglo-American model of capitalism, which was the least suitable one, given the incompatibility of the free markets and the post-communist political institutions and culture (Gray 1993: 26).[21] One aspect of this incompatibility became clear early on: instrumental attitudes to law, and a *legocentric* belief that changing the law will be enough to achieve certain objectives such as economic growth and a flow of foreign investment. The prolific, yet chaotic output of the Sejm in first years of systemic reforms is indicative of both the above attitudes. Kolarska-Bobińska quoted a Polish MP as saying: 'The law is to serve us, to be for us. It is not that we are to serve the law. We are the makers of the law, and not its slaves' (1993: 304).[22] The overproduction of laws and regulations in Poland created a highly fragmented patchwork of legal rules, which do not amount to a legal system (Staśkiewicz 2009: 56), and whose quality was poor (Zirk-Sadowski 2006: 303). According to the media and academics, the proliferation of legal regulations in new Poland has reached elephantine proportions and created a 'legal crisis' (Kochanowski 2003: 79). Morawski further claimed that the lack of coherence and clarity make the law appear unpredictable and instrumental; they also undermine the democratic bases of legitimacy of law (1993: 19).

In line with Morawski, Zirk-Sadowski makes a direct link between quality of democratic discourse and the quality of legislature and legislation that such discourse leads to. He argues that only by improving the democratic process of articulation and communication of political, social and economic interests, the quality of legal acts can be improved. That is because the law represents a translation of those interests into legal categories: the clearer the expression of interest the better these are likely to be represented in legal acts (2006: 302). Consequently, by-passing the democratic process in the early 1990s for the sake of the efficient and quick establishment of a good-quality regulatory environment needed as a stimulus for the economy, produced at best mixed results.

---

21   Compare with Van der Pijl (2006) passim.
22   See also Morawski (1993) on instrumental use of law in Poland after 1989.

It is clear by now that the systemic reforms driven by economic imperative were not entirely effective in erasing old political and legislative practices such as instrumental uses of law, poor legislative technique, and overproduction of legal acts without considering the practicalities of their implementation driven by legocentrism. What also survived was the patronising attitude towards society based on the projection that society was going to evolve away from the passive *homo sovieticus* towards a more liberal species that would be less likely to fall for populist and possibly authoritarian politicians once it starts experiencing material prosperity. As discussed in Rose, Mishler and Haerper (1998: 178), a study by the New Democracies Barometer (NDB) of economic conditions and democracy in 135 countries seems to confirm this hypothesis, at least initially. Some of the key findings of this study identified a noteworthy influence of material conditions on the rejection of undemocratic alternatives, that is, the lower the household income, the greater the level of material deprivation and greater the likelihood of voting for undemocratic alternatives. However, Rose et al. point out that when political measures are added to the study, economic factors lose their dominance. Hence, the inevitable conclusion is that although economic attitudes exert some influence on political outlook, 'politics matters more' (Rose et al. 1998: 178). In light of this, it appears that even if the choice of the neo-liberal model for reforms has been highly controversial, on balance, it seems that more damaging for the long-term democratic revival was the undemocratic politics and the process of implementation of reforms, or the 'when and how' (Schmitter 2001: 4–5) that failed to activate and politically engage society. The initial high levels of support for democracy and democratic institutions[23] that occurred at constitutional moments of RTTs and the first phase of transitions have turned into a growing disappointment with democracy across CEE.

The Politics of Implementation of Reforms; the Role of Solidarność

As already argued, the implementation of reforms was the second 'constitutional moment' (Schmitter 1993: 5) in the early history of Polish transformation after the RTT. The political strategy of that moment defined the power relationship between the state and the people for years to come, particularly so, since it was the government that was primarily responsible for designing the new political and economic order. Even if the shape of this strategy was, in part, a result of pressure from money-lending institutions and guidance of Western advisers (Rose et al. 1998; Gołębiowski 1995), the final and most decisive were the policy choices of the Polish political elite, which included the top members and advisers of Solidarność. If there can be no doubt that the strategy chosen at that time by the political elites resulted in an undisputed success of delegitimisation of state

---

23   Sixty to 80 per cent of the ECE population accepted the idea of democracy (Miller, White and Heywood 1998: 143). Krzemiński and Śpiewak (2001: 69), arrived at similar results in relation to Poland.

socialism at the institutional level (rejection of command economy and single-party system), this was somewhat undermined by reverting to a *etatist,* or *statist* style of governance (Schöpflin 1993: 288–90; Kolarska-Bobińska 1993: 305) by the same elites.

A typical *etatist* feature of the new political order was the dogma of neo-liberalism underpinned by an idealised, utopian concept of democracy, which drove governmental policies, and projected society as an obstacle to the introduction of these ideas: 'a paradoxical situation arose in Poland in which social order that was to be based on grass roots initiatives and groups' self-organization was introduced from the top downwards with the passive consent of a part of society' (Kolarska-Bobińska 1993: 305; Zirk-Sadowski 2006: 299). Szacki argued that in part it was the eagerness to demonstrate the rejection of socialism, and everything even remotely related to it, that facilitated this ideological zeal (1994). Such demonstration was designed to convince the Poles that socialism was truly over, but also to prove to the West and the global financial institutions that there was no going back. In a sense, de-communisation was used as a political weapon to protect the policies of reforms against dissent or doubt as well as to demonstrate that Poland should be perceived as a haven for safe investment, deregulation and powerless trade unions.[24] In what is probably one of the greatest paradoxes of this time, Solidarność played a leading role in this process. Its 'unconditional commitment to whatever reform the new government chose to introduce' (Ost 2005: 53), pledged regardless of the impact of such measures on the interests of workers, can be interpreted as at attempt to pre-empt any possibility of being seen as a remnant of communism. In another ironic twist, Solidarność resorted to a communist-like strategy to achieve this goal. Why and how was this possible? And how can we understand the anti-labour stance taken by the leaders of Solidarność given their success in organising labour until 1989 within the tradition of semi-constitutional restraints initiated by KOR?

Ost (2005) provided probably the most comprehensive insight of how this happened, based on his thesis of the failure of the Solidarność leaders to organise worker's anger after 1989.[25] Ost is right in calling this failure 'a major political blunder' which was to have disastrous consequences for labour's ability to organise collectively within a framework of democratic mechanism of interests articulation, or in Ost's words 'emancipatory narrative of civil society' (2005: 191). Ost is also correct in stressing the role of the elites in shaping politics, but not entirely convincing in explaining the reasons behind the elites' failure to support grass-root democracy. Securing a stake in the post 4 June 1989 government and in the Sejm by Solidarność is clearly an important factor, but, I suggest, of limited

---

24   These conditions are already attracting foreign capital predominantly focused on short-term profit and minimising costs. See for instance Dziadul (2003), Orenstein (2009).

25   I do not entirely agree with the 'workers' anger' framework used by Ost, since at least at the beginning of the RTT the strong support for the imminent reforms and the high levels of trust in the Solidarność leadership tell a story of hope and positive mobilisation.

explanatory power. Committed democrats rarely shed their democratic clothes once they become part of the government. Unless their democratic convictions were skin-deep, which, I believe might have been the case.

Solidarność: Constitutionalism Versus Democracy

There is strong evidence of limited constitutionalism in the functioning of the political opposition stretching back to KOR and continuing throughout the 1980s. The RTT and the negotiated transition were possible partly thanks to the self-limiting strategies used by both sides of the political divide in Poland at the time. Some crucial elements of democracy, on the other hand, were largely absent from the modus operandi of Solidarność, already in the 1980s. In contrast to Ost, who links the demise of democracy within Solidarność to the changing perception of its intellectual leaders and advisers on labour and democracy which occurred in the mid-1980s, I suggest that Solidarność has hardly been democratic in its programme and internal functioning from the start. The origins of Solidarność go back to the opposition movement of the 1970s and to KOR, when the protection of workers' interests was the main objective, not the creation of a democratic state.[26] Neither in August 1980 nor in 1989, after its re-legalisation, was democracy a priority. Overwhelmingly, the main task of Solidarność was set by its leaders – who became increasingly alienated from the concerns of the rank and file – and that was the renewal of national identity and dignity based on the teachings of the Catholic Church (Koczanowicz 2004: 92). Hence, the role played by the Church and religion in inspiring workers to rise against the state and then the hijacking of this agenda by the Solidarność leaders, must be a part of any discussion of Solidarność's role in the first years of transition.

The Pope's visit in 1979 is widely seen as playing a vital part in bringing communism down, and crucial in inspiring the mass movement against the government.[27] It would be impossible experientially to verify those claims; however, the immense symbolic appeal of the Pope's pilgrimage, as evidenced by the massive crowds participating in the visit, cannot be denied. The Pope's sermons were constructed around such key phrases as solidarity, dignity, national and Christian revival – all of which formed the foundations of the Solidarność political programme. Wałęsa's visit to the Vatican in 1981 was also a manifestation of the movement's commitment to catholic values. Wałęsa himself, 'received by the Pope like a son' (Davis 2001: 365), cemented his position as a symbol of national and spiritual revival. The strong presence of catholic values has been on show in all the strike and protest actions in the1980s which entailed celebration of mass and singing of religious hymns (Koczanowicz 2004: 92). Such evidence supports the claim that Solidarność's core values and outlook were firmly rooted in the

---

26	As explained in section Constitutionalism before 1989, above.

27	According to CBOS (2009g: BS83) 78 per cent of Poles are convinced that the first visit of the Pope contributed to both the establishment of Solidarność and to freeing Poland from communism.

symbolic national and catholic identity. These values, rather than democratic ones, were to form the main substantive basis of national consensus. As suggested by Koczanowicz, Wałęsa's saying that 'two Poles will always find a way of reaching an understanding' (2004: 92) well illustrates this approach.[28]

This alleged weakness of democratic commitments of Solidarność might seem difficult to accept, since, undeniably, the mass character of the movement is irrefutable evidence of its democratic credentials (Koczanowicz 2004: 94). This was seized on by many scholars who related the re-emergence of the concept of civil society to Solidarność (Ost 2005: 3). However, this mass support for Solidarność could be also interpreted as a certain political capital of trust and social mobilisation that was just an initial condition for the establishment of more sustained democratic politics. By far more decisive was the way this enormous, but also fickle social/political capital had been steered by its leaders. And, on that score, the evidence overwhelmingly suggests that the Solidarność leadership showed many signs of constitutional restraint, but not much evidence of respect for democratic process. In some way the democratic neglect was forced on Solidarność by circumstances, but in part it was a matter of deliberate choice:

- by prioritising the nationalistic/religious framework, the concept of democratic engagement has been defined predominantly within the set of national/religious symbolism and unity in rallying around these symbols;
- the necessity to avoid confrontation with the state, backed at that time by the might of Russia's military power, meant that dissent and diversity of opinion had to be kept in check (Davis 2001: 16–17, 413). In the face of such powerful threats, Solidarność had to be organised around the trust in its leaders and respect for organisational hierarchy;
- the 'non-violence' doctrine preached by the Pope was taken seriously. This meant that avoidance of confrontation took priority over open, transparent negotiations.

All the above lead me to claim that the seeds of undemocratic practices so apparent at the RTT and in later developments were sown into the foundations of Solidarność's early existence. Deeper and more systemic reasons for the democratic ethos weaknesses relate to the utopian concept of democracy which the elites themselves propounded. This is in line with Schöpflin, who argued that

---

28   I believe that this argument holds despite the fact that Solidarność acted as an umbrella organisation, as it attracted a number of political orientations, and, as suggested by Davis, the restoration of traditional political parties was 'only a matter of weeks away' (2001: 158), before the Martial Law was declared in 1980. So, whether it was a matter of developments which would have eventually led to a democratic revival being cut short, or whether if was a matter of dominance of nationalistic, catholic values that did not encouraged democratic process, the result was similar: democracy has not been the top political objective of Solidarność.

'the postcommunist elites were themselves unable to deal with challenges and criticism; they tended to regard the normal workings of democracy as a hostile conspiracy rather than as a fairly routinised process of give and take' (Schöpflin 1994: 136).[29] In Heller's words

> In totalitarian times the ECE [CEE] intellectuals viewed democracy in a rosy light. It stood for perfect political order. By realizing that the new democratic order is imperfect, the answer is readily at hand: it is not democratic enough. (2000: 11)

If democratic politics and its 'disorder' and uncertainty were not easy to accept in other than predominantly formal, declarative manner, constitutionalism – in the sense of rules that regulate and limit the exercise of power – seemed much closely aligned with the political instincts of Solidarność leadership.

Instrumental Use of Democratic Discourse
There is practically no evidence that democratic support for the reforms has been sought either directly via public debate, or through party politics or the trade unions, including Solidarność. The introduction of the first package of reforms has not been debated, even with the experts.[30] Hausner noted that from the beginning, Balcerowicz took a stance against negotiation and social agreement. This has become a trademark of the government's attitude towards the democratic debate on reforms or the idea of social contract (Hausner 1992: 70–71). Such a stance attracted widespread criticism not just from academia but also from people and bodies connected with the government. Interestingly, the nature of the criticism from the government-connected group confirmed the existence of some of the pervasive faults in Polish politics – elitism, authoritarianism and lack of respect for democratic processes. Alongside statements condemning the lack of social consultation, however, these groups attributed a purely instrumental value to the social dialogue by depicting it as a socio-technical supplement to a programme of reforms that has no ready alternative anyway (Hausner 1992: 71).

The post-communist elites pushed the workers into positions of the 'played', not the players, on the assumption dictated by the devious logic comparable to that used by the communists seizing power after the second World War, that only the elites knew what was in labour's interest (Ost 2005: 58). As a result, in the process of taking crucial decisions on re-shaping the state at the RTT and in its aftermath, the workers were reduced to disempowered objects and treated 'as

---

29   Some scholars point to the fact that the Polish political elite originates predominantly from the intelligentsia, whose ethos stresses the notions of 'collective mission' and 'didactic role', concepts which go against the basic elements of democratic culture such as individualism, adversarial politics, participation and so on.

30   Bożyk (1997: 64), for instance, argued that the shock therapy, introduced spontaneously, without theoretical grounding or debate, led to a deep economic crisis.

a dangerous antidemocratic force with instinctively illiberal predilections' (Ost 2005: 190). Ost rightly concluded that the marginalisation of working people from the post-communist democratisation discourse, in which Solidarność played such a prominent role, is one of the most remarkable developments in the history of political sociology (2005: 18). The spectacular failure of Solidarność to listen to and represent workers' concerns in relation to rapidly growing poverty and economic want and to defend the workers' economic interest, alienated the movement from its rank and file and started its irreversible decline (Ost 2005: 53). In the long term, the likely effects of Solidarność's conduct, coupled with its unreserved support for neo-liberal market capitalism expressed in democratic language, was to forge an understanding of democracy as grounded in market economy and private property, rather than active, republican citizenship.

Capitalist system, socialist method?
The post-communist governing elites in 1989 and 1990, formed partly by the leaders of Solidarność, resorted to the communist matrix of leadership that bore many similarities to the ideological offensive carried out by the communists in the late 1940s.[31] Both types of approach amounted to the exclusion of society from the political process: the communists could not trust the people to vote for them, the post-communists were unwilling to let the people take part in political decisions which were, instead, to be taken by the politicians voted in by the people. Such exclusion was based on the assumption that Polish society was deeply conservative, closed in character, badly educated and hostile to democracy (Schöpflin 1994: 136), hence not fit to participate in a democratic process. This also signalled an authoritarian manner of 'doing politics' from the outset of systemic reforms. With the benefit of hindsight, this approach proved to be one of the strongest indications of the problems which were to haunt Polish politics in the next two decades, as it has reinforced, rather than eradicated, the socialist-like style of communicating with society by presenting decisions taken on behalf of the people as the only and the best way forward.

The policies that the post-communist elites were promoting and the trust and popularity that they still enjoyed sets them apart from the communists of 1940s. However, as argued above, the support for change in 1989 was driven strongly by the state of semi-revolutionary social mobilisation *against* the party-state, as well as by a positive political programme, which, although it remained weakly defined, it was rooted in the core demands for political freedom and the rule of law. Since the programme of change has been only gradually taking shape at the RTT and in the Sejm, such social mobilisation represented floating political

---

31   Szacki points out that the liberals, as did the communists in the 1940s, held a passionate belief in an idea and a deep conviction that their policies were in the best interest of the people. In addition, Schöpflin argued that the concept of society which the elites propounded was curiously like the one Marxists had put forward forty years earlier. (Schöpflin 1994: 130).

capital partly expressed as a high degree of trust in the politicians and leaders of Solidarność (Ost 2005: 58), and partly as a strong identification with the outline of the policies that were communicated to the people by using the rhetoric of 'democracy', 'freedom' and 'prosperity' (Ost 2002: 115–17).[32] By propounding the notion that the workers' participation in political decision-taking is dangerous to democracy (Przeworski 1986: 63; Ost 2002: 117, 2005), the elites might be accused of abusing their own legitimacy rooted in such trust. Their chosen strategy was one of pre-empting any opposition to the 'only and best' programme that, as it was assumed, soon would be positively verified by its own success.[33] That also meant speed in carrying out the reforms and the use of propaganda in rallying for support, an approach that earned it the label of 'new totalitarian temptation of Lesseferist variety' or bolshevism, according to Bugaj, the leader of one of the factions of Solidarność (Szacki 1994: 189). Moreover, as noted by Schöpflin, the omnipresent references to the dogma of free-market ideology and the labelling as democratic the authoritarian policy-making amounted to an imposition on society of the 'utopian, homogenizing and idealised concept of democracy' and the squandering of social trust (1994: 130).

Clear parallels that can be drawn between the political fallout of the communist and neo-liberal reforms – both excluded social participation, and neither saw the need for explanation or debate. Both were elite-driven, imposed on society from above and implemented by state bureaucracy; the possibility of democratic dissent was precluded. Both fed into and reinforced traditional, structural weaknesses of Polish political and social cultures, that is, their ritualistic character and ethos-based social relations where society is mobilised around symbols and rituals rather than interests. Both developments were characterised by a deep rift of hostility and alienation between society and the government, where only the appearance of due political process was upheld.

Politics of Reforms and Democratisation

Democratisation is not a self-contained topic in this discussion, but since it underpins the functioning of democratic constitutionalism, it should be given a short assessment in light of constitutional law and policy-making at the breakthrough of 1989/90. This section will discuss the impact of the politics of implementation of the first wave of systemic reforms on the social and political values relevant to democratisation. 'Democratisation' is used here in the sense of attitudinal and social consolidation, which goes beyond the creation of democratic institutions, and which is necessary for creating a long-term prospect for the effective functioning of democracy. One of the measures of this type of democratisation is the dominance of 'democratic frame of mind' in society, which

---

32   Compare with Herman and Chomsky (2002).

33   Compare with Bihari's thesis that capitalism itself might be the greatest threat to democracy (1991: 287).

has been recognised as crucial for long-term democratic prospects (Berglund et al. 2001: 29). In Ost's words, 'democracies need democrats' (Ost 2002: 65).

Participation in Politics

The party-state communist political system in pre-1989 Poland created mechanisms of intimidation and blackmail to secure participation in political events, including the elections and political rallies. Those strategies in effect annihilated 'public space' and resulted in the withdrawal of individuals into their private lives. Almost two decades after the collapse of the one-party political system the question must be asked whether the politics of transition had a positive effect on the willingness of people to engage in either political process or in civil society structures. I will focus on just two broad factors relevant to fostering a more participatory society: the level of social and political empowerment, that is, a sense of having influence on political and economic policies and attitudes towards the government.

Theoretically, the political freedoms established under the post-communist system such as freely contested elections and freedom of speech and association, should have led to a visible increase in political activity. And in some sense that was what happened. The number of parties and other political groupings rose rapidly and soon the whole spectrum of political views was represented on the Polish political scene. This polarisation and crystallisation of political views was, in a sense, a long-overdue process of political maturing of society and building up of a pluralistic political culture. However, these processes have failed to produce a more politically and socially engaged society. According to the research findings of Miller, White and Heywood (1998: 100), the change of regime produced a society that was *less participant* and *less satisfied with participation* than before 1989.[34] One reason for this might be that the majority of the mainstream parties were created from above, not by the grass-root movement. However, the decline in active participation in politics and civil society can hardly be explained in relation to party politics alone, since it extends to non-political organisations. Moreover, this state of 'uncivil society' (Miller, White and Heywood 1998: 100) does not correspond to the high support for democracy confirmed in a number of empirical data. Miller, White and Heywood also confirmed that the political values of ECE societies are not much different from the old established democracies like Britain.[35] So if the 'political values in CEE were part of the solution, not part of the problem' (Miller, White and Heywood 1998: 28), what was the problem?

---

34   Author's emphasis. The statistics are as follows: 63 per cent of people in CEE took less part in political life and 70 per cent took less part in non-political organisations (civil society structures) than under the communist regime.

35   Although their understanding of democracy and related ideas is certainly not the same due to different lived experience.

The Gap Between Society and the Governing Elites

I suggest, following a number of scholars (Hausner and Marody 2000; Kaldor and Vjevoda 1999; Mokrzycki, Rychard and Zybertowicz 2002), that part of the explanation lies in the problematic relationship between the governing and governed, shaped by specific history and tradition and also developments which took place after 1989. Such an argument finds support in, among others, Miller, White and Heywood (1998: 41–2), who stress the vital role of the historical experience that has shaped political culture at the popular level and at the level of political elites, in explaining the establishment and maintenance of democratic government. The character and behaviour of the Polish political elite can be partly related to the ethos of the gentry and intelligentsia and to the peculiar tradition of democracy, the so-called 'gentry democracy' (Gomulka and Polonsky 1990). Both the gentry and the intelligentsia have been credited with the survival of Polish culture and national identity under the partitions. The intelligentsia of the communist era (who originated mainly from the ranks of the gentry) continued this tradition. The charisma and reverence surrounding the intelligentsia found perhaps their clearest expression in the high percentage of votes that it received in the first Polish free elections of 1989. This high workers' support for the intelligentsia has been interpreted as a sign of alliance between the two. But, even if this was the case, its lifespan was very brief.[36] The political turn of 1989 and, in particular, the politics of the first years of systemic reforms, led to a breakdown of the co-operation between the workers and politicians, which was soon replaced by open hostility between the two. Since the mid-1990s, when the scale of social and political costs resulting from the introduction of market policies became visible, the workers started voicing their discontent. By then, however, the structures 'normally' used for protesting against government policies (the trade unions) were rendered in effect impotent (Ost 2002; Gardawski 2001). The great betrayal of workers by the elites had taken place (Ost 2005). As so often in Polish history, grass-roots interests were sacrificed for the elite vision of the state and society

This strategy was considered a betrayal of workers' trust, since the rhetoric of democratisation used by the politicians 'pushed Solidarność into support of a radical marketisation programme whose true social cost they [the ideologues] disguised in order to secure that support' (Ost 2002). Yet, the CEE politicians' economic views were more ultra-liberal than the CEE public and the public and politicians in Britain, as showed by Miller, White and Heywood (1998: 392).[37]

---

36   The political struggle against the communist regime throughout the era has been significantly weakened by this rift. Only the first phase of the Solidarność movement, in 1980 and 1981, is an exception. Unlike in 1968 and 1970, the two sides co-operated closely. Even if the events leading to the 1989 Round Table agreement were built on close alliance between the two camps, subsequent developments such as the open warfare between Wałęsa and the group of intellectuals (Michnik, Kuroń, Mazowiecki) destroyed this unity.

37   For instance, 99, 65 and 90 per cent of British politicians agreed that the government should be responsible for health care, employment and adequate housing, respectively, to

Their rejection of the welfare state, regulation of the economy and overwhelming commitment (or naïve enthusiasm) (Miller, White and Heywood 1998: 393) to privatisation were described as extreme even by British standards. After almost two decades, these do not show any signs of abating. The eruption of uncritical enthusiasm for Anglo-Saxon neo-liberalism also in popular and academic writings that started in early the 1990s continued throughout the next decade. Any attempt to critically discuss concepts such as the free-market or democracy, and any suggestions of political and economic alternatives were dismissed as 'populism, utopianism, and irresponsibility' (Żuk 2004: 48).

This type of naivety of the Polish political elites was not surprising given their lack of experiential knowledge of both the neo-liberal market system and democratic politics. What is, however more difficult to excuse is the elites' acceptance of extreme variety of free-market dogma, and an attempt to impose this dogma on society, as the best solution to Poland's economic and political problems. Such attitudes feed into the traditional traits of Polish politics – its elitism (we know best) and arrogance (forcing certain policy choices without understanding their nature). Both excluded the populace from participation in politics, but rallied for popular support using rituals and national symbols, creating in this way a façade of a democratic process.[38] Both led to the reinforcement of the schism between the governing and the governed (Mokrzycki et al. 2002: 139; Hausner and Marody 2000: 122), which was the hallmark of communist party-state years. At that time, however, opposition to the government fulfilled a much more positive role socially and politically, as it allowed to claim a high moral ground against the corrupt party-state regime.

The current social perception of state power as an alien outside force,[39] hostile and deceptive, is arguably more damaging in transition countries which are trying to rebuilt social trust in democracy and constitutionalism. What stands in the way is corruption, still relatively pervasive and common on central and local levels of public administration – as well as a growing lack of social discipline which leads to factiousness, particularisms and *liberum veto*. These phenomena have been deepened by the 'negotiative' pattern of political relations described by Mokrzycki et al.[40] 'Negotiative' politics employs techniques of placating selected interest

---

81, 30 and 40 per cent of politicians in CEE (Miller, White and Heywood 1998: 392).

38   See also Kowalik (2004) for an idea of oligarchic democracy, as an outcome of oligarchic-corrupt type of capitalism that has been established in Poland over the last two decades.

39   Liberals often see the mistrust of the state as a positive mechanism of democratic control of its powers, hence, as evidence of robustness of democratic control of state power. I do not think that this logic can be applied to the Polish situation where the immature democracy is yet to create a sense of governance which could be said to be representative or responsive.

40   This means the bypassing of constitutional mechanisms of articulation of interest that have been replaced by direct negotiations with the most powerful interest groups. Even though such dealings are clearly unconstitutional and illegal, the principle of 'negotiative politics' takes precedence over official policy of the state and the rule of law (2002: 141).

groups by, for instance, manipulations of state budget, random tax concessions and arbitrary application of Criminal Code; it sanctions unconstitutional and undemocratic dealings that have become inherent features of political life in Poland. Yet the minimum standards of propriety and morality in conduct of the government are not just a necessary part of the doctrines of democratic political system upholding the rule of law. Miller, White and Heywood's (1998: 29–30) 'democratic precedents' in government, which he saw as a necessary part of democratisation in CEE, are needed to prevent the 'normalising' effect of such behaviour on society by labelling it as not acceptable. The visibility of democratic precedents in CEE increased considerably since 1989, but it is all too often overshadowed by the party patronage, favouritism, and other malpractices that survived from the old era.[41]

Democracy and Constitutionalism After the Introduction of Reforms: A Summary

The discussion of constitutional moment of changing the political and economic system of the Polish state identified some of the root causes of the weakness of democratic constitutionalism. The neglect of democratic and social commitments within the agenda of economic reforms as well as the top-down, undemocratic manner of the politics of their implementation were partly responsible for the derailment of the democratic process within mainstream politics. By feeding into some of the existing weaknesses of Polish political and social cultures, the damaging effects of the first years of reforms led to the entrenchment of undemocratic practices and networks within the political process (Zybertowicz 2002). Annihilation of the mechanism of articulation and representation of interest through political parties and trade unions resulted in a syndrome of 'abandoned society'. Further entrenchment and institutionalisation of such weaknesses within the democratic process have led to a more permanent state of unconsolidated democracy as its dominating form.

The political capital of social mobilisation based on trust in individual politicians and the expected revival of democracy have turned into political disengagement and disillusion with both domestic politics and political leaders. The major steps on the road of changing the fundaments of the Polish state, which began with the strikes organised by Solidarność in August 1980, the RTT and the negotiation and introduction of the first packages of reforms, were carried out with

---

41   The most spectacular illustration must be the PiS take-over of most of higher managerial positions in central and local public institutions and state enterprises after its election victory in Autumn 2005, under the pretext of waging offensive against the '*uklad*'. The following positions were secured by the PiS for the party appointees: National Broadcasting Council, National Judicial Council, Ombudsman, the head of the Institute of National Memory, many positions in provincial governments across the country, management of state enterprises, and state radio and television, and state agencies. The scale of this take-over was similar the PUWP's system of nomenklatura appointments [Gwiazda 2008: 814–21].

observance of a quasi-constitutionalism that started developing in Poland after the signing of 1975 Helsinki Final Act, and KOR's appearance on the Polish political scene. Its main tenets were the self-restraint by both sides of political divide in the type of demands that were put on the negotiating table and responses to those demands. Yet, given the drift towards elitist and secretive decision-making at the RTT in which the first sets of systemic reforms was agreed, it is difficult to resist the temptation to draw a parallel with the tradition of Polish constitutionalism stretching back to the 3 May 1791 Constitution. Then, as in 1989/90, the rhetoric of saving the country took hold. The drafters of the 3 May Constitution pre-empted any possibility of dissent by misleading the political opposition as to the date of the final Constitutional debate. Different tools have been employed at the RTT, but the end result was the same – exclusion from the constitutional decision-making of the parties whose vital interest were at stake in the outcomes of such decisions.

Two decades ago, the governing elites, in a clear show of lack of trust in the society, negotiated a secret deal which was to have a dramatic impact of the lives of most people without allowing their views to be voiced and their interests represented. The quasi-constitutional constraints within which the RTT and the first reforms were introduced can probably be credited with preventing potential violent internal conflict and ensuring the self-limiting character of the transition. Whether the distrust of the democratic process and the by-passing of democratic constitutionalism, in the sense of popular participation in taking the core decisions, was a fair price to pay for such an outcome will never be known. Opinion polls suggested that 74 per cent of Poles believe that the RTT facilitated bloodless transition (33 per cent very positive and 41 positive) (CBOS 2009e: 8). What is certain is that the undemocratic introduction of the 1989/90 reforms squandered the political capital of that particular 'constitutional moment' and laid the foundations of political system that is neither entirely constitutional nor truly democratic. This conclusion links to the negative assessment in opinion polls of the functioning of democracy in Poland with the exclusion of society from political process and the little sense of political influence that people feel they have (CBOS 2009c: 12). The majority of Poles consider the two issues as the most important problems that Poland faces (Jarosz 2007: 53). The opinion poll in which 50 per cent of Poles declared that the opportunities that transition presented have not been fully realised (CBOS 2009b: 13), echoes these sentiments.

The main 'sins' of the Polish politics of reforms revealed in opinion polls not only overlap with, but seem to be rooted in systemic problems that were identified by politicians and scholars: badly functioning state's institutions, alienation of society from the governing elites, too high and not fairly shared costs of reforms, weaknesses in democracy and political scene, underdeveloped (or largely absent) civil society (Jarosz 2007: 54). The most detrimental, however, for the prospects of democratic development must be the growing popular disappointment with democratic institutions, as it might, potentially lead to disillusion with democracy itself – in a reversal of 1989, when political freedom and democracy were declared as most important values by the majority of Poles (Kolarska-Bobińska and Kucharczyk 2009: 7).

The Redrafting of the Polish Constitution: The Politics Behind the Process[42]

The April and December 1989 Amendments

The RTT not only sealed the agreement on introduction of reforms, but also gave the first impetus to the redrafting of the 1952 Constitution. Even if only some provisions agreed then found their way into the final text of the 1997, the political contract on power-sharing between the Party and Solidarność opened a new epoch in Poland's political history (Garlicki 2008: 18). The amendments of the Constitution promulgated in April and December 1989,[43] and other legislative measures taken at that time set Poland on a road of piecemeal constitutional change, culminating in 1997 with the new Constitution of 2 April. There is no need to re-trace in detail the process of constitution-making nor to analyse the substance of specific Constitutional rules, as this has been already done by many scholars: see for instance Gralczyk (1997), Brzeziński (2000), Sanford (2002), and Chruściak and Osiatyński (2001), Osiatyński (2003). Instead, I will focus on the politics behind the drafting and only its most relevant aspects for constitution-making from the point of view of democratic constitutionalism, that will allow to assess the political legitimacy of this process.

The first constitutional amendments of 7 April 1989 implemented some of the decisions taken at the RTT: a new electoral law guaranteeing 'legal pluralism' was passed; the Senat – the upper chamber of the Parliament – was restored, as was the office of the President. The powerful position of the President led Garlicki to point out that the powers of the President were potentially outside of the Sejm's control, putting a question mark over constitutional and democratic standards of this first attempt at re-writing the foundations of the state governance. Garlicki further suggested that these early amendments should be seen as a reflection of competing objectives of the two parties of the RTT, rather than an attempt to lay the foundations of the democratic state (2007: 18–20). Despite those issues, the amendments of 29 December, followed by the ones in March 1990, amounted to a complete redrafting of the first chapter of the Constitution, changing drastically

---

42   The discussion that follows is based on the Stenographic reports (Sprawozdania stenograficzne) from the sessions of the Sejm and the National Assembly Constitutional Committee between 1989 and 1997, available at http://orka2.sejm.gov.pl/Debata1.nsf., as well as on the first-hand account provided by Chruściak and Osiatyński (2001) – both authors had taken part in work of the Constitutional Commissions. The interpretations and arguments are my own.

43   For an outline and discussion of 'April Amendments', see for instance Garlicki (2008: 18–20); Brzeziński (2000: 83–7); Gralczyk (1997: 71–86).

the axiological and political foundations of the state. Poland has been defined as democratic rule of law state, based on the principles of social justice. New articles introduced the protection of private property; political pluralism; freedom to pursue economic activity as well as reactivated the local self-governance (Sejm 1989d). These attempts to patch up the 1952 Constitution did not lead to promulgation of a new Constitution, as it became clear that achieving this might take longer than initially anticipated and that a temporary constitutional document will be needed. All this led to the initiation of work on the Small Constitution announced on the 17 October 1992.

The Small Constitution of 1992

Serious problems appeared from the start: new rules of re-drafting the Constitution were needed, but the weak legitimacy of the Sejm – which was at first Party-dominated and then only 'contractual' before elections of 1991– meant that it was unclear who should be asked to draft them. One of the questions was whether to follow art. 106 of the 1952 Constitution, which conferred the constitution-making power on the Sejm, or whether to replace the Sejm with both chambers acting as National Assembly. The RTT agreement was silent on procedural constitutional rules. The uncertainty turned into an open conflict between the Sejm and Senat and led to the breakdown of communication between the two chambers. The main underlying reason for this schism, according to Chruściak and Osiatyński, and other scholars, was the Senat attempt to score political points, and to the avoid being 'used' as a legitimating force of the contractual Sejm, by co-authoring the constitution, yet not having enough control over its content (2001: 40–41). At the end, the two chambers drifted into working on the constitutional drafts through their respective Constitutional Commissions: a solution without legal base, but whose lack of legality was neither raised or questioned (Chruściak and Osiatyński 2001: 41).

In a curious twist, the Sejm, undemocratic at that time, behaved in a more democratic manner than the democratically elected Senat which rarely used expert opinions and mostly debated behind the closed doors. The Sejm, in contrast, opened the debates to experts. Both chambers failed to communicate with society – proceedings published specially for that purpose failed to give much sense of what was discussed, or why and by whom decisions were taken (Chruściak and Osiatyński 2001: 43). Emphasis on the symbolic role and meaning of the constitution dominated the proceedings. One of the objectives was to have a complete draft of the new constitution ready for the 200 anniversary of the 3 May Constitution and for the next Pope's visit which was to take place in June 1991. Chruściak and Osiatyński suggested that the new Polish constitution was to be a 'constitution for the Pope' [*konstytucja dla Papieża*] (2001: Chapter 2).

It certainly looked this way at the time, given the Senat's Commission manner of working closely with Catholic Church authorities. Visits to the primate, Józef Glemp, and inviting bishops to take part in the work of the Commission became part of its modus operandi. The reverence of Senators for the Church resulted in Byzantine situations where the debate was stifled or halted as senators did not dare to speak after the Bishops (Chruściak and Osiatyński 2001: 46–57). The Pope sent letters blessing the Senat's Constitutional Commissions, and the Senat's leader participated in the Conference of the Polish Episcopate. The final draft of the constitution was submitted to the National Assembly and the Polish Primate. Curiously, the Senat's draft was not submitted to a vote, and was accepted only by a resolution. This can be seen as a pragmatic step taken due to an increasing polarisation of views and the realisation that the majority, needed to pass the draft, would be impossible to secure. Alternatively, this can be interpreted as a political manipulation, aimed to achieve a designed outcome regardless of procedural impropriety.

The Senat's work on the new constitution in both process and substance reflected the changed political face of Solidarność[44] that became clearly visible in the mid 1990s and was represented by a decisive turn towards the Church and religious values (Ost 2005: 66, 84–6). The Sejm, which only after the Autumn of 1991 elections could claim full legitimacy, produced a draft that was impossible to reconcile with the Senat's.[45] This has created another constitutional headache, since there were no rules in place on who should take responsibility for finding a compromise between the two drafts, not an easy task, especially since the two chambers of the National Assembly remained in a state of 'war'. In effect, the work of both chambers on the drafts was wasted, as only very few aspects of the texts have been used for the drafting of the Constitution of 1997.

The work on the Small Constitution stayed within the RTT paradigm of imposing limits on state power and the neglect of democracy-building. The suggestions of academics such as Gwiżdż to involve society in the preparation of the constitution by publishing the first draft and generating a public debate were defeated by the National Assembly. The Act that established the drafting procedure and the manner of promulgation the Constitution, was passed in April 1992. It limited the role of society to the right of vote in the national referendum, leaving the substantive decision on the content of constitution to the specially established Constitutional Commission (CC), comprising forty-six MPs and ten Senat members (Sejm 1992). The work of the new CC received scant attention in the press and media. On the whole, the few meetings between the members of the CC and the public failed to raise issues related to the Constitution. Instead, these were used as occasions for ritualistic celebrations rather than discussions about the details of constitutional arrangements. Chruściak and Osiatyński conceded that the debate on the Constitution has been very limited, and amounted to a lost

---

44   Out of the one hundred Senators, ninety-six were elected from the Solidarność supported list.

45   For texts of both drafts, see for instance Kallas (1992).

chance to educate the public in constitutional matters (2001: 73).[46] If the public ignorance of constitutional matters is problematic, but not unusual, the same cannot be said about the lack of awareness of the drafters. Yet, that precisely was the case with the Polish MPs and Senators in the CC. They refused to acquire a degree of understanding of constitutional doctrine even when that was offered, and also rejected the use of expert opinions and reports in their work.[47] Osiatyński commented, 'The Constitution become divisive, did not teach any lesson to anybody and it did not work' (2003: 267).

Individual Rights and Freedoms

The re-drafting of constitutional provisions on individual rights and freedom has not been treated with the same urgency as other constitutional matters (Winczorek 2000: 213). Only the 1997 draft of the final document contained a revised section dealing with rights and freedoms. That meant that for the first eight years of systemic reforms, sections of the 1952 Constitution on fundamental rights were still applicable. There were some limited reforms: the April and December 1989 constitutional amendments amounted to ridding the text of remnants of the party-state system by introducing a general provision guaranteeing rule of law, democracy and describing the nation as a source of political power; shortly after the RTT, the Sejm passed a series of laws introducing the very basic political rights such as freedom of association, the right to form political parties, as well as changing some of the most politically repressive provisions of the Criminal Code (Sejm 1989a).

Poland acceded to the European Convention of Human Rights in 1992. In the same year, Wałęsa introduced in the Sejm his 'Charter of Rights and Freedoms'. At the time, the Charter sparked a lively debate, mainly among the experts, which, in part, became a polemic about the very shape of Poland's future economic system and direction of reforms.[48] The neo-liberal lobby supported by the Western advisers argued strongly against social, positive rights being included in the Constitution

---

46   Compare with Winczorek, who states that the process of constitution-making in Poland was open and inclusive since 'numerous non-governmental organizations, the Catholic Church, other churches and religious organisations participated in the work of the Constitutional Commission', only to contradict this by observing that 'constitution-making process was conducted in an atmosphere of societal indifference and insufficient knowledge among the public' (2000: 212).

47   According to Chruściak and Osiatyński, the publication of the Bulletins of Constitutional Commission – which were invaluable as sources of information on the theory and practice of constitution-making directly relevant to the issues which needed to be solved – have not been read by the MPs and Senators (2001: 73 and 76).

48   This was a recurring theme in the debates on the amending, and later drafting of the new Polish constitution. See Sprawozdania stenograficzne z prac Sejmu 1 i 2 kadencji, i Komisji Konstytucyjnej [Reports of from the sessions of the Sejm of 1st and 2nd term and the Constitutional Commission] available at: www.sejm.gov.pl.

(Elster 1995; Gralczyk 1997: 157–65; Brzeziński 2000: 121–2; Schwartz 2000: 63–6). That went against the overwhelming views of the Poles, whose preference for social equality and welfare support have remained very strong (CBOS 1994a; CBOS 1994b).[49]

In the end, the catalogue of individual rights included in the 1997 Constitution is generally considered generous, and includes several positive economic and social rights, particularly art. 64–76 (Sejm 1997a). However, many provisions are not self-standing, and referrals to implementing legislation do not always define the parameters and principles which such legislation needs to respect. In addition, the enforcement of constitutional rights is weak; only the judicial review type of action in the Constitutional Tribunal is allowed (see Chapter 4), as is a complaint to the Ombudsman. The inadequacy of these provisions is reflected in the very high volume of Polish cases lodged at the European Court of Human Rights in Strasbourg.[50]

Wałęsa's Charter of Rights itself fell victim to party politics and work on it was terminated in 1993 after several meetings of the Special Parliamentary Commission. Particularly contentious was the class of individual rights underpinned by ethical and moral values, such as rights of the unborn child, discrimination based on sexual orientation and family rights. Interestingly, the Charter has been taken out of the normal constitutional procedure, which meant that only the Sejm and the Senat could propose changes and that a referendum was not needed for the promulgation of the Charter. Yet, as the name of this document suggests, the Charter should be seen as the most relevant part of constitutional regime from an individual's point of view. Consequently, the almost total exclusion of the people from having a say in the amendments, or even by the limited means of a vote in a referendum, amounted to one of the most blatant disregards for some of the basic principles of democracy and the rule of law. As a result of the Charter's failure, Poles got their catalogue of rights and freedoms only when the 1997 Constitution was enacted. Such a delay is, to some extent, understandable, under the condition of 'rebuilding the ship at sea'. That is, accepting that fundamental reforms of the political and economic system should have taken priority over issues of rights for individuals. However, treating this area of constitutional provision as *the lowest* on the list of priorities for almost a decade can be interpreted as an indictment of a state which has been propelled to a democratic plane by the people whose democratic constitutional rights have been, thus, neglected.

---

49   See also Sejm (1994a, 1994b) for examples of debates in the Sejm on this controversial issue.

50   Data for Poland: in 2009 – total judgements 634, pending applications 3516, violations 551. Compare this with France 740, 2421, 556; Germany 136, 2488, 81 respectively. Given that both Germany and France have been members of the Council of Europe since 1950, the data for Poland mean that the Poles suddenly became very litigious or that domestic human-rights protection is poor.

Path to the 1997 Constitution: Democratic and Constitutional?

It is clear that the democratic standards, in the sense of allowing direct involvement of constituent power in the drafting of the constitutional amendments of the early 1990s and the Small Constitution of 1992, were observed only ritualistically. The drafts were neither well publicised nor were time and opportunities created for people to have their say. In contrast to this view, some commentators blamed the slowdown in the work on the Constitution on the fact that there was *too much democracy* in the NA, which led to too much diversity of the interests at play (Geremek 1996). Contrary to Geremek, I doubt whether some of the events which contributed to a number of conflicts and parliamentary battles such as the war between the Sejm and the Senat or Wałęsa's 'acceleration'(*przyśpieszenie*) could, indeed, be understood as a democratic struggle between competing political interests. I suggest that it would be difficult to ascribe democratic quality to such interests, as the political groupings in the Sejm and Senat at the time could hardly be considered as representing anything much else beyond their own party/group interests. I develop this point later under the 'Political parties' subheading.

Equally problematic will be to agree with, for instance, Brzeziński, who suggested that the power holders were committed to the principle of rule of law and carefully followed constitutional procedure (2000: 105). We have already established the lack of both, the knowledge or experience of democratic constitutionalism of the National Assembly tasked with drafting the new constitution – as evidenced by the lack of clarity of setting the initial rules of constitution-making and in rejection of experts' opinions and reports. Not surprisingly, there were many documented instances where even the most fundamental principles of constitutional doctrine and procedure were misunderstood, misapplied or simply bent (Gralczyk 1997; Chruściak and Osiatyński 2001; Wołek 2004). Gralczyk observed 'In constitutional and political practice (of even the most successful constitutional democracies) only rarely the formal rules are followed to the letter. However, the divergence between constitutional law and practice rarely is as extreme as it was the case in Poland between the establishment of Tadeusz Mazowiecki's government and the passing of constitutional amendments in December 1989' [*Nigdy się nie zdarza, by formalnie (określone konstytucją i najważniejszymi ustawami) ramy ustrojowe wystarczały do opisania reguł życia politycznego toczącego się w tychże ramach. Rzadko jednak rozbieżność pomiędzy prawem konstytucyjnym a praktyką konstytucyjną jest tak wielka, jak było w Polsce, w okresie pomiędzy utworzeniem rządu Tadeusza Mazowieckiego we wrześniu a nowelizacją konstytucji w grudniu*] (1997: 82).

This lack of respect for constitutional procedure, which continue beyond the initial, and probably most extreme phase described by Gralczyk, needs to be seen against the background of a highly fragmented and unsettled political scene. The first freely elected Sejm of Autumn 1991 illustrates this fragmentation – twenty-nine different parties and groups were represented. The election of Autumn 1993 partly remedied this by introducing a five per cent threshold which limited the number of political groupings represented to seven, but this did not eliminate the political instability, as evidenced by the three changes of government in 1993 and in 1994. To appreciate more fully the impact of the weakness of polity, further factors need to be added: most political parties and groups have been established by the former Solidarność leaders and small groups of their supporters. Such top-down imposition of political structures of interest representation meant that those leaders represented mainly themselves and their narrow group interests – they did not have to worry about being accountable to their electorate – which, due to the almost complete absence of an electoral base, simply did not exist in the standard meaning of this term.[51]

1997 Constitution: Legitimacy of the National Assembly

The perils of entrusting constitution-making to the National Assembly resurfaced yet again in 1993.[52] After the Autumn 1993 elections, the Sejm and the Senat were less fragmented than previously due to the introduction of the five per cent threshold, but less representative, as many of the smaller parties/groups failed to win seats. Hence, questions of legitimacy were raised again. Partly to alleviate such concerns, the invitation to take part in the debate and to submit drafts were extended to national trade unions and religious organisations (Sejm 1994d). This was an improvement on the first legislation on the procedure for preparing the new constitution which listed only three types of subject with a right to submit drafts proposals: the Constitutional Commission, the fifty-six members of National Assembly and the President of the Republic (Sejm 1992: art. 2). Smaller or regional parties and groups were to be kept in the information-exchange loop by the Constitutional Commission. Altogether this amounted to eleven political parties, sixteen national trade unions and eleven religious bodies (Chruściak and Osiatyński 2001: 225). All in all, it took a handful of amendments to both the Statute of the Procedure for Amending the Constitution [*Ustawa o Zmianie Konstytucji Polski Rzeczpospolitej Ludowej*] (Sejm 1992), and the Rules of Procedure [*Regulamin Zgromadzenia Narodowego*] (Sejm 1994c) to rectify some of the most blatant shortcomings. In the final version, the Rules of Procedure

---

51   In the 1990s, one of the most fundamental problems, as observed by many commentators, was the lack of grounding of political parties in society (Hausner 1992: 66; Urbański 1994: 132). That was the case even with Solidarność. Many of the leading parties did not have local branches for years after 1989.

52   Compare with Holmes and Sunstein, who argued that political infighting in the National Assembly, or the politicisation of Constitution-making 'was the result of a need for public legitimation', otherwise difficult to achieve 'of a constitutional revolution delivered unexpectedly from abroad' (1995: 380). I suggest that the lack of representativeness of the political parties and their unwillingness to involve the people in debates of constitutional matters challenge this argument. Since the parties represented mainly their own interests, and not that of their electorate, this process falls short of what can be considered as 'public legitimation' of constitutional revolutions.

provided that the Constitutional Commission would be sitting in public. It also allowed the organisations/trade unions which submitted drafts to take part in the sessions and to participate in the debate (art. 7. s. 4). The reports of Constitutional Commission were to be made public (art. 9 s. 3), and the sessions open to the public and the media (art. 23).

Those provisions aimed at demonstrating the legitimacy of the Constitutional Commission, but had a limited effect of the actual procedure, as they failed to placate those political parties which did not win any seats in either chamber of the National Assembly. Those parties refused to participate in the works of Constitutional Commission, and created their own Constitutional Commission outside the National Assembly, claiming that as a result of the September 1993 elections, 35 per cent of the electorate was not represented in the National Assembly. Even if the 'beyond the Parliament' status of this grouping meant that their participation in Constitution-making would have been illegal, its existence sparked a debate which led to the amendment allowing for submission of the citizens' drafts (1994d). More significantly, the very existence of this grouping re-opened the question of legitimacy of the Parliament in its role as constitution-making National Assembly and the thorny question of the society's more direct involvement in constitution-making.

One of the most fundamental and primary issues, which has not been satisfactorily tackled and which combines the question of representation and empowerment in constitutional matters, was whether the Parliament elected in the course of party-political competition should also be given the task to draft the new constitution.[53] Such an issue would not have been raised by Bellamy, for whom everyday democratic politics is at the core of constitutionalism (2007: 8). However, the exceptional conditions of Poland's polity at the beginning of the 1990s must be factored in any discussion of this kind. It was not just a matter of the change in electoral law that impaired the Parliament's representativeness by introducing the 5 per cent threshold. Much more significant was the *degree of representativeness* that political parties could have reasonably asserted, as well as the willingness and their ability to rise above their party interests and political squabbles of everyday politics. There is sufficient evidence to suggest that the political parties in existence in Poland in the 1990s would have failed on most of these scores. Factors such as the mode of establishing the parties from above meant that most failed to develop a grass-roots base and mechanisms of interests articulation and representation. Another reason was that the 'new parties emerged as a result of personal conflicts, animosities, and ambitions, rather than differences of ideas, programs, or interests' (Osiatyński 1993: 315). For the vast majority of party activists, politics is a career, not a kind of public service, hence they rarely notice preferences of their electorate. Even today parties are elected

---

53   Compare with Elster, who stated 'The most important is perhaps that to reduce the scope for institutional interests, constitutions ought to be written by specially convened assemblies and not by bodies that serve as ordinary legislatures' (1995: 395).

on the popularity of their leaders rather than on attractiveness of their political programmes. All in all, the idea of entrusting constitution-making to a Parliament rather than a constitutional convention specially elected for this purpose is bound to be seen as controversial in most cases, but, in the specific conditions of Poland's early transition, this seemed like a recipe for allowing party-interest politics to dominate this process. And that seems indeed the closest to the reality of the 1997 Constitution-making. Arato confirms similar problems across the CEE:

> As these parliaments are deeply involved in the processes and conflicts of ordinary politics, and are in the position to tailor constitutional requirements to party political needs […] it is indeed an open question whether such bodies can generate democratic legitimacy for the constitutions they produce. (1992–93: 680–81)

During the first phase of work on the new constitution the Parliamentary debates focused on addressing the perceived problems with National Assembly legitimacy by mooting the idea of pre-referendum that later led to the the the amendment of 22 April (Sejm 1994c), allowing for submission of the citizens' draft. Chruściak and Osiatyński described this outcome as an 'exemplification of time wasted on quarrels only seemingly related to the constitution' [*Znowelizowana ustawa, która tego dnia weszła w życie, stanowiła niemal symboliczną egzemplifikację traconego czasu i zbędnych sporów, tylko pozornie związanych z nową konstytucją*] (2001: 239–40). Osiatyński commented further 'In fact, however, politicians used the referendum campaign for a constitution to win support for their own parties rather than to solidify a constitutional compromise' (2003: 267).[54] Clearly then, the real struggle that was taking place under the veneer of constitution-making was the competition for votes and popularity between the parties and promotion of the parties' political interests.

The next section is organised around three themes that emerged as problematic from the 1997 Constitution-making: the citizens' involvement in the process, the power brokers behind the process, and the perceived and real legal and political impact of the final text.

The Pre-referendum and the Citizens' Draft of the Constitution

The debates that took place in the National Assembly and in the Constitutional Commission indicate that two mechanisms of involving citizens in constitution-making were considered: the pre-referendum and allowing for the submission of the Citizens' draft of the constitution. No other ways of facilitating such involvement have been seriously considered. The debate on the pre-referendum went on for over two years, and the idea was finally rejected on 21 June 1996. However, the

---

54   See also Gonenc, who suggested that one of the causes of the 'tragic result in the referendum […] was the over-politicization of the referendum campaign' (2002: 133).

choice of proposed questions that should be asked was interesting: these were mostly related to the core issues of the division of governmental powers and the acceptance of the Senat. Those matters that were likely to affect the electorate more directly, such as individual rights and freedoms, the place of Catholic Church and religion in political life or abortion rights were not included (Sejm 1994e).Yet, the opinion polls confirmed that clearly prioritised by the respondents were the latter type of issues over the former (CBOS 1998: 7–9). In any event, the usefulness of a pre-referendum would have been limited partly due its nature and the narrow scope of the issues that could have been covered. In addition, there was a danger of party popularity context taking over any public debate of that sort.

The idea of allowing for a citizen's draft to be submitted was first introduced by Wałęsa under the pressure of the political groupings that were not represented in the Sejm. The National Assembly passed a motion allowing for such submission in April 1994. The citizens' draft was to replace, in a sense, the failed pre-referendum (Sejm 1994c). It was presented by the MP Gwiżdż (Sejm 1994f) as a more effective way of involving society in the process of constitution-making. The threshold of 500 000 signatures needed for a citizens' draft seemed rather high in a society barely able to self-organise in the wake of being betrayed by the Solidarność leaders (Ost 2005). After all, this was a society that has just emerged from an era where the choice between centrally organised parties and dissident activity created a syndrome of escape into privacy. Moreover the time-scale was tight, the draft needed to be submitted within tree months from the date that the 1994 Act came into force, that is by 6 September 1994. Not surprisingly, only one draft emerged, that of the independent trade union Solidarność, which had been in preparation from December 1993, and which became known as the 'Citizens' draft'.

Despite the success of the signature-collecting action – more than 950,000 signatures were obtained – the extent to which this draft should have been seen as actually reflecting the wishes of the citizens is not entirely clear. Two factors in particular support such a suggestion – the very low knowledge of the draft content in society, and the active involvement of the Church in promoting it. I start with the first factor. In the opinion poll testing knowledge of the draft conducted in February 1997 only 6 per cent of respondents declared very good or good degree of such knowledge. In March 1997, another opinion poll asking the same question found that on a scale of 1 to 7, where 1 indicated no knowledge and 7 indicated good knowledge of the draft, the overall score for the Citizens' draft was 1.83. These findings allowed the pollsters to conclude that among politically engaged people the degree of awareness of what the draft contained was very low (CBOS 1997a: 6–7). If we factor in the politically passive citizens who were among the signatories, the score will be even lower.

The second factor that influenced the level of support for the Citizens' draft was the active involvement of the Catholic Church in its promotion. A number of bishops publicly pledged their support, and instructed the parish priests to do the same. Both *Gazeta Wyborcza* and *Rzeczpospolita* reported on this. The action of collecting signatures has been conducted mainly in Churches (Gralczyk 1997:

152–3). This level of Church involvement in promoting the Citizens' draft should come as no surprise given that this project contained a high number of regulations that clearly originated within the ranks of the Polish Catholic Church hierarchy. None of the other drafts submitted to the Constitutional Commission went as far in promoting the right to life from conception to natural death, the right to religious education in public schools, and placing natural law on top of the hierarchy of sources of law. The preamble contained purely religious *invocation Dei*. Marian Krzaklewski, Wałęsa'a successor as the leader of Solidarność, when presenting the draft to Constitutional Commission re-stated that the preamble refers to the Christian concept of man and society, but rejected the claim that a constitution based on such foundations will only be inclusive of Christians. In contrast, according to him, Christian values are the most humanitarian and inclusive, essential in any authentic democratic order, and fundamental in any concept of natural and indivisible human rights. Krzaklewski went on to distinguish three types of values underlying the draft: 1) Christian, based on the social teaching of the Catholic Church, 2) patriotic and national and 3) social values rooted in social rights of the citizens. He concluded his speech by stating that this should be the constitution for the Pope (Sejm 1994f).

The catholic-clericalism of Solidarność espoused by Krzaklewski led to increasing alienation of Solidarność rank and file from its leadership. Ost (2005) suggested that Solidarność betrayed the workers and alienated the middle classes and intelligentsia, hence lost the legitimacy to act as representative of those parts of electorate. The Church never possessed such legitimacy in the first place[55] since the Poles consistently express a strong disapproval of the Church's involvement in politics.[56] Hence, the heavy involvement of the Church in promoting the draft and shaping its content, and the negligible level the Poles familiarity with the draft makes it difficult to see this document as *Citizens' draft* in much more than its title.

Power Brokers Behind the Constitution: The Church

In contrast to the weak public engagement in Constitution-making, and in constitutional politics more generally, the Catholic Church's role can be described as strong and often authoritative. This does not come as a surprise, as it fits with the more general picture of the Church's powerful influence on Polish politics during the last two decades, depicted by Michnik as totalitarian in substance, in the sense of trying to impose a 'clean vision of the world' (1995: 655) and

---

55	The Church hierarchy claimed that it often needs to 'step in' in voicing opinions on public matters due to the weak civic engagement of the Poles (Mazurkiewicz 2003: 202–3). This clearly amounts to the usurpation of the power to represent the Poles.

56	Opinion polls consistently evidence the opposition of the Poles to the substantial political engagement of the Church, which, despite this, does not show any signs of abating (Gazeta Wyborcza 2010; Szostkiewicz 2010).

authoritarian/insidious in form.[57] Historically, the Church's active presence on the Polish political scene has been the most enduring and continuous of any public institution. Even after WWII, with the ascent of an inherently anti-religious communist state, the Church was the most powerful power broker outside the structures of the PZPR (Polish United Worker's Party). Given the mass support that the Church enjoyed, in democratic terms, the Church clearly outpaced the Party in moral and also political standing in Polish society, becoming the 'most powerful institution in the country' (Eberts 1998: 817).

This powerful position the Church retained, and in some respect built up, through the upheavals of drafting the 1997 Constitution. By then, the initially open political activism of the Church during the Round Table talks and in the early 1990s, was replaced by a more secretive, if no less effective, participation in state politics.[58] As noted above, not only were the Church's representatives invited to take part in the works of Constitutional Commission, the drafts were sent to the Pope and the Primate for consultation and approval.

It was mainly in the manner described by Eberts as secretive, manipulative and instrumental (1998)[59] that the Church succeeded in forcing numerous changes of law and policy after 1989 (Sadurski 2008: 24). No public debates were held on the issues forced by the Church and the basic legal procedures and constitutional process were frequently breached, with Parliament often by-passed altogether.[60] Curiously, the CCRP's challenges of legislative decisions clearly driven by the Church agenda, and, arguably, breaching the rule of law, were dismissed by the Constitutional Tribunal (Gowin 1995: 142–3). Even the Sejm was overruled by the CT's judgement on abortion, which, in effect, endorsed the Church's position, but went against public opinion (CBOS 1998). Although the Church was less successful in installing its own candidates in the Polish Sejm, the eagerness of the decision makers to appease the Church's leaders more than compensates for this in ensuring the Church's influence in shaping law and policy. It is widely accepted

---

57   For an overview of the role of the Catholic Church in Polish politics, see Eberts (1998).

58   The attempts by the Church to openly engage in politics have been badly received by the Poles, who in the early 1990s voted overwhelmingly against the Church's political role (only 38 per cent of Poles were happy with public role of the Church in 1993, a drop from 90 per cent in 1989/90). Since 1995 this percentage was rising steadily to reach 68 per cent objecting to the Church's involvement in politics by 2002 (Mazurkiewicz 2003).

59   The true cost to the taxpayer of Church privileges – such as subsidies to Church schools and educational institutions, subsidies and maintenance of Church buildings and works of art – is not widely known or publicised. Sadurski (2008: 23) raised the issue of the allocation of 20 and 40 million złotych in 2006 and 2007 for the building of the Temple of Gods Providence [*Świątynia Opatrzności Bożej*] in state budget as against constitutional values and norms: 'Współfinansowanie tego przedsięwzięcia z budżetu państwowego nie jest uprawnione z punktu widzenia wartości i norm konstytucyjnych.' [Co-financing of this endeavour from the state budget is against the constitutional norms and values.]

60   For instance, the teaching of Catholic religion in public schools was introduced by Ministerial Instruction.

that the Church exercises influence through unofficial links with political parties, some of which adjusted their platform to conform to the views of the Church (Derleth 2000: 297).

From a constitutional-theory point of view such a manner of participation in political life fits with Loewenstein's concept of the 'invisible, non-official and non-legitimate power holders' (1965: 16). According to this theory, the reality of the power process suggests the existence of the official, legitimate, visible power holders (the Government, Parliament, the Courts and the electorate) and those 'that influence the power process unofficially, indirectly, and often extra-constitutionally – the unofficial and invisible power holders' (1965: 14). The discovery of such power holders can be accomplished only by 'analysis of the reality of the power process' (1965: 16). I suggest that the evidence presented above is sufficient to claim that the Catholic Church in Poland is the invisible power holder.[61] Direct statements in the academic literature further reinforce this claim:

> The voice of the Church has always been an important one in Poland and [...] usually has considerable influence on Citizens' attitudes and it also exerted such influence on the manner of adopting the Constitution and its contents. (Winczorek 2000: 214)

As suggested above, such influence on constitutional politics might be considered a breach of the rule of law and also of basic principles of democratic constitutionalism. What makes this situation even more problematic is that, in specific Polish conditions, an effective legal remedy to challenge such breaches might not always be available given the poor record of the Constitutional Tribunal.[62] In light of this, the expectations articulated by Walker (2003: 383) and Weiß (2005: 11), that 'the constitutional courts of the new member states might gain an important role' and that the new constitutional development might take place – one that will be less tied to vested national and institutional interests – took some bashing. The Polish Constitutional Court's clear support for the entrenched Catholic values, indirectly upholding the institutional power of the Catholic Church, amount to a strong re-assertion of both national and institutional interests, contrary to the suggestion of both authors.

The political influence of the Catholic Church in Poland might not be that unusual in comparison with Churches and religion in other countries.[63] According to Habermas, the recent growth of the influence of religion over public opinion can be explained by the increasing split over 'value conflict in need of political

---

61   Compare with Holmes and Sunstein (1995: 305), who recognised the potential danger of non-democratic sources of legitimacy, such as the traditional Catholic Christianity, that might threaten to eclipse democratic ones in legitimating the governments in CEE.

62   Sadurski described the striking down of a liberal abortion statue in May 1997 as 'the most outrageous and illiberal decision of any constitutional court in the region' (2003: 162).

63   See further Madeley and Enyedi (2003).

regulation (2008: 64). However, troubling are not just the scope and extent of the Church influence but the manner of their transmission: secretive, handed down as a non-negotiable dogma, not to be subjected to any debate. These diktats often lead to formation of policies that challenge the foundation of constitutional state, as they affect fundamental rights of individuals and society's core values. Some of those that seem to become entrenched are the following: Church's success in excluding its activities from the jurisdiction and oversight of the state[64] (Burnetko 2008); covert fusion of the agenda pushed by the Church with the political stance of decision-makers;[65] the ease of by-passing not just the public and the courts, but also often the Sejm in pushing through policy measures that are either fundamentally unconstitutional, or which facilitate unconstitutional practices. One of the most obvious is a threat to the religious neutrality of Poland and the separation between the Church and the state guaranteed in art. 25 of the 1997 Constitution. So is the provision of equality of all religions in Polish state. No other religious figures, apart from the Catholic Church dignitaries, took part in preparing the drafts of the 1997 constitution. The Citizens' draft of the constitution has been endorsed by Catholic parish priests, who coordinated a signature collection. Publicly endorsing certain political formation and influencing political choices of the parishioners by spiritual blackmail and religious threat has become a firm part of the daily worship of the Catholics. Even the recent Presidential elections after the plane crash in Smoleńsk on 10 April 2010 were accompanied by a political campaign conducted in Catholic Churches across the country (Szostkiewicz 2010). Only the Catholic religion is taught in public schools and only Catholic priests are employed as teachers, in police stations, fire services and hospitals: paid from the public purse. That such positions exist and in which numbers has never been made public, nor has the huge financial burden that these wages represent for taxpayers (Siedlecka 2010e).

Some commentators write about the bargains that the political elites and the Church entered into that might help to explain why such law- and democracy-defying conduct is allowed to continue: in return for calming the social mood in the early 1990s, the Church secured the restrictive abortion legislation; in return for endorsing the Constitution – it got the Concordat; for its support of joining the EU – the Church's estates were returned (Janicki and Władyka 2009). Even if the precise reasons for the current status quo are not entirely clear, there is a broad

---

64 Only recently some of the instances of the Church's fraudulent dealings were uncovered. See for instance: Kursa (2010), Kursa, Pietraszewski, and Skowrońska (2010), Kursa, Czuchnowski, Pietraszewski (2010) and Wiśniewski (2010).

65 More general evidence of such influences are the frequent audiences with the Pope, public declarations of faith, participating in mass, allowing crosses in most public buildings, inviting priests and bishops to most state and local events to bless new public buildings, projects and so on, pilgrimages of the voivodes to Jasna Góra, Suchocka's entrusting the Polish nations to the care of the Mother of God, and suggesting that Jesus Christ should be the Polish King (Gralczyk 1997: 222; Burnetko 2008; Janicki and Władyka 2009).

agreement that the insidious influence of the Church on public life, and on the politicians as the agents who make sure that the Church's wishes are implemented in law and practice, has become one of the most entrenched and problematic aspects of Polish democratic and constitutional politics of the last two decades (Eberts 1998; Burnetko 2008; Janicki and Władyka 2009; Markowski 2010). The rushed decisions of constitutional importance such as the Concordat; the opt-out from full applicability of the EU Charter of Rights; the allocation of funds in the state budget for Catholic Temples, schools and colleges (Sadurski 2008: 24); the tax breaks secured by the Church as early as 1989 (Sejm 1989b); obtaining publishing and broadcasting space; the right to deliver religious instruction in public schools; (Sejm 1989c); all these concessions were granted without any public debate. As argued by Janicki and Władyka, the Church secured all that it was asking for in the areas of ideology, worldview, and in symbolical and material sense (2009). Even though the relations between the Polish state and the Church are much closer to non-democratic than democratic patterns of religious-state relationship, according to a classification suggested Stepan (2005: 8–9), none of the suggested there criteria, however, cover the true nature and the extent of the Church's influence on Polish politics.

Strikingly absent from Polish politics is the debate of both the issues ring-fenced by the Church, and the place of the Church in constitutional and democratic politics. The former might be due to the success of the Church in defining the parameters and limits of debates related to the areas and matters that are of particular interest to the Church, in such a way as to, mostly, eliminate such debates. 'All methods of the Church's struggles lead to prevention of meritorious debate' (Karnowska 2008: 241).[66] As suggested by Janicki and Władyka, the main blame for this falls on the deference of politicians who treat the Church's voice as *cause finita*, instead of as one voice among many equal ones in public debates (2009) acknowledging the importance of the Church's political leverage for their own interests (Karnowska 2008). Similarly, in debates on the Constitution, the MPs often did not dare to say anything after the voice of the member of the Church hierarchy was heard. This stays entirely in line with the Church's position, which is primary geared towards defending religious dogma. Since dogmas are there to be accepted and not disputed, the debate is neither needed nor allowed.

The real power of the Church as the 'non-official and non-legitimate power holder' (Loewenstein 1965: 16) is perceived by the politicians as more decisive in keeping them in office than the power of the electorate. Clearly the link between parish priests, who, following the directions from the bishops are effective in instructing their flocks who to vote for, is much closer, and definitely more effective than that between political parties and their constituents. Behind these

---

66   One of the examples of how far some politicians are prepared to go to secure the Church approval is the Polish PM Tusk who, despite being already married in a civil ceremony for more than 20 years, wed his wife in Church, couple of weeks before the general elections in 2005.

assertions lurk complex arguments relating to the issues of obedience to the Church's hierarchy, which is easier to secure than support for political programmes of political parties, as these are challenged and contested. In contrast, the Church's pronouncements are mostly just followed, since they are clear, decisive and do not allow dissent or contestation. The powerful position of the Church within the Polish political power structure is clearly bolstered by staying behind the scenes, away form open political competition, thus avoiding any form of democratic scrutiny.[67] As argued by Markowski,

> no normal criteria of the rule of law state and democracy such as transparency and public good relate to the Church. Even asking about the Church's finances, for instance, is impossible. [...] Most interesting is not the fact that Church acts in this way, but that it is allowed to do so due to the high degree of social acquiescence and opportunism [*Do Kościoła w Polsce żadne normalne kryteria państwa prawa, transparencji, demokracji, dobra publicznego się nie odnoszą. Jako obywatel nie mogę zadać nawet pytania o finanse tej instytucji, a są one zupełnie nieprzejrzyste. Słynna Komisja Majątkowa zwracająca majątki Kościołowi, gdy obywatelom II RP wmawia się, że nie mogą odzyskać swej własności, jest daleko posuniętą nieprzyzwoitością. Ale nie sam fakt takiego postępowania tej potężnej instytucji jest ciekawy, tylko zakres społecznego przyzwolenia i oportunizmu. Jestem ciekaw, czy to się teraz zmieni*]. (2010)

From this perspective, the need for a Christian party – or any other mechanism of bringing the Church into an open political arena where it would be forced to compete for votes and support – is greater than ever. In the continued absence of such political mechanisms, the prospects of weakening of the unconstitutional and undemocratic nexus of power between the Church and the state seem remote, and so are the hopes of making the political and constitutional process more transparent and accountable.

The Political Parties and Democratic Constitutionalism

Most scholars agree that the development of representative parties must be seen as a critical condition for democratic consolidation in CEE (Innes 2002; Grzymała-Busse and Innes 2003; Paczyńska 2005; Rose-Ackerman 2007). Under the specific circumstances of the early period of systemic change, where fundamental decisions were taken on the future shape of the state, ensuring public input and control over such decisions through the political party representation should have been a fundamental rule of post-communist politics. The evidence confirms that this was not the case, and that despite the institutional provisions of free and pluralist elections, electoral rather than political accountability has been

---

67　Compare with Stepan's idea of democracy as 'a system of conflict regulation that allows open competition of values and goals that citizens want to advance' (2005: 5).

secured (Grzymała-Busse and Innes 2003: 66; Rose-Ackerman 2007: 33; CBOS 2007c). That means that the electorate could elect different parties, but it could not influence effectively their policies. This has created a sense of powerlessness and alienation in the CEE societies (Kiss 1996), as well as deepening of popular disengagement from political life and the growing rift between the governing elites and the electorate. And, most crucially, it resulted in the exclusion of majority of social groups from having a say in constitutional matters which were to have an impact over their lives.

When, as was the case in most of CEE, the drafting of new constitutions is entrusted to National Parliaments (Holmes 1993: 22), issues of party representativeness and the parties ability to rise above party-politics acquire additional importance. In Poland the first decisions of constitutional importance were taken during the negotiations between the governments and the organised opposition. As argued above, the openness and accountability of these processes and the representativeness of the parties at the negotiating table were at best limited. There was no attempt to consult or communicate with the rank and file of Solidarność, or with the wider society. Work on reforms needed to institute the systemic change continued in National Parliaments also responsible for constitution-drafting. Not surprisingly, the volatility, fragmentation and major fluidity so characteristic of the political competition between the parties at that time (Lewis 2007: 175) has been imported into the processes of constitution making.

Interestingly, the Polish Sejm enjoyed popular approval of more than 65 per cent in 1989, which declined to the more recent 71 per cent of negative opinions about the Sejm in 2000 and about the same (70 per cent in March) in 2010 (CBOS 2010e), with a rising rate of positive opinions around the time of promulgation of the 1997 Constitution. The initial enthusiasm for the Sejm might have been a part of the elevated social mood in the constitutional moment of the early transition. In part, this was surely the credit of social trust usually occurring after elections, the so-called political honeymoon. However, the rapid diminishing of this credit and the fact that the Sejm never recovered social trust, might mean that this amounted to a persistent, systemic failure and cannot be treated as just a glitch of early post-communism. As observed by Osiecka and Karpowicz, the general opinion about political elites and other institutions of government, and not just the functioning of the Sejm, are decisive in shaping social perceptions of the whole political system (2001).[68] So, the issues identified as problematic in relation to the Sejm can be applied to the whole political system, as it fails to provide mechanisms of inclusion and representation. This seems justified in light of the public opinion polls which consistently identify issues related to democratic representation and exclusion of society from political process as the most important of Polish problems (Kozarzewski 2007: 52–3).

---

68   According to this report, only 16 per cent of Poles were satisfied with the functioning of the Sejm in 2001.

Famously, 29 parties and groupings won seats in Poland's first democratic elections. When the number of parties was limited to seven in the second elections in 1993, that led to charges of exclusion of 34 per cent of the electorate who voted for the parties which failed to secure seats. But even among the electorate of the parties who regularly win seats the sense of powerlessness dominated: in 1992 only 7 per cent of Poles felt that they had a sense of influence on the country's affairs (CBOS 2007c). This did not improve much – in 1999, 87 per cent declared to have no influence over such matters (Paczyńska 2005: 604). Most observers stress that parties represent only their own interest and that of the party functionaries (Chruściak and Osiatyński 2001: 119, 151; Paczyńska 2005: 602). Party membership is very low: only 1.5 per cent of the population carry a party card of any kind (Lewis 2007: 207) and there is almost no connection to the societal grassroots. Involvement in civic activities or associations, as an alternative to party membership and support, is almost completely lacking (Paczyńska 2005: 607). All this amounts to a widespread sense of abandonment and alienation from political life, since the articulation of interest has no transmission to government (Paczyńska 2005: 607; Kolarska-Bobińska and Kucharczyk 2009: 7–9).

A crucial additional factor is the deep distrust and disrespect of politicians and parties, that has been very high since the beginning of 1990s. Part of the explanation for this links to the existence in Poland of a *multiparty nomenklatura,* where party patronage and rent seeking is central to understanding of the system. At the extreme, political parties have been accused of morphing into joint-stock companies of the party apparatuses (Szahaj 2004). A more balanced view is based on the party-patronage thesis, which gained wide support recently (Grzymała-Busse and Innes 2003; Paczyńska 2005; O'Dwyer 2004: Rose-Ackerman 2007; Kozarzewski 2007: 56–7; Gwiazda 2008: 802) and which is a more accurate interpretative tool here. Both the opinion polls and academics agree that the political parties are successful in marginalising the preferences of the electorate and in replacing those by party interests in shaping short- and long-term directions of governmental policies.

Most scholars stress the top-down imposition of democratic institutions, including the parties, as the underlying cause of the systemic weaknesses of democratic politics. Ost (2005) blames the betrayal of the workers by Solidarność. Despite declaring support for market reforms in the first years of transition, and despite demands to have a voice in the politics of their implementation, the workers have been marginalised and reduced to passive recipients of those policies. All major power brokers – the Church, the Sejm, the parties and the unions involved in the decision-making process during the constitutional moments and constitution-drafting in the 1990s – acted mainly as defenders and representatives of their own group interests, leaving the majority of Polish society alienated and disempowered.

Constitution and Polish Society

The disappointingly low turn out in the constitutional referendum, at 43 per cent, contrasts with declarations of the importance of the constitution in the lives of Poles – 74 per cent (CBOS 1994a). Fifty per cent are happy with the 1997 Constitution, a percentage higher than that of people who took part in the constitutional referendum (CBOS 2002b). Unequivocally confirmed by most opinion polls is the firm conviction of the Poles of the importance of having a Constitution, both for the country and for their own lives – 52 per cent saw it as a source of rights and freedoms, 30 per cent considered it the most fundamental legal document, source of all the laws (CBOS 1994a). On the whole, respondents were assessing those types of constitutional regulation as the most important that have most direct impact on their lives, such as individual rights and freedoms, social rights and the existence of the CCPR (the Ombudsman). Much less important were issues related to the structure of Parliament – with or without the upper chamber. Identified in these opinion polls most salient constitutional priorities stay in exactly reversed order to the questions that the National Assembly considered as worth asking in the pre-constitutional referendum (Sejm 1994a and 1994b; *see above*).

More pertinently, 86 per cent declared their knowledge about the constitution as non-existent in 1994 – this fell only slightly in March 1997, to over two-thirds (CBOS 1997b). Both scores should be seen against the high proportion of society who declare that knowing the content of the constitution is very important – 87 per cent in 1994 (CBOS 1994b). Yet, only 7 to 9 per cent of people were well informed and 11 to19 per cent were averagely well informed about the constitution in February and March 1997, just before the referendum. Even these scores should be taken with some caution, as detailed questioning revealed that declared knowledge is often an illusion as it does not correspond to the actual familiarity with the content of the constitution.[69] The picture that emerges from the data is one of a society well aware of the existence of constitutional rights and their theoretical/potential significance, but having only a limited understanding of how those rights can be claimed. Many declared that the constitution is having a crucial influence on their lives despite having only a weak idea about its content. Most are pleased to have a constitution, but also see that the state can function without it – 37 per cent (CBOS 1997a) – a drop from 79 per cent, who in 1994 considered that no state can function without a constitution (CBOS 1994a). It was, undoubtedly, the long time that was taken to promulgate the new constitution that proved that the state could exists without one. But this result might also be interpreted as a reaction to the nature of the process of constitution-making and as evidence of the devaluation of the importance of a constitution for running the country. That 74 per cent of the Polish population considered the constitution as very important for them as individuals but have only a vague idea of its content, might mean

---

69　61.3 per cent declared good knowledge of the constitution yet between 39.9 and 63.9 per cent of those got very simple questions about its content wrong (Pentor 2007).

that the constitution is perceived mainly as a symbolic, rather than actual legal document. It also means that neither the sense of entitlement to protection of constitutional rights, nor accepting the constitution as a guide for one's conduct has been developed to any sufficient degree.

There is evidence to suggest that the paradigm of law and the constitution as not applicable to direct one's conduct is still playing a role in shaping attitudes towards law and the social perception of law in Poland. 'Law is a collection of texts, a source of certain goods but it is not a duty. If it works, it happens only through the assistance of the state coercion' (Zirk-Sadowski 2006: 307). As observed by Kurczewski, 'the Constitution has not become the political frame of reference for the politicians or for the public' (2003: 179). Winczorek observed

> both those who supported Constitution and those who were against it, did not know its content. The final result of voting (bearing in mind the low attendance) was rather a consequence of voters' attitude towards the political authors of the Constitution than to the content thereof. (2000: 218)

In the context of the Polish experience, this kind of perception was most likely reinforced by the exclusion of the electorate from debates at the constitutional moments of the RTT and systemic reforms where the fundamental decisions were taken. This prevented the development of a sense of popular influence that might have led to a closer identification with this document. The actual process reinforced the elitism of the political system, and a sense of popular alienation, as things were done in the name of the people only. Public participation in the constitution-making has been limited to a vote in the referendum – an important, but mainly symbolic gesture. Even though, as observed by Arato: 'Special legislatures and expert commissions involved in constitution making need not isolate themselves from ongoing public discussion in which those most concerned can participate in an organized fashion' (1992–1993: 670).

The neglect of provisions related to individual rights and freedoms, and effective ways of accessing/enforcing those, confirm that there were other priorities than the position of an individual in the political and legal restructuring of the state order.[70] The political infighting that was the constitutional debate and the accommodation of the Church agenda by the National Assembly did nothing to dispel the perception of an elitist nature of the process which end result was to legitimise the gains of power and influence of political classes and not the entrenchment of rights (Kurczewski 2003: 173, 179). The instrumental use of law and procedure added to this less than inspiring picture. It seems that even the constitutional tradition that links back to the 3 May Constitution has

---

70   Compare with Zirk-Sadowski, who argued that 'in the public consciousness legal obligation continues to be treated as a derivative of coercion, and legal rights were perceived as a kind of good' (2006: 301).

been weakened by such a spectacle, at least temporarily, as support for 1997 Constitution dipped to its lowest level in 1997 and only recover some years later.

Politics and Discourse of Constitutionalism in 1990s in Poland: Politicisation, Legal Instrumentalism and Symbolism

Most, if not all, constitutions' symbolic power transcends their practical significance (Grey 1984; Monaghan 1981: 356; Ackerman 1983) – it is the 'power which lurks beneath [...] values' (Weiler and Wind 2003: 17). The first constitution of the free Poland is no different. It had been presented to the electorate as, foremost, a symbol of national identity, rather than a legal document and a source of rights. The rush to promulgate it on the bicentenary of the 3 May Constitution and the almost immediate, after the RTT reinstatement of the 3 May as public/religious holiday confirms a strong political will to keep alive both its symbolic and historical link to the Constitution of 3 May 1791. Forging such a link, however, exposes a huge contrast between the negligible practical impact of the 3 May Constitution, which was defeated before it could influence the practice of government, and its status as the most cherished state document in the memory of the Poles. Kurczewski wrote about the 'constitution of the heart' (1993: 370) to capture the importance of its symbolic appeal during the partitions of Poland. The contemporary disparity between the low awareness of constitutional provisions and the declared importance of constitution in peoples' lives suggests that the paradigm of constitution as a symbol continues to dominate public perception.

There is a strong tradition in Polish legal and political theory of conceptualising law as a spiritual, intuitive phenomenon. Such an approach is partially the product of Polish history where the Poles lived for long periods under the occupation of states whose oppressive laws needed to be negotiated by the spiritual sense of legality and upholding of national symbols and rituals.[71] This type of constitutional tradition, steeped in national language and culture, functioned as a mechanism for national and cultural survival in the nineteenth century as well as during and after WWII.

The persistence of the paradigm of the 'constitution as a symbol' relates to wider cultural trait that links also to the perception of law as an abstract phenomenon, which, in turn, carries a number of important consequences for both shaping the approach to constitution making and the type of legitimacy that such constitution attracts. The drafting of constitution-symbol is more of a battle of competing ideological/value-laden agendas, rather than one of democratic deliberations on the best legal and political settlement of a state's order and fundamental rights. The acceptance of such constitutions will be necessarily limited to, mostly, an emotive support of its emblematic value.

It must then be seen as regrettable that the new constitution of free and democratic Poland failed to break away from the 'constitution as symbol'

---

71   The best-known proponent of the intuitive law theory is Leon Petrażycki (1955).

tradition. The finished document remains largely unknown and irrelevant in practical sense of legally enforceable catalogue of rights. It its making, it failed to give the people a sense of influence over the fundamental issues that were going to affect their lives. Creating such agency might have helped to develop within society a sense of ownership of the constitutional document and its perception as effective in defining and sustaining the legal and political position of individuals within their state. In other words, the type of constitutionalism developing in Poland did not entirely live up to its promise of creating a new type of citizenship: democratic and politically engaged. Instead, it legitimised the post-1989 settlement between the main power-brokers that emerged: the new multiparty nomenklatura and the Church.

The Accession to European Union: One More Lost Chance to Democratise Polish Constitutional Politics?

The lack of consultations and lack of popular engagement and/or input into the process of accession to the EU is one more example of a constitutional event of recent Polish history that fed into the more general dynamics of failure of democratic politics after 1989. Sajó commented

> Given that accession was a unilateral process and very much one that an elite governmental bureaucracy carried out, without ever allowing for genuine public discourse, one cannot be surprised that there was little popular enthusiasm when, very late in the game and hastily, an opportunity for plebiscitarian approval was granted to the public in accession referendum. (2005: 252)

Particularly problematic in this context was the elitism and authoritarianism of the accession politics, strongly reminiscent of the first years of systemic reforms. The pragmatic stance of the Poles, bolstered by the Pope's strong encouragement, produced a positive result. But this happened despite the absence of the democratic process of debate and consultation. Yet, the accession to the EU had been a momentous event in Polish history, as was the political breakthrough of 1989, both rare historical occurrences, and both potentially capable to mobilise and engage the people in democratic politics. It seems, though, that at both of these historical junctures the chance to democratise Polish society and politics has been missed.

The prospect of joining the EU raised high hopes for improving and consolidating democracy in the new Member States of the CEE.[72] This was confirmed in opinion polls in the late 1990s (Sadurski 2003: 33). More recent opinion polls also confirm that such expectations towards the EU continue to be high and that they are partially based on the belief, that gained support in Poland, that the EU institutions function well, and that the quality of EU governance should be copied on domestic level (CBOS 2005). This suggests that the Poles' appreciation of the state of democratic governance in the EU is rather poor, so

---

72   Compare with Albi (2005).

such hopes of consolidation of democracy under the influence of the EU are based on myth rather than evidence. One likely explanation behind this over-inflated trust in the EU is the persisting disappointment with the state of Polish democracy and the functioning of the Sejm (Osiecka and Karpowicz 2001).[73] Seventy per cent of Poles are dissatisfied with the state of Polish democracy, and a still higher percentage believe that Poland is closer to a non-democratic than to democratic system (CBOS 2006). These results remain consistent for the best part of the post-1989 era.

It is clear by now that democratic procedures were neglected in the pre-accession and accession stages. This was partly a result of time pressure and a desire to join as quickly as possible. There was no debate, not even in the Polish Parliament (Sejm), and little information was available in the mass media on European matters.[74] EU membership was presented as the only possible way forward. As a result, apathy rather than hostility threatened a negative outcome and was the main problem in the accession referendum. The Pope's intervention was one of the most decisive factors behind Poland's 'yes' vote. This seems a reasonable explanation given that the publicity campaign in 2003, prior to the accession referendum, was described as 'patronising' and one-sided (Marody and Wilkin 2004: 172), so unlikely to entice an informed, engaged type of voting. Not only such campaign failed to ignite popular interest in the EU, but it further alienated the governing elites from the people,[75] and did nothing to stop the rather extreme, in the sense of political orientation, changes of governments, as the fate of the government which took Poland to the EU confirms: the SLD lost the elections in 2005 by a big margin, to be replaced by PiS, one of the most extreme right-wing, conservative political formation.[76]

---

73   Sadurski claims that this phenomenon is not confined to Poland: 'Citizens of the CEE do not trust and do not like their own states: fourteen years after the advent of democracy the belief in their own institutions is very low' (2003: 35). These negative opinions of domestic democracy continue (CBOS 2008).

74   '... after the tense accession referendum, the more specific issues associated with Poland's participation in the EU practically vanished from the media and politicians' statements, although even beforehand they had not occupied much space, if one discounts the purely emotional appeals calling, on the one hand, to defend national sovereignty and, on the other, to not squander the opportunity to accelerate civilizational development. [...] This ... can be explained by the low familiarity with internal EU issues, not just among politicians but also among their broader support structure' (Marody and Wilkin 2004: 193). President Kwaśniewski lamented: 'in this huge country of 40 million people I found seven individuals with knowledge of agricultural issues and European policy' (Gazeta Wyborcza 5–6 July 2003).

75   Compare with Pridham (2002: 954).

76   The SLD [Sojusz Lewicy Demokratycznej] lost 35 per cent of mandates in comparison with the elections in 2001. The winner of the 2005 elections, the PiS [Prawo i Sprawiedliwość] moved up from 9.6 to 33, 7 per cent in 2005. Data available on the Sejm web-site at http://www.sejm.gov.pl.

Despite many failures of popular democratisation on accession, but also more generally, Poland passed the EU criteria for democracy on entry to the EU.[77] This was helped by assessing the level of compliance according to mainly formal/institutional indicators of democratic governance (Kochenov 2007; Pridham 2002).[78] The weakness of such a mode of assessment is revealed by comparing the Commission's report of 1997 (DOC/97/16) and a number of Western academic texts asserting the consolidated state of Polish democracy, with Polish academic publications and Polish opinion polls that paint a much more pessimistic picture (Jarosz 2007; Kolarska-Bobińska 2008, Kolarska-Bobińska and Kucharczyk 2009). Both the direct democracy, in the sense of facilitating an informed popular participation in the issue of accession to the EU, and the indirect, institutional involvement in the process were affected by lack of attention to basic democratic standards. The rushed adaptation of laws resulted in an over-inflated role of the government of the day and a diminished role of the Parliament. This strengthened the tendency to concentrate power in the executive branch which continue to dominate the political process today.[79] The current Polish Constitution stops short of providing the Sejm with the power to be included in European policy-making. (This obviously goes against the spirit of the ToA 'Protocol No. 1 on the Role of National Parliaments in the EU' as revised by the Treaty of Lisbon.) The only formal mechanism open to MPs is a routine question to a minister within the framework of parliamentary question time.

The high moral authority and democratic legitimacy that the EU enjoys in Poland and other CEE states, particularly as an overseer and guarantor of democratic standards, contrasts with the weaknesses of democratic politics on accession. In 2010, 86 per cent of Poles were pleased with Poland's membership in the EU (CBOS 2010c). Trust in the EU institutions is also high: 49 to 55 per cent positively assess their functioning (CBOS 2009d). This might be interpreted as yet another myth that Poles are clinging on to, given their poor familiarity with the EU matters (CBOS 2005; Popławska 2008: 283). The relative power of such myth means that the identification with the EU is predominantly symbolic, rather than informed and engaged – not a great prognostic for hoping that the Poles will become the active and interested EU citizens.

---

77   Poland was one of the first ten candidate countries which had satisfied the EU Political Conditionality (Articles 6 of the and 49 of EU Treaty) and the Copenhagen criteria, according to which a candidate country should be a stable democracy, respect human rights and the rule of law and protect minorities; have a working market economy; adopt the common rules, standards and policies which make up the body of EU law.

78   See also Kochenov (2007) on the failure of the EU conditionality.

79   The Freedom House report pointed this out as a reason for worse rating of Polish national democratic governance (2006: 2).

Conclusions

The neglect of the democratic process at the constitutional moment that marked the beginning of the deep systemic change resulted in a lasting derailment of the democratic process and pluralistic debate, and was instrumental in facilitating the rise of politics dominated by party-political and Church interests. The exclusion of the Polish society from active participation in shaping its destiny amounted to a failure to harness the force of democratic social mobilisation that started with the Solidarność strikes of 1980 and culminated in the establishment of the new political and economic system in 1989. Instead, old style authoritarian and patronising political process returned where the political parties imposed from the top failed to built their grass-root bases and turned into a multiparty nomenklatura, characterised by party patronage and rent seeking. Solidarność, in effect, disappeared from the political scene. The negligible presence of trade unions in the increasingly privatised economy left large sections of society without effective representation – creating a state of abandoned society.

The drafting of the new constitution turned into a power play between party interests and was dominated by the Catholic Church whose agenda strongly influenced both the process and the substantive provisions of the 1997 Constitution. The absence of public debate and disproportionate attention devoted to the symbolic dimension of the new Constitution fed into the historic traits of Polish constitutional culture which defines constitution as a symbol of Polish nationhood grounded in Catholic religion, rather than a source of fundamental rights. Instrumental in those processes were the formal/charismatic type of legitimacy that was secured in the heightened state of social mobilisation that was the constitutional moment of RTT, and in constitutional referendum. Such legitimacy was more likely to occur also due to the forged link between the promulgation of the 1997 Constitution to that of the 3 May 1791.

The failings of both RTT and constitution-making to include the constituent power in shaping the new state order have been legitimised by the apparent constitutionalisation locking in the limited nature of democratic politics behind those events. Thus established constitutional status quo amounts to a lost opportunity of forging a more politically active and involved type of citizenship, depriving the system of constitutional democracy of one of its most important corrective mechanisms – that of democratic constitutionalism.

Chapter 3

Democratic Constitutionalism in Poland After 1989: External Influences

Introduction

In this chapter I discuss the impact of international and European pressures and conditionality on Polish democratic and constitutional development. In particular, I will examine the claim that the external pressure from international organisations such as the IMF, the World Bank, the Council of Europe and the EU have been overwhelmingly beneficial for the democratic consolidation of Poland and other CEE countries.[1] To do so, I use Whitehead's classic work on the international dimension of democratisation: contagion, control and consent (1996a: 4) and theories and perspectives on Europeanisation (Schimmelfenning and Sedelmeier 2005a; Schimmelfenning 2007; Featherstone and Radaelli 2003) and on EU conditionality (Kochenov 2007; Grabbe 2006). In contrast to the prevailing approaches, I will focus on the dynamics of the processes through which the external policies directed at Poland and other CEE countries have been created and carried out, and less on the substance of these policies. I will be asking what was the impact of external policies aimed at achieving democratic change in Poland given that the creation and delivery of those policies not always followed democratic and constitutional standards. This approach[2] differs from those accounts that consider the socialisation and social learning models in context of legitimacy of external conditionality (Schimmelfenning and Sedelmeier 2005b: 18–190; Sedelmeier 2009: 12, 26) in that it considers the impact of political conditionality as a process of *learning through observing*, which fits neither the rationalist nor the constructivist explanations that prevails in such accounts. A broader question that I would like to pose is if the success of external policies aimed at achieving

---

1   Note the existing critical accounts on EU conditionality of Grabbe (2006), Hughes et al. (2004), Schimmelfenning and Sedelmeier (2005a).

2   I call 'learning-by-observing' an approach rather than a model to make a distinction between these two concepts: models are theoretically sophisticated constructs with their own internal organising structures, principles and logic that assist us to make predictions about (in this case) the behaviour of societies/states. An approach, on the other hand, is a perspective, a way of making sense of the phenomena under investigation; in our case, the impact of aid and conditionality and delivery practices of external actors on the democratic learning of the target countries.

democratic change in specific domestic contexts depends on whether those policies were created and delivered in a democratic and constitutional manner.

The rationale for such an approach is grounded in the assumption that in countries which have not experienced a functioning democracy and constitutionalism – such as the CEE transition countries – the first 'live' encounter with the process of delivering aid and conditionality amounted to an immense learning experience which was bound to leave a deep imprint on the political and constitutional practices of these countries. I suggest that learning-by-observing and being on the receiving end of aid, assistance, and conditionality, should be seen as at least equally important as the content of those policies. Support for this logic comes, in some measure at least, from Vojtech Cepl:[3]

> Political and legal changes can be modelled on the systems of Western democracies. In contrast, rules of human conduct are learned by observing societal conduct and are not changed by amendments to legal text but only by people actually modifying their behaviour. (1995: 3)

The actual practices of the external actors in their roles as aid providers were the most obvious, clear and readily available manifestations of 'democracy in action'. Observing the donors in action should be seen as also effective in shaping the understanding of what democratic standards look like in practice and, so, it is likely to allow for less ambiguous assessment of the delivery of external policies from the perspective of compliance with democratic and constitutional standards. And that is because the assessment of such standards based on documentary evidence and/or the discourse accompanying aid delivery and conditionality is bound to be much more uncertain, particularly, since there is often discrepancy between the content of the conditionality policies and the declared and practised standards of behaviour on the part of the external actors. Such a perspective therefore should contribute to developing an understanding of how democratic and constitutional learning of the CEE countries might have been affected not just by the content of external policies, but also by the manner of their design and delivery.

This perspective does not fit well within the existing approaches to democratisation from international influence perspectives: modernisation, transition and the structural approach (Grugel 1999: 23), and only weakly relates to Whitehead's contagion model. Nor does the literature on Europeanisation cover the procedural and experiential aspects of it – in the sense mentioned above.[4] To

---

3   Quoted in Pogany (1993: 569).

4   Among the many models suggested by the literature of Europeanisation and conditionality Featherstone and Radaelli (2003), Schimmelfenning and Sedelmeier (2005b); Schimmelfenning (2007); the closest is the social learning model which focuses on a correlation between legitimacy (in the sense of quality of rules that are made in democratic and constitutional procedure; are equally applied to all, and are set in deliberative and consensual way) and conditionality. In contrast, the democratic precedents

fill in this gap, I will attempt to develop further the understanding of the impact of 'democratic precedents' Miller, White and Heywood (1998: 29–30) or their absence from practices of the external actors engaged in direct assistance in CEE, by looking into the type of relationship between the international actors and the target countries, and the domestic responses to conduct of external actors. In sum, I will be asking if the democratic consolidation and democratic constitutionalism were likely to be weakened by the poor democratic practices in application of conditionality, and delivery of aid by external actors.

These questions imply procedural perspective, in the sense of procedures employed in practical application of conditionality, and delivery of aid by external actors and impact of those on target countries perceptions and understanding of what a democratic practices should look like. Consequently, answering them should lead to uncovering the dynamics between external influences and domestic democratic development and consolidation as the necessary pre-conditions for democratic constitutionalism to take root. Even though such processes are impossible to quantify and even though the relations between the domestic and international will often be inferred, this type of analysis is yet capable of illuminating both the historical and current experiences of this dynamics.[5]

In the first part of this chapter I re-examine concepts of internationalisation and Europeanisation in relation to political and social reality of Poland before and after the 1989. I first discuss the meaning of both concepts. Then I attempt to analyse the dynamics between the external influences and internal processes which might have been affected by those influences. Finally, I discuss the impact of external policies, including the Western aid and EU conditionality, on the internal democratic constitutionalism in Poland and other CEE countries.

Behind the Iron Curtain: Limited Internationalisation and Europeanisation of Poland Before 1989 – The Concepts and Their Use

Most books and articles that discuss the internationalisation of CEE countries concentrate on their economy or political economy. The impact of international factors on the polity and society on their own do not receive that much attention. Exceptions to this are the edited collections by Pridham and Vanhanen (1994), Pridham, Herring and Sanford (1994), Whitehead (1996a), Grugel (1999) and (Zielonka: 2001). These focus on the 'after 1989' period, and mostly avoid concept of 'internationalisation'. Instead terms such as 'international context' and 'international dimension', or 'international factors' are used in discussing the international impact on political and social processes. This may be so because, as suggested by Schmitter,

---

and constitutional practices in my 'learning-by-observing' approach relate to the actual behaviour of the external actors as observed by the target countries.

5   Compare with Whitehead (1996a: chapter 1).

> international context is notoriously difficult to pin down [...] On the one hand, it is almost by definition omnipresent, since very few polities are isolated from its effects. However, its casual impact is often indirect, working in mysterious and unintended ways through ostensibly rational agents. (1996: 28)

As this quote suggests, bar the economic regulations forced on countries by WTO, IMF and the EU, the impact of other international factors – which may be a part of external assistance on polity and society – is much more diffused and difficult to capture in a logic of causality.

Often, work on internationalisation includes European organisations such as the EU, OSCE, the Council of Europe, which suggests that there might not be much of a deviding line between the two phenomena. This might be due to the following reasons: before 1989 neither European nor international factors had much of a direct impact on the functioning of the CEE countries due to the relative isolation of those countries behind the iron curtain; after 1989, when this influence became much more direct, most policies, even those that originated in the World Bank or the IMF, were coordinated by the EU. Placing the EU in the driving seat of external policies in the CEE chimes with Schmitter's suggestion that the really effective international context that can influence the course of democratisation has increasingly become regional, not bi-national or global (1996: 40). This also means that 'internationalisation' should be seen as part of Europeanisation, not the other way round, to reflect the strong regional impact of the EU.

The international action directed at the post-communist transition countries soon after the 1989 revolutions was complemented by the political conditionality of the Europe Agreements, PHARE and TACIS programmes in the early 1990s, and the Copenhagen criteria since 1993. It seems then that for the purpose of the current analysis it makes more sense to settle the following two points: the term 'Europeanisation' should replace both 'Europeanisation' and 'internationalisation' in the discussion of the impact of external factors on Poland and other CEE countries; and secondly, that a chronological line – that is, pre- and post-1989 – rather than thematic one should be drawn to reflect the qualitative change in the effectiveness of the international influences after 1989 following the end of the CEE countries' isolation from the rest of the world. This will be in keeping with both Whitehead and Schmitter, who suggested that there is a great deal of overlap between the four types of international influence: contagion, control, consent and conditionality. Hence, instead of trying to ascribe particular effects to specific influences, it seems more productive to assume that all of those become more relevant after 1989, although each in a different way. Contagion was clearly a more relevant type of influence before 1989, the 'diffusion of experience' took place through the informal channels from the West to the CEE countries, whereas consent and conditionality played a much bigger role after the opening of 1989 when the CEE countries expressed the will to democratise and were then 'helped along' this road by EU conditionality.

Democratisation and Constitutionalism in Poland Before 1989: External and Internal Influences

In order to present a fuller picture of external influences, the implications of Poland's position between the East and the West must be examined, as it was one of the strongest factors influencing not just political history, but also her national culture and societal outlook. Historically, one of the most enduring political and social aspiration of the Poles was to be seen as part of the West, to belong to the civilised part of Europe, and to distance itself from Russia – the East. The development of Poland's variety of the persistent ideology of 'return to Europe' should be seen in this context. The 'return' symbolises the resistance of the Poles to the threat from the 'barbaric' East and to German expansionism from the West. It also refers to the symbolic dimension of Poland's Partition;[6] two of the three occupying powers, Germany (Prussia, at that time) and Russia, are Europe's two extremes representing the West and the East or, in other words, Western Civilisation and Eastern Despotism (Zarycki 1997: 97).

As summed up by Pravda and Zielonka, the 'pull' from the West was complemented by the domestic 'pull' away from the East (2001: 2). Poland's aspiration to be part of the West fits well with the idea of the pull, but it also relates to the Polish inferiority complex, which has its roots in Poland's economic underdevelopment, lack of democracy and political freedom and being firmly classed as belonging to the *East* of Europe (Tazbir 2007).[7] This sense of inferiority deepened after the second world war with the rapidly growing civilisational distance from the West. The distance had been predominantly economic, since culturally, Poland's intellectual life was robust, sustained by the charismatic intelligentsia. The Poles enjoyed a relatively rich diet of Western films, books and music subsidised by the state. Part of this openness to the West were the links with the Parisian 'Culture' and other networks supporting political dissidents and artists.

The 'pull' of Europe – or the civilised West – had been a strong force shaping the aspirations of the Polish elites and the people well before any formal relations between the European Community and CEE were established. The romanticised vision of the Western paradise, as symbolised by the EEC, functioned in popular discourse in the East as a frame of reference used to contrast, favourably, Western

---

6   Poland was occupied from the end of the eighteenth century until 1918 by Russia, Germany and the Austro-Hungarian Empire.

7   J. Tazbir commented that the French 'Histoire de l'Europe', which was going to be the prototype of the textbook on the history of Europe sanctioned by the European Union, mentions Poland only sparingly and only as a country on the periphery of Europe proper. Tazbir points out that almost all texts on the history of Europe, including the French 'Histoire de l'Europe', stop on the Elbe line. Anything beyond this is the 'far provinces of Europe'. Curiously, Poland and Baltic states are placed in Central Eastern Europe, France and Germany belong to Western and not Central-Western part of the continent.

reality with the most absurd aspects of everyday reality under socialist systems. The saying popular in the old system 'this would not have happened in a "normal" (Western) country' captures this well. However, the attractive qualities of such 'normality' have been assumed rather than verified by experience. Hence the ideas about and perceptions of the West have existed in post-war CEE mainly as abstract concepts. Their powerful grip on the public imagination might have much to do with their abstract quality, particularly in those cultures which, as the Polish one, had historically developed heightened receptiveness to symbolic meanings rather than experiential reality.

Schmitter described this type of Eastern European turn to the West as the best case of 'contagion', in other words, 'diffusion of experience through neutral, i.e., non-coercive and often unintentional, channels from one country to another' (1996: 40).[8] Contagion affected both the elites and the society through 'culture, travel, consumption patterns and a proliferation of other demonstration effects' (Whitehead 1996a: 388). The main problem with this type of external influences is that, as observed by Whitehead, they are difficult to specify and evaluate even if their impact is obvious and powerful. In relation to the CEE countries, this difficulty was further compounded by the inverted dialectics between the attractiveness of the relative unknown West and its romanticised vision on the one hand; and the Soviet Union, rejected and opposed on a societal level but politically dominant, on the other.

Despite the strong anti-Russian sentiments, the elites were, on the whole, supportive of the close strategic links with the Soviets for reasons of security since, historically, the West was seen as failing to defend Polish interests for the sake of preserving its own power.[9] Another element was daily life in Poland which, in contrast to the projected idealised vision of the West, often appeared more unattractive in societal discourse than the everyday reality would suggest.[10] All in all, it would appear that the assessment of the overall impact of external influences under the 'contagion' label is more complex than both Schmitter and Whitehead allow. This might partly be due to their focus on the international and European politics and lesser attention afforded to societal level and cultural influences. Yet without fuller account of the two: societies and culture, the picture is less clear. The CEE countries' specific geopolitical position between the East and the West was a firm, and enduring point of reference of a distinct strand of

---

8   Featherstone suggested the term 'cultural diffusion' to capture this type of Europeanisation (2005: 5).

9   The hostility towards the Soviet Union might partly explain why the West appeared so attractive for the Poles despite the 'sell out' of Poland to the Soviets at Yalta and despite the lack of concern for Poland's fate in 1939 (Whitehead 1996: 375), memories of which are kept alive in Polish popular discourse.

10   Compare with Pravda and Zielonka (2001: 2), who suggested that 'The West also stands as a pole of attraction because many East Europeans, especially the elites, wish to identify with what they see as the heartland of European Civilization.'

political and societal discourse. The governing elites' propaganda used the West as a favourite target for mud slinging. The crudeness of such attacks, however, fed into the deference for the West within society and strengthened the tendency to exaggerate the West's achievements. As a result, on societal level, the West was glorified as a symbol of civilisation, freedom and prosperity. So, the influences of the West under the model of contagion should be seen as mediated by domestic responses rooted in cleavages of regional history, political systems and societal cultures of the CEE countries.

In the next section I will identify and discuss Polish domestic responses to international factors by analysing constitutionalism and the discourse of rights in CEE, and Poland in particular, before 1989. The three models of contagion, control and consent will be used in a limited manner only, since their power of explanation is limited by the diffused and contingent nature of the processes under investigation.

Constitutionalism in Poland: External Influence, Internal Responses
As outlined in Chapter 2, the development of Polish constitutionalism can be traced to efforts to create a more palatable international image of Poland in the early 1970s[11] aimed at Western money-lending institutions.[12] Both the state, and the dissidents increasingly used the idea of constitutionalism by, for instance, framing many of their political objectives in the language of rights, particularly in the 1970s and 1980s.[13] This strategy received a significant boost with the signing of the 1975 Helsinki Final Act of the OSCE Conference on Security and Co-operation in Europe,[14] which, for years to come, served as a frame of reference for political opposition, and, later, dissident-supporting organisations such as the Helsinki Human Rights Foundation.[15] In the context of European politics towards the CEE countries, the significance of the 1975 Act appears truly momentous. According to one interpretation, the Act constituted an international treaty which specified a 'coherent and disputed set of Western requirements, incentives, and reassurances [...] that shaped Moscow's policy options' and played a crucial role in the democratisation of CEE' (Whitehead 1996a: 378).

---

11   Earlier efforts, such as the 1952 Constitution, have been described as meaningless in constitutional terms (Brzeziński 2000: 1), hence cannot be considered as instances of constitutionalism proper.

12   Edward Gierek's regime borrowed heavily from the West to boost the supply of life-style goods. This often created a bad impression in the prevailing conditions of permanent shortages of basic consumer goods.

13   The Solidarność movement is probably the best known example of a political movement which placed fundamental rights demands on its banners. Kurczewski, for instance, suggested that civility and political rights and HR have always been part of the struggle against the communist regime (1993).

14   Helsinki, 1 August 1975.

15   Active in Poland from 1982 as a dissident organisation, it was officially established in 1989. See http://www.hfhrpol.waw.pl/.

In line with Whitehead's suggestion, Davy claimed that by helping to legitimise Western intrusion into the Soviet sphere of influence, the Final Act also paved the way for setting up structures alternative to the old regimes (Davy 1992: 25, 263) – such as KOR in Poland and Charter 77 in Czechoslovakia. I suggested earlier that apart from allowing political opposition to acquire institutional form, the Act also provided a legal frame of reference and a language that both sides – the government and dissidents used as a mechanism of containment, facilitating in this way a smoother transition. This processes, I further suggested, should be seen as a fundamental turn in constitutional thinking by the main political powers in Poland at that time (Garlicki 2008: 15).

The nascent constitutionalism developing in Poland since the late 1970s has clearly helped to avoid major confrontations during the events leading up to the signing of the agreement between Solidarność and the government in 1980. It also reassured the Soviet Union that the PUWP was in control of the situation, helping to pre-empt the need for military intervention. In a sense, this dynamics amounted also to a continuation of the European détente (Whitehead 1996a: Chapter 13) as it widened the channels available to Western pressure and strengthened the hand of pro-reformist faction in the Soviet Union. This development created the impression that the fall of the communist system was precipitated by the authoritarian Russia – 'the most powerful autocratic state' – not the democratic West (Schmitter 1996: 34). In reality, without the Helsinki Final Act, Western influence by contagion and later, direct pressure, Gorbachev's perestroika might not have happened. The indirect Western influence has therefore been decisive – if not immediately apparent – in this final act of the Cold War.

The drive to legitimate the Polish state domestically and internationally continued also through institutional developments such as the establishment of High Administrative Court, the Tribunal of State and, perhaps most significantly, the Ombudsman, otherwise known as the Commissioner for Citizen's Rights Protection (CCRP) in the late 1980s. All in all, the institutional reforms which were initially undertaken to improve the international image of Poland, and were, in some measure, designed to remain more fictional than real, in fact boosted Polish constitutionalism and influenced practices of public institutions (Brzeziński 2000: 131–63).

Constitutionalism and the Discourse of Rights

Although the state's and the dissidents' use of discourse of rights and constitutionalism as a legitimising platform[16] was clearly a win-win game, it created its own problems affecting the creation and understanding of rights and constitutional principles. One such issue was the understanding of law and rules

---

16   My argument goes against Přibáň's thesis that 'living in truth' was the main legitimating value and not the rule of law (Přibáň 2002: 52), but it aligns with Grudzińska-Gross (1997), who suggested that discourse of rights was part of the 'Polish constitutionalism' which began in the 1970s.

as imposed in a top-down, authoritarian manner, formal/positivistic in form, that this particular discourse of rights facilitated. Neither the state, nor the dissidents attempted to subject their ideas of what the rights should be to a public debate – for obvious reasons. It was beyond the modus operandi of the socialist state to do so, and the dissident movement – which was not an official part of political landscape – simply could not conduct any wider public debate. As a result, rights functioned in an elitist discourse of the government and the opposition, with the exclusion of the rest of society. Rights were projected as idealistic aspirations whose practical meaning and application were beyond discussion. As suggested by Přibáň and Sadurski, 'the culture of rights that already existed was more [...] culture of the "idea" of rights' (2006: 197).

To sum up, the diffused and uncertain growth of Polish constitutionalism before 1989, which took place largely, but also indirectly in response to, international pressure, in which the 1975 Helsinki Final Act played an important role, developed a number of characteristics. Most of these corresponded to a number of historically conditioned tendencies: the elitist character of the process; the heavy reliance on formal as opposed to substantive reforms to create the right impression externally and to encourage positive social responses via the symbolic appeal of such reforms; and the abstract understanding of democratic and constitutional rights by the Poles that could not easily be remedied due to lack of life-experience of democratic and constitutional system.

The developments analysed in this section do not fit the three models of international influence very well: *contagion*[17] – since the domestic change was mainly driven by the need to create the appearance of constitutionalism, which gathered momentum of its own and turned into a more effective process than was envisaged. This was clearly far away from the 'diffusion of experience through neutral means' that this model presupposes. *Control* – the external influences were much too indirect and diffused to satisfy this type of mechanism, which requires 'explicit policies backed by positive or negative sanctions'. Finally, *consent* – hardly applicable to Poland, as it is based on 'complex interactions between international processes and domestic groups that generates new democratic norms from below' (Schmitter 1996: 30).

After 1989: International Assistance and Conditionality

The opening that was the 1975 Helsinki Final Act which allowed the West access into the CEE countries widened considerably during Solidarność strikes in Poland in the 1980s. The international support and cheering on of the Solidarność movement turned into more concrete steps in response to the imposition of Martial Law in December 1981 and the banning of Solidarność. Throughout the most acute period of economic crisis in 1982–1983 the Poles were supported by a huge inflow of aid (food and other essentials) mainly coordinated by charities, private

---

17   All references in this paragraph are to Schmitter (1996).

organisations and individuals in the West. Some countries took in members of Solidarność released from internment camps. The award of the Nobel peace prize to Wałęsa was clearly designed as a slap in the face of Jaruzelski's regime and an expression of international recognition of the importance of Solidarność struggle against the authoritarian rule of the PUWP.

The Round Table Talks and the first semi-free elections[18] marked the start of systemic reforms and the so-called transition or transformation[19] to a market economy and democracy. The formation of Mazowiecki's government in August 1989 and the election of Wałęsa as President in Autumn 1990 completed the transfer of power, at least in a formal sense. This chain of events opened the door to Western states and organisations and allowed a flow of massive effort of assistance and support for Polish economic and political reforms.[20] The main actors in these efforts were the individual states, primarily the USA, and European organisations, most crucially the EU, which co-ordinated most of the actions. Other organisations involved were the Council of Europe (CE), NATO, Organization for Security and Cooperation in Europe (OSCE); and other bodies: International Monetary Fund (IMF), European Bank for Reconstruction and Development (EBRD), and the World Bank (WB). The latter group of organisations were mainly involved in economic reforms, whereas the EU, representing the most powerful engine for economic change through the pre-accession and accession economic conditionality, used policy instruments specially designed to promote democracy, human rights and the rule of law.[21]

To assess the impact on democracy and constitutionalism of this wave of foreign aid, the two types of influence will be discussed separately: the indirect ones, through financial/technical aid, coordinated mainly by the USA, and the ones directly aimed at encouraging democratic development – for which the main responsibility fell on the EU. The main instruments that the EU used were, initially, PHARE (Poland & Hungary Aid for Restructuring Economy) and TACIS (Technical Assistance for the CIS) trade and aid programmes, followed by the Europe Agreement, the Copenhagen criteria of pre-accession conditionality and the Accession Partnerships from 1998. I will not discuss the substance of those programmes here since there is a rich body of literature covering this. Instead, I will focus on the manner in which they were designed and delivered. The reason

---

18   There are numerous books that analyse these events in detail. See for instance Sanford (1994, 2002); Brzeziński (2000).

19   Neither of the two terms used in the literature is accurate: transition – because of its predetermined end destination – transition to a specific other form; nor transformation – as some crucial aspects of political system, for instance, continue from the previous era and are hardly changed. Others acquire a new, or transformed form, but those new forms do not comply with the end results that the use of the term implies: democracy is but one example.

20   Economic reforms fall outside the scope of this work and will be refereed to only as a subsidiary matter.

21   See also: Dembour and Krzyżanowska-Mierzewska (2004).

for this is that, in line with my argument, it is not just the content of policies that determines the effectiveness of the programme of external assistance. The process of putting those policies together and their implementation is at least as crucial, if not more decisive, in shaping the recipient country's ideas of democracy and due process. The linkage between the manner of international aid delivery and democratic learning might seem, initially, tenuous. However, it is supported by Radaelli's idea of horizontal Europeanisation through diffusion of ideas and notions of 'good policy', that is:

> Processes of (a) construction, (b) diffusion, and (c) institutionalisation of formal and informal rules and procedures, policy paradigms, styles, 'ways of doing things' and shared beliefs and norms which are first defined and consolidated in the making of EU public policy and politics and then incorporated in the logic of domestic discourse, identities, political structures, and public policies. (2003: 30)

In addition, the agency-centred approach of sociological institutionalism supports the idea of learning through 'resonance' with domestic practices (Olsen 1996: 272). Following this, I argue that in many ways the process of learning-by-observing the practices and behaviour of the principal deliverers of political aid, assistance and conditionality – that is, the representatives of Western government and agencies and the EU – is at least as important as the substance of external assistance and policies of conditionality.

I further suggest that the receptiveness to external influences is heightened in times of critical and profound changes. Actions aimed at assisting the fundamental reforms of the state and also targeted towards reviving devastated economy, are surely of huge and unique significance, and fit into the concept of 'critical and profound' change, a characteristic of constitutional moments (see Chapter 1). Consequently, the first-hand exposure to the practices of EU at such a juncture of the CEE states' history was more than likely to set precedents of behaviour and to shape the hosts countries' perception of due process, transparency and inclusiveness in policy-making and implementation of the targeted aid delivery.

The scope and type of aid which included the transfer of specialist expertise, consultancy and training, apart from credits, trade incentives and money – meant that this was one of the first meetings on that scale of the Western experts, policy makers and consultants with their Eastern counterparts. Since the scope and potential benefits of external aid were crucial for the success of the reforms in the CEE countries,[22] the unspoken expectation was that the allocation of incoming resources and the selection of domestic partners should have been based on both strategic and equitable criteria. It seems logical to expect that the behaviour of the Westerners, who were representing governments and governmental agencies, would reflect their domestic governmental standards and ways of doing things, so

---

22　It must be noted that Czechoslovakia refused US aid.

the host countries would learn not just about economic efficiency, but also about the political process which underlies decisions on the aid content and practice of its delivery.

The next section outlines the *how* of the Western assistance delivery in the first years of reforms in CEE and gauges what was the likely impact of the actual manner of aid and assistance delivery on democratic learning in the CEE countries. The process of aid delivery will be analysed from two perspectives: firstly, as a process designed by the donor countries, and secondly, the actual aid delivery and its reception as evidenced by the behaviour of the experts, consultants and policy makers on both sides.

Foreign Aid and Assistance: The Process. Implications for Democracy

The majority of writings on international promotion and consolidation of democracy in the CEE countries through foreign aid and assistance assert its relative success (Whitehead 1996b; Smith 2001; Pridham, Herring and Sanford (1994); Pridham and Vanhanen 1994; Radaelli 2003; Schimmelfenning et al. 2005). Most scholars stress that it was not just the beneficial influence of the West, but that domestic conditions which favoured democratic development – including the strength of the 'pull', or openness to Western influences – played a crucial role (Smith 2001: 57; Pravda and Zielonka 2001: 2). With the benefit of hindsight, I think that a more balanced account of those processes is in order.[23]

To provide such a re-balanced account I begin with distinguishing two stages in the process of democratisation: democracy promotion and democracy consolidation. Promotion is the more elusive, but also more straightforward, phenomenon in relation to CEE countries such as Poland, Hungary, Czechoslovakia and Slovenia: it is the convincing of the target countries that they should strive towards democracy. The CEE 'leaders' in democratisation – Poland, Hungary, Czechoslovakia and Slovenia – did not need much convincing, mainly because their desire to democratise had already been strong. At the earliest opportunity they expressed the wish to re-join the democratic family of states. The aspiration to live in democracy and freedom drove the democratic protests that led to the political breakthrough in the first place. Hence, at the beginning of the systemic reforms there was a strong drive to democratise both at the grass-root and the elite level – the chances for democratisation looked promising (Grugel 1999: 8). Under these conditions, Western assistance and pressure for democratic reforms and Western models of democracy played a positive role in establishing the institutional foundations for democratic and constitutional order in the initial period of democratisation, as they fed into the domestic contexts favourable to democratisation.

---

23   Grabbe (2006) is one of the few scholars who provide such balanced account, but the focus of her work differs from my own.

However, when it comes to the more critical stage – the consolidation of democracy, in the sense of creating a political culture which would support the development and functioning of democratic institutions – the picture becomes less clear. Yet the crucial importance of such a culture of consolidated democracy is accepted across the literature on democratisation and democratic theory (Grugel 1991: 12), perhaps most strongly in the writings influenced by structuralism. It has been also widely recognised that weak culture and democratic consolidation might cause democratic institutions to act in a non-democratic way (Grugel 1991: 9) and lead to serious pathologies and distortions in the way that political systems work.

Promotion of Democracy from Outside the CEE

There are grounds to suggest that beyond the success of promotion of democratic development, international influence on democratic consolidation is, at best, mixed.[24] The most problematic aspects of this influence can be grouped under the following headings.

1. Unbalanced power relations between the West and the East. Top-down process: dialog and deliberations between the foreign actors and target countries largely absent.
2. No clear or well-defined plans for the promotion of democracy. Neoliberalism informing the general direction of policies.
3. The process of selection of recipients of aid and assistance lacking in transparency and accountability. In many cases this led to selection based on the existing, usually *clientelist*, networks, instead of selection on merit – which lead to the legitimisation of those networks. The substantive choices of the donors meant that groups associated with neo-liberal market reforms were promoted to the exclusion of others. For instance, only the post-Solidarność groups got funding, the opposition did not.
4. NGOs – established and financed by Western donors. Not sustainable – many disappeared once foreign funding ended.[25] Many surviving NGOs started functioning as 'hedges', focusing on their own survival, not on social/public goals.

Each of the above points have been already elaborated in existing literature. In the next section, I will develop these points above only from my own narrow perspective and only to the extent necessary to further my main argument.

---

24 See Grabbe (2006) for a similar view.

25 This way of establishing NGOs resulted in the façade-type of NGO which did not take root and disappeared once funding was terminated, or transformed into 'hedges', focusing on their own survival (Nowicka 2010).

Patterns of Aid Delivery

One of the most common matrices for international aid delivery is that of Western help in the developing countries of the Third World.[26] Evidence suggests that this matrix has been used in taking aid to CEE countries despite their very different socio-political make-up and needs. Shöpflin, for instance, observed that Western practices have been imposed on CEE in a colonial fashion (1992: 40). Yet this clearly misguided approach had not been challenged. One of the reasons may have been the persisting perception of the West as a benevolent empire willing to extend a helping hand, and the needy CEE, grateful for help and eager not to upset the generous host.[27] Such dynamics fed into existing cultural traits on both sides: West and East. It bears recognisable traces of the Polish tradition of great willingness to accept a benevolent paternalistic authority that grants favours (Osiatyński 1993: 314). On the other hand, it reflects the decades (if not centuries) of mutual lack of interests and understanding between the two parts of Europe. The unequal power relation that became obvious in the design and delivery of the programme of assistance for the CEE countries was partly a reflection of those systemic features of the West–East relations, but partly also reflected the high priority given to the West's own interests: security and economic gain. Despite these obvious aspects of realpolitik, there was more than a grain of belief in the target countries that a Marshall-plan-type aid package was on offer through which the West would finally compensate for the sell-out in Yalta in 1945.[28]

More crucially for the prospects of democratisation, these unbalanced power relations between the donors and recipients meant that the partnership and dialog was not to be the main modus operandi in the way that aid was designed and delivered. On the contrary, the picture that emerged was that of the donors acting in a manner of an enlightened planner, in a way, a replacement for the Communist party whose task was to set targets. The recipients had little input into the decisions and were often not even communicated to them. Not surprisingly, their response to the objectives set by the donors often amounted to the 'please the donors' practice, which meant replacing reality with fictitious success stories and outcomes (Wedel 1998: 73). This practice was mastered to perfection under the previous system of a centrally planned economy and it proved very useful in the aid-programme reception: since both sides needed to show good results, they colluded in exaggerating the success of many such programmes. As demonstrated by Wedel, much of the reporting of the progress of reforms was an eyewash (1998: 73).

---

26   See for instance Sørensen (1993).

27   Compare with Schöpflin (1992) and Zielonka (2008).

28   Compare with Sørensen, who actually used the term 'new Marshall plan' for the 1990s (1993: 63).

Economy as Basis for Democratic Development: Neoliberalism
As far as the strategic planning for the promotion of democracy in the CEE goes, Western consensus did not translate into a coherent strategy of how this could be achieved (Smith 2001: 33). One of the more widespread assumptions that informed Western action was that free-market economy reforms will eventually lead to democratic consolidation.[29] Most academics also supported this idea (e.g. Pinder 1994; McMann 2006).[30] This belief was elevated to a dogma by neoliberal ideologists and informed many of the economic policies imposed on the CEE countries. 'Spectrum of political debate has been constrained by the international and domestic consensus for neoliberal market' (Grzymała-Busse and Innes 2003: 66). To what extent this neoliberal push produced the expected results is an open question and one that lies beyond the scope of this chapter.[31] However, the neoliberal flavour of the approach of Western donors clearly influenced the manner of aid delivery. Of particular significance was the separation of economic aspects of aid delivery from the political process, in other words, the exclusion of aid allocation from democratic political controls – in line with one of the fundamental tenets of neoliberalism. On a bigger scale of systemic reforms a number of important consequences followed. Little direct assistance went into establishment or support for democratic institutions and procedures.[32]

The neoliberal agenda also lead to the strengthening of the phenomenon of political capitalism (Staniszkis 1991) which had already started taking root in Poland, by excluding from democratic control the politics and policy of economic reforms, including privatisation. This, in turn, paved the way for the flourishing of the mutually parasitic relationship between the donors and the new Polish owners/ businessmen: the consultants representing the donors made sure that the donors' strategic goals were achieved; the new Polish businessmen used the consultants to establish contacts, links and to seek investors. Wedel (1998) gives such an example of collusion between the donors and the local entrepreneurs: the consultants often deliberately understated the value of companies which were considered for privatisation. The buyer – that is, a Polish or foreign entrepreneur – did not object,

---

29   This approach refers to the so-called modernisation approach to democratisation, associated with the work of Lipset (1960).

30   These assumptions are increasingly challenged. See for instance Orenstein, who suggests that neither free-market reforms nor democracy are decisive in ensuring stable conditions for economic growth. Instead, geopolitics – in other words, either good relations with Russia or EU membership – are much more decisive factors (2009).

31   One possible outcome was suggested by Ganev (2005: 371), 'the East Europeans were willing to take neoliberal money and run with it in nonneoliberal directions'. See also Orenstein (2009).

32   Compare with Rengger, who argued that over-emphasising state-building at the expense of grass-roots democratisation was likely to 'lead to decreasing support for the "democratic" institutions on which they had pinned so much hope' (1994: 72). Almost two decades later, opinion polls confirm that the trust of the domestic governing institutions has been extremely low for a number of years.

since the benefits of buying the company cheaper was an obvious incentive, while the national treasury suffered a loss.

In substantive terms, the aid delivery practices of the donors driven by the neoliberal blueprint[33] created a snowball effect of facilitating the establishment of like-minded elites whose power was bolstered not just by financial resources, but also by joining 'the only game in town', that is, neoliberal reforms (Żuk 2004: 48). It also contributed to a failure to establish a constitutional mechanism of governance in a wider sense of limiting economic self-interest of the governing elites. The enhancement of elite-power strengthened the hierarchies of patronage and personal connections, that is the feudal-like social stratification characteristic of communist systems. In addition, the use by donors of the established network of informal, clientelist relations and communist-style organisation and practices helped to legitimise those networks and those practices (Wedel 1998: 189).

Yet another doubtful consequence of the neoliberal policy bias was that the donors choose to assist those CEE groups that were associated with a similar ideological orientation in promoting market reforms. In this way, many decisions on aid, even those which were said to be about democracy, pluralism and civil society, were determined by the economic agenda of the donors (Wedel 1998: 99). Not only did this lead to resentment of the losers and their constituencies, but it also undermined democratic learning by attaching a label of democracy to undemocratic practices of what amounted to a selection based on political orientation rather than on merit. One of the pathological outcomes of such aid allocation was that financial aid often benefited informal groups that formalised themselves as NGOs and used the aid only for the benefit of the group. Almost two decades later this trend continues: most NGOs in Poland and other CEE countries have been described as 'hedges' whose main raison d'être is to secure, usually, public funds to ensure their continued existence rather than to engage in social or political missions. Since the security of funding became their main activity, these NGOs have become on the whole more successful in competing for funds against other, socially engaged organisations, pushing them out of existence (Nowicka 2010). It is difficult not to attach at least some blame to the donors for the degeneration of the idea of civil society as their actions in this area had the power of setting examples of good practice in countries where the idea of civil society and NGOs was yet to take roots.

Part Summary

I believe that it is reasonable to assume that the politics of aid delivery and the conduct of the representatives of the Western democratic states, the experts, advisors and consultants, shaped the public perception of democracy and capitalism in the transition countries of CEE. It was, after all, the first close encounter between the

---

33   Compare with, for instance, Whitehead (1994: 68–9), who questioned the suitability of market-driven reforms for CEE countries.

democratic practices of the West and the post-communist reality. In these countries, where democracy and constitutionalism were still mostly empty concepts, filling those concepts with meaning and substance for the first time, and on such a scale and scope can be compared to chiselling permanent traces on the system, which, at that time, was particularly receptive to such a process.

I suggest that aspects of this process and politics of the delivery of Western aid, both economic[34] and directly targeted at democracy promotion, has been a lesson damaging to learning about the need for dialogue, transparency and accountability. Greater openness to Western influences (the strength of the 'pull') of countries such as Poland might have, paradoxically, contributed to a more profound subversion of democratic development as these countries were more likely to be less critical of the undemocratic practices passed on to them under the banner of democracy by the Western donors. Moreover, the patronising and often self-serving style of delivery of some aid programmes, particularly at the beginning of the CEE reforms, reinforced and, in some ways, legitimised many of the undemocratic practices of the old political system. It seems fair to conclude that the delivery of Western aid succeeded in neither creating new precedents of democratic practices in post-communist countries nor in changing the undemocratic and unconstitutional practices well-established in these countries.

Transition and Accession to the EU: Political Conditionality

Europeanisation and the 'Return to Europe'

A number of academics have pointed out that CEE's Europeanisation is a potentially confusing concept. According to some scholars this is so because it implies the process of joining the EU,[35] but also the much wider phenomenon of the 'return to Europe' (Grabbe 2006: 4–5; Cremona 2005: 8). Both terms are problematic, to say the least, and not very precise on a practical or a conceptual level, as calls for 'EU-sation' imply. Despite this, both concepts capture reasonably well the re-setting of the boundaries of Europe and 'within Europe' in more than a geographic sense (Cremona 2005: 8). However, this metaphorical movement is rooted in a set of implied, rather than tested or justified, political and developmental criteria.

---

34   The question might be asked why economic aid should be delivered in other than an efficient manner. I suggest that the meaning of efficiency in this context presupposes that resources are well-targeted. The way to ensure this under conditions of competition for aid is to enter into a dialogue and transparent process of resources allocation. So, the aim might be economic, but the process should be based on democratic criteria such as equal treatment, transparency and accountability.

35   I use the term 'EU' even though before the 1992 Treaty of the European Union (the Maastricht Treaty), 'EEC' is the correct term.

Conceived in this way, the semantics of 'return to Europe' and Europeanisation reinforce this asymmetry of preconceived assumptions between the civilised, developed Europe and its backward periphery (Tazbir 2007). The post-communist countries are denied their Europeaness until they reach the standards set by the true Europeans – the West. Hence, in both political and cultural terms, Europeanisation and the return to Europe indicate a relation of power and domination vis-à-vis the weakness and aspirations to re-join the site of highly desirable attributes such as modernisation, civilisation and development. The 'return to Europe' framework is the more emotive of the two, indicating the movement from inside the transition countries.

Such dynamics of EU and the CEE relations helped to shape the perception of the policies imposed on the CEE as part of Europeanisation as directly beneficial for both the CEE countries and the EU. Acceptance of this perception has led some scholars to concentrate on Europeanisation as EU rule adoption, which in turn led those scholars on a search for models and mechanisms to help to explain such processes (Schimmelfenning and Sedelmeier 2005b). Other schools took a broader view of Europeanisation as 'a response to the policies of the EU', or, more specifically, as a process of institutional adaptation and as adaptation of policy and policy processes (Featherstone and Radaelli 2003: 2–5). Generally, most of the Europeanisation literature concentrates on trying to ascertain how rule adoption or policy and institutional adaptation takes place; which model is closest to capturing such processes, and under what domestic conditions Europeanisation is most likely to be effective. A sub-genus of this strand of Europeanisation literature evaluates the real and potential gains for both the CEE countries and the EU.[36]

I will not engage in this type of discussion directly, as my approach is mainly procedural. My main question relates to the potential benefits of learning by exposure to the way in which the EU has been dealing with the CEE countries in delivering aid and assistance and in implementing conditionality. The following are some of the pervasive issues which dominate this dynamics between the CEE countries and the EU, in the sense of practices and procedure and their domestic impact.

1. The EU – similar to the international aid donors discussed above – was placed in positions of benevolent authority (empire) whose motives and means of acting were beyond discussion as they were assumed to be beneficial for the target countries. Practical help and assistance were dispensed by the EU on empire-like terms in a top-down process.[37]

---

36   The vast majority of writings, particularly those on the role of the EU in post-communist transformations, focus on substantive, positive outcomes – mainly economic, but also political – of the EU's and other international pressure and assistance for the recipient countries.

37   A remark made at one of the University Association for Contemporary European Studies annual conferences summed up this way of thinking: 'Why we should pay those

2. CEE countries were placed in a position of subjects rather than as partners to this imperial benevolence, so the possibility of voicing concerns or/and discuss suitability of certain solutions was limited.[38]
3. There was a lack of benchmarks and clarity of meaning of the terms on which the EU political conditionality was based and lack of clear standards of assessment.
4. Delivery of conditionality took place through mainly technocratic process led by the Commission.

Pre-accession Conditionality: Tools

Conditionality was probably the strongest of the policy instruments used by the EU in trying to encourage domestic change, and it played a decisive role in both processes: the 'return to Europe' and Europeanisation. The rich literature on EU conditionality can be divided into two basic strands: appreciative of the, on balance, great benefits of conditionality while admitting that not all was well (Hughes et al. 2004; Vahudowa 2005; Schimmelfenning and Sedelmeier 2005b; Grabbe 2006);[39] and the second strand, which sees conditionality essentially as a failure, mainly due to the lax standards used to assess the state of democracy and the Rule of Law in the candidate countries by the Commission (Kochenov 2007). My own argument focuses on the undemocratic application and enforcement of conditionality, as one of the possible causes of the damage inflicted on the democratic learning of CEE societies and governing elites. To navigate between those competing stands, I start by placing conditionality within the context of pre-accession politics.

The EU has been perceived as a powerful and potentially very influential actor in the CEE transformations, mainly in appreciation of its economic and political power, confirmed by the desire to join, expressed by a number of the CEE countries very early on in their 'refolutions'. The decades-long quest of 'returning to Europe' bolstered this perception by projecting the EU as a powerful symbol of freedom and prosperity; joining it was a way of reclaiming a place in the civilised family of nations. This 'pull' was met, initially, by the EU PHARE programme created in 1989. Also in 1989, the EU Commission was tasked to coordinate the aid from the G24 (including the OECD, World Bank, IMF and the Paris Club).

---

countries for doing something that they should be doing anyway'. This observation did not attract any critical comments, which probably means that the majority of the audience agreed with that point of view. See for instance Zielonka (2008), where the term 'Europe as Empire' occurs.

38   Sajó commented: 'The acqui was imposed unconditionally and in the most extended sense, and many people in the East considered it a kind of dictate' (2005: 252).

39   One of the most recent contribution is Přibáň, who acknowledges 'a very mixed results' of the Copenhagen criteria on democratic constitutionalism proceeds to assert 'its enormously positive and stabilizing effect' (2010: 16–17).

Even though this package of powers placed the EU 'in a position to channel a wide range of policy advice about transition, both from its own resources and also the international financial institutions and other bodies' (Grabbe 2006: 8), initially EU influence was limited to economic matters. Only with the signing of the Europe Agreements[40] did the first timid formulation of political conditionality appear in the suspension clause which linked trade and cooperation agreement to five conditions: rule of law, human rights, a multi-party system, free and fair elections and a market economy.

Copenhagen conditions set more specific requirements, of which the following were the core of political conditionality: stability of institutions guaranteeing democracy, rule of law, human rights and respect for and protection of minorities. The Partnership Agreements, which were offered to the candidate countries between 1998 and 2002, contained more specific and explicit conditions, although these were mainly related to economic integration. By 1999 a group of ten CEE candidate countries were judged to have met the initial political conditions, which propelled them into the accession negotiations proper. The signing of the Accession Treaty[41] and the successful referenda in all accession countries completed this stage. 1st May 2004 was set as the official date of accession for the ten new member states.

The brief outline of the main steps leading towards full membership of the CEE countries will be developed in the next section with the aim to offer insight into the nature of the process behind the completion of each of those steps. The main questions, in keeping with the general focus of this book, will relate to the democratic constitutional standards: was the process of the EU political conditionality deliberative and inclusive of the main participants? Were the criteria clear? Was the auditing process carried out according to set and agreed criteria? In short, was the implementation of EU pre-accession/accession political conditionality an effective lesson in democratic and constitutional learning?

Pre-accession and Accession Conditionality: Process and Effects

The next section will evaluate the process of setting the criteria and will follow the applying/enforcing the conditionality based on those criteria. For the sake of clarity, economic conditionality must be distinguished from political conditionality as it is more intrusive and based on a pre-judged model of economic policy, so potentially more problematic from the point of view of adjustment costs expected from the candidate states. Even though on substance, economic conditionality lies outside the scope of this project, the politics and application behind this conditionality arguably illustrate the type of dynamics that developed between the EU and the candidate countries and the politics and process behind it. Moreover, the importance of two types of conditionality should be appreciated more generally,

---

40   No longer in force, replaced by Accession Treaties.
41   Treaty of Athens, signed on 16 April 2003. See Hillion (2004) for a comment.

since they relate to many of the most fundamental functions of the modern state. Recogniticn of this justifies the insistence on democracy and constitutionalism in designing and delivering those policies, as their potential to influence the political and economic systems of candidate countries must be seen as considerable.

In contrast to those expectations, the setting and defining of criteria of conditionality, both political and economic, have been criticised as one-sided, non-transparent, and not accountable (Cremona 2005: 17). The instruments containing conditions and expectations were created by EU institutions without much debate or accommodation of the needs of the candidate countries. Grabbe observes that 'by arguing that the CEE had to be ready to join, the EU put emphasis on the applicants conforming to the EU, rather than the EU reforming itself to fit the new members' (2006: 29). Grabbe goes on to say that

> The conditions were presented as if they were self-evident, with no ackncwledgement of the policy debates going on in the EU and outside about the appropriate role of the state in the economy and alternative models of corporate governance. [...] no rationale was presented publicly. Even though *this was such a wide agenda from such an important external influence*, there was no detailed justification for these demands beyond the fact they come in the name of joining the EU. (Grabbe 2006: 25) [*emphasis added*]

In keeping with the above assessment, the candidate countries were not invited as partners to the negotiating table and their preferences were often marginalised. Grabbe (2006: 193–7) asked why the CEE countries only rarely challenged EU demands that were so clearly going against their vital interests. She provided five levels of explanation, the most relevant of which – from this book's perspective – related to the weakness of the CEE states, both in the sense of bargaining power vis-à-vis the EU, and due to the systemic upheavals they were undergoing. Also, since many areas of state activity related to private economy were either non-existent or underdeveloped, there was a genuine need for solutions and models to be imported from outside. Such importation, however, often amounted to wholesale transplantation since the power relations between the EU and the target countries impaired more sensitive adjustment to local conditions.[42]

The unquestioning acceptance of even detrimental measures of the EU's conditiorality policy by the CEE candidate countries should also be seen as indicative of the power relations between the EU and those countries, and the way those were mediated by domestic political practices. The policies were known only to a small group of policy makers and not publicly discussed, yet, the need for debate and transparency might have been further reduced by the willingness of national governments to take the blame for potentially unfavourable outcomes of those policies. Such submissiveness of the CEE countries, made the possibility of

---

42   On the perils of forcing Western models on post-communist countries of CEE, see for instance Wedel (1990: 238); Wälde and Gunderson (1994).

challenging the EU for not designing its policies in line with local needs unlikely. The lack of such a challenge may also have indicated a lack of appreciation in the candidate countries of the complexity of what was required. The reasons behind this might have been the lack of competence and knowledge related to the 'low capacity in terms of comprehension and access to expertise' in domestic Parliaments:

> The *Sejm* will soon be flooded by EU legislative proposals, but it does not have the technical or intellectual capabilities to deal with them. [...] Please do not confer upon the parliament any additional oversight functions with regard to our accession to the EU, because *Sejm* is incapable of performing even the most rudimentary oversight functions in internal policy. (Sadurski 2003: 53)

Sadurski further suggested that the level of competence of parliamentarians in other new Member States is probably not much better (2003: 53). This was almost certainly the case, as confirmed by Kochenov, who quoted a Romanian MP: 'Please do not debate: this is an international provision in the EU and so we just have to put it in the law as such' (2007: 157).

I suggest that the problems with the National Parliaments participation and the lack of oversight of the European Parliament over the process further weakened the democratic and constitutional credentials of conditionality. This, however, is not a generally accepted view. Schimmelfenning et al., for instance, offer a contrasting explanation of the passive acceptance of conditionality by candidate countries. According to him, and following the 'external incentives' model, 'the desire to join the EU was so strong that it overrode any concerns and criticisms the candidate countries might have had with the appropriateness of EU conditionality' (2005: 32). This view refers the unequal power relations, but in an accepting rather than a questioning manner. In line with this, the high domestic costs, rather than concerns with legitimacy of conditionality might have been 'the only reason' of non-compliance. In contrast, I am suggesting that the candidate countries would not have dared to voice concerns for fear of rejection, which led to badly designed package of policies, lacking in legitimacy and constitutional credentials. By developing 'coping' strategies, the perception of EU conditionality effectiveness was created, but this undermined in large measure its real effectiveness and, crucially, weakened the potential to set democratic precedent.

In his later paper Schimmelfenning once more relates the effectiveness of conditionality to:

> a credible conditional perspective of admission to the most attractive organisations [...] an open invitation to all European countries to become European Union and NATO members once human rights and democratic institutions are firmly established has the strong potential to lock in democratic reforms and *'civilize'* authoritarian, nationalist and populist political leaders and parties. (2007: 138) [*emphasis added*]

The cringe-worthy reference to cold war rhetoric of the civilised West and the barbaric East which can be civilised by joining NATO and the EU hides a number of doubtful assumptions. But it also goes some way towards explaining the prevailing justification of the clearly hegemonic position that the EU asserted in CEE accession conditionality and the disparity between the expectations towards the old, presumably already civilised, MSs and the candidate countries. The lack of democracy in the process of the pre-accession conditionality design and application compares unfavourably with previous accessions, where the scope for negotiations and derogations was much greater. The clear asymmetry in power relations not just between the EU and the CEE candidate countries (Zielonka 2008: 476) but also between the old MSs and the aspiring candidates excluded the chance for a dialogue-based partnership, the lack of which, under conditions of clear dominance and discrimination, was unlikely to lead to most productive outcomes. As argued by Zielonka

> the EU's exercise of power should not have been chiefly about indoctrination and subjugation, but about promotion of policies, procedures and rules that lead to empowerment of other actors, however weak. (2008: 484)

The candidate countries were hardly empowered by policies that were not consulted and imposed in a top-down manner, hence, not likely to accommodate the needs and specific conditions of the applicants. This was made even more problematic by the EU's acting on the assumption that the *acqui* offered a universal model for the establishment and functioning of markets, and that pre-accession conditionality constituted the most suitable package of political objectives. The strong drive to join might have lead to practices designed to create compliance, at a superficial level at best, but without creating a supporting culture or entrenchment necessary for lasting and meaningful change. If this last effect cannot be dismissed as totally unworthy, since even the superficial effects might turn into a profound change with time, this seems a rather long-winded way in comparison with one which would lead to the creation of an appropriate adjustment strategy in the first place. So, contrary to Schimmelfenning, the 'locking in of democratic reforms' (2007: 138) could have a better chance if carried out in a responsive rather than a top-down fashion.

Inequality of Treatment
The disparity of the Commission's expectations between the existing and the prospective member states (MSs) under conditionality is yet another of its problematic aspects. At the centre of this is art. 5 TEC,[43] which limited EU competence to monitor the existing MSs only in the fields covered by the 'conferred powers' principle under this article. The limitation of Commission's powers did

---

43   Art. 5 TEU, as amended by Lisbon Treaty, Official Journal of the European Union C 115/19.

not apply under art. 5 TEC, to, at that time, candidate countries (Albi 2009). That meant that what was expected of the candidate countries might not have been yet achieved in the existing MSs, nor in the EU, as problematic record on human rights[44] and persisting accusations of 'democratic deficit' imply. It would be difficult to avoid the conclusion that the candidate states were expected to comply with standards that barely existed in the EU, and compliance with which might have varied across the MS. This inequality of treatment had more substantive consequences, since, as suggested by Grabbe the accession process pushed the CEE countries towards greater convergence with particular policy models than had occurred within the old MSs (2006: 42). Yet, the evidence that emerges from Poland confirms that the EU's policies and regulatory models might not have been the most appropriate for the CEE transition countries (Skąpska 2009; Kowalik 1994; Poznański 1999). The question should be asked, why the CEE countries accepted those models in the face of their doubtful suitability and also given that the old MSs were not under the same obligation? The perceived lack of domestic solutions[45] that created the need and receptiveness to external policies definitely played a role, but the weaker bargaining position of the CEE countries and lack of debate were also important factors. Even if it would be difficult to link directly the weakness of democratic and constitutional standards in EU with the undermining of the legitimacy of conditionality, the inequality of treatment between the old and prospective MSs seems to provide such a link; it makes those deficiencies visible in a particular set of practices that the EU developed and implemented.

Indeterminacy of Conditionality
Another problematic aspect of political conditionality was, as argued by Kochenov (2007), the lack of any clarification of what were the very standards that the CEE countries were expected to satisfy and the lack of clarity on how the Commission conducted its assessment of compliance with those standards.[46] There are at least two ways in which this happened; first, it was the lack of precision in the use of terminology on which accession conditionality was based and secondly, the lax manner of auditing compliance by the European Commission.[47] Radaelli noted

---

44   The persisting debate and questioning of the EU's commitment to HR lost its most acute edge with the passing of Lisbon Treaty, which prepares the ground for the EU's accession to the ECHR. See for instance Arnull (2003) for an outline of the main issues in this debate.

45   The internal politics of most CEE countries precluded any form of public debate on such choices. This was partly due to the rejection of the public preferences which were scorned as those of homo sovieticus, that is, demanding regulated capitalism with well-developed welfare provisions and egalitarian society.

46   Kochenov's convincing argument on the failure of conditionality is based on this thesis. My own approach is to argue that the unbalanced power relations between the EU and the CEE and the less than democratic manner of accession preparation, including conditionality, were equally, if not more, important for this failure.

47   As persuasively demonstrated by Kochenov (2007).

that 'concepts that are not well-defined lead to confusion and elusive language [...] and generate mistakes in terms of "ladder of abstraction"' (2003: 28). The absence of definitions in the Commission's documents did create a semantic confusion and its own ladder of abstraction.

Since democracy and rule of law are essentially contested concepts, their blurred meaning arguably becomes even more uncertain when applied to countries which for at least the past five decades did not experience a functioning constitutional democratic system, and for whom those meanings were more abstract than for other MSs. The way the Commission proceeded with its auditing activities, on an *ad hoc basis*, compounded this semantic confusion even further. By arbitrarily neglecting some fundamental elements of the governmental function of the state while focusing on others (Kochenov 2007: 191, 305), the Commission lent its authority to legitimise even the unchecked aspects of the system. Stamping its seal of approval on doubtful practices and institutions most likely perverted the substantive meaning of the basic democratic terminology. Democracy and constitutionalism might have been devalued and disconnected from their substance. On an operational level, the elites might have lost the incentive to continue with bettering the system, since the limited reforms were approved as sufficient by the Commission and the public received a lesson in democratic posturing which was presented as true democracy.

In contrast with the above, Schimmelfenning et al. accepted the existence of the lack of 'determinacy and legitimacy' of EU political conditionality but dismissed its relevance (2005: 32). According to this, the absence of determinacy was offset by a concrete demand for changes in state rules and behaviour. This argument is not fully convincing. The Commission selectively assessed only the arbitrarily selected institutional elements of the democratic system: the composition of the parliament, the efficiency of parliaments, and the compliance of the legislation with the *acqui*. It neglected such fundamental phenomena as how the party system functioned, parliamentary representation and the electoral process (Albi 2009: 987). Even within this narrow focus there are doubts as to the Commission's accuracy: its positive assessment of parliamentary efficiency contrasts sharply with native accounts.[48] In a wider perspective, focusing on institutional aspects of democratisation leads not only to simplification of the concept of democracy, but often also to taking the existence of institutions for democracy itself (Grugel 1999: 4).

More crucially, Schimmelfenning et al. does not pay much attention to the essential elements which democracy needs if it is to evolve and consolidate: accountability, inclusion, representation and transparency.[49] So the Commission's feedback might have been clear on points related to the functioning Parliaments and the number of Acts of Parliament which were passed in the implementation of the *acquis communautaire*. However, the lack of attention to the absence or serious

---

48   Sadurski (2003: 53), quoted above.

49   Those criteria break down into much more detailed factors too numerous and complex to discuss here.

weaknesses of other fundamental elements of democracy in the implementation of the *acquis* challenges the view that determinacy of conditionality has been 'indeed high' (Schimmelfenning et al. 2005: 32).[50]

In summary, conditionality might have been more detrimental to democratic consolidation in the CEE countries than is acknowledged. The lack of clear standards, benchmarking and haphazard auditing by the Commission may have led to a mainly formal type of implementation, undermining the effectiveness of conditionality. The technocratic nature of the conditionality implementation contrasted with the basic democratic criteria of transparency, accountability and responsiveness. More crucially, the meaning of democracy and rule of law communicated to the CEE countries through the Commission's actions and through the lack of definitions of those terms created semantic confusion which not only negatively affected the cognitive and normative dimension of Europeanisation, but potentially undermined the legitimacy of the values that conditionality was aiming to uphold.

The Case of the EU Charter of Fundamental Rights

The inclusion of the non-binding Charter of Fundamental Rights in 2000 Treaty of Nice was an important step in the EU constitutional development. The Charter's soft power helped to solidify the EU's perception as a beneficial influence on Member States. However, in contrast to this perception, the evidence that the EU had been focusing more on symbolic effect than on the legal content of rights during the drafting of the Charter attracted accusations of instrumental use of the Charter to strengthen the EU's legitimacy and to alleviate the fear of the existing MSs towards the Eastern enlargement (Goetz 2005: 257). Such accusations need to be taken seriously, since the Charter, in contrast with the political conditionality which was aimed at a broad range of systemic adjustments, goes to the heart of democratic constitutionalism as it focuses on the rights of individuals. It follows that the Charter's drafting and debating process should have been inclusive and responsive. The reality shows that this was not the case. Not only did the drafting process struggle to live up to basic democratic expectations, but also the potential significance of the Charter was partly lost in the politics surrounding it.

Not all share this view: De Burca, for instance, positively assessed the nature of the drafting process, particularly the involvement of civil-society organisations and 'relatively deliberative and open forum for constitutional debate' (2001: 138). The majority of scholars, however, beg to differ. Schonlau stops short of anti-democratic charge, but raises questions in relation to representativeness of the members of the Convention drafting the Charter, the role and accountability of the presidium, and the quality and quantity of civil society, that was to play crucial

---

50   Compare also with Sedelmeier (2009: 21), who noted the level of difficulty in assessing *actual* as opposed to *formal* compliance.

role in consulting and advising the Convention.[51] The lack of any challenge to the proposed text itself might be taken as evidence that a robust debate did not take place. Hence, the *'sense* of popular legitimacy' and *'symbolic appeal'* are probably key phrases helpful in understanding the impact of the work of the Convention.[52]

From the perspective of the (then) candidate states of CEE, the drafting of the Charter may have represented yet another instance of the top-down exercises that were so characteristic of the process of accession; they were included in the drafting, but only in a 'little more than symbolic' manner (Sadurski 2002: 346). The outcome of the one and only 'audition' that the candidate countries were granted resulted in a 'nil' impact upon the Charter (Sadurski 2002: 348). Such treatment was unfortunate, as these countries were at that time, and still are, struggling to learn their democratic ways; and particularly regrettable since the Charter was to become a yardstick to test the HR credentials of those countries (Sadurski 2002: 342). It seems then, that the relations between the EU and the candidate states of CEE on the drafting of the Charter fell into the pattern set during the earlier design and application of conditionality. Exclusion rather than participation and no real input into the debate over the substance of the Charter send a confused message – neither the process of drafting the Charter, nor its substance seemed that important.

Opting Out of the EU Charter of Rights: Conditionality in Reverse?[53]

Poland's position vis-à-vis the EU evolved from the keen acceptance of the EU conditions in the early 1990s to increasingly hardened stand on Union policies after the Commission's report of 1997 (DOC/97/16) which confirmed Poland's readiness for membership and opened accession negotiations. Was this yet another case of gradual reassertion of bargaining power which reflected much more strongly preferences of domestic politics 'once the accession was "in the bag"' (Ágh 2003: 113)?

The evolution of Poland's position on the Charter of Rights suggests that this might have been the case. Poland's contribution to the 2000 Intergovernmental Conference contained the following statement:

---

51   A number of academics point to the problematic nature of civil society organisations in their role as political actors. See for instance Dobson (2007).

52   Compare with Schonlau (2005): 'It is the perception of the citizens which is the main target of the project of drafting the Charter according to the Cologne mandate, not the substance of the rights concerned' (2005: 82).

53   Poland is not the only new MS who secured the opt-out: Czech Republic followed. See for instance Flash News (2009). For comment on both opt-outs see for instance Shuibhne (2009: 816) who asked if the 'the possibility of opting out has been reduced to political game-playing?

> For obvious reasons, connected with Poland's historical experiences and efforts
> to ensure the maximum guarantees of fundamental rights, [...] Poland supports
> the work on the Charter.[54]

This supportive statement was replaced by the Polish opt-out of the Charter in 2007 as a rather extreme turn around of Poland's position; the statement did not give any indication of such change. The 'historical experience', referred to in the statement, implies the awareness of the neglect of fundamental rights in the communist past and, presumably, heightened efforts to provide their effective protection in free Poland. In contrast, Poland's declaration 61 annexed to the Final Act puts the 'sphere of morality, family law, as well as protection of human dignity and respect for human physical and moral integrity' (2007/C 306/02) at the centre of Poland's rights policy. By taking a firm stand on rights in 'sphere of morality' in declaration 61, Poland might have been restating the need to ground the EU values in catholic doctrine, a move similar to the 2003 campaign for 'Christian roots' in the preamble of the Constitutional Treaty.

The timing of rolling out the agenda of Christian morality as a justification for Polish opt-out from the Charter provides an interesting comparison with Poland's negotiations over the Constitutional Treaty; the latter occurred after Poland's accession to the EU was secured, the former was and an act of a full member of the EU. It seems that once the membership was 'in the bag', Poland tried to establish a more assertive position towards the EU institutions and other MSs (Friis and Jarosz 2000: 31), in a clear attempt to be seen more as a 'policy-maker' or 'uploader' of her preferences on European level than as a 'downloader' (Goetz 2005: 255) – a reversal of power relations that were shaped by the EU conditionality. The 'Nice or death' slogan under which Poland entered negotiations over constitutional Treaty, 'Ioannina compromise', Kaczyński's attempt to secure more voting power for Poland using the 'war dead' (Traynor 2007) argument can be interpreted as European power games played for the benefit of domestic audience. But only the opt-out from the Charter – a continuation of such politics – has clearly demonstrated the influence over Brussels, since the other battles never amounted to a clear win. From this perspective, hence, the opt-out can be construed as a show of strength towards the EU.

On domestic level the politics of the opt-out from the Charter followed the undemocratic blueprint so characteristic of EU accession. There was no public debate on the opt-out, not even in the Sejm. The undemocratic domestic process behind the opt-out, and the politics of power towards EU may be interpreted as a failure of conditionality, since respect for fundamental rights was one of its key criterion, and democracy clearly suffered in the process of deciding on the opt-out. But also, this can be seen as Poland turning tables on EU by acting towards it in the same high-handed style as did the EU when designing and applying political conditionality. As argued by Schimmelfening and Sedelmeier:

---

54   CONFER/VAR 3967/00.

a top down, hierarchical rule transfer suffers from a legitimacy problem as the candidates had no say in creation of the rules, and thus lack 'ownership'. Once on the inside, resentment against such rules can therefore not only lead to strategic non-compliance, but to an open backlash against rules that are perceived as unfair external impositions. (2004: 676)

Even though Schimmelfening and Sedelmeier meant non-compliance in the sense of implementation and enforcement of the main body of EU law, the opt-out from the Charter fits the idea of 'strategic non-compliance' and 'open backlash' surprisingly well. The 'external impositions' in the context of the opt-out from the Charter refer to the competing vision of morality that clashed with that of Catholic Poland – which is a different type of imposition to what the authors had in mind. However, the general point that this quote illustrates is that the lack of input from the subjects to whom the rules are to apply under both types of conditionality – related to the *acquis communautaire* and political conditionality – is likely to produce similarly problematic results. The occurrence of such problems can be understood as a confirmation of the viability of the learning-by-observing approach, in that the undemocratic inclinations of Polish politicians were reinforced rather than undermined by the conduct of the EU officials in the practical application of conditionality that they observed.

Part Summary

Polish opt-out of the EU Charter of Fundamental Rights can be interpreted as a failure of important part of the EU political conditionality. It is likely that the hegemonic process by which political conditionality has been designed and applied failed to facilitate political change in post-communist part of Europe able to sustain and support true commitment to human rights protection. But this is not just the matter of substantive commitment: the shift in Poland's position from eager compliance with conditionality in pre-accession to a decisive opposition to the Charter of Fundamental once Poland's membership was secured, points to manipulative behaviour which has not much in common with democracy or constitutionalism. Since this opt-out has been verified neither by public debate not by prevailing social views, the domestic politics underlying the opt-out also scores very weakly on those credentials. It seems that not just fundamental rights agenda suffered from the lack of attention to democratic procedures in the Charter's drafting and enactment but equally affected was the wider process of EU constitutionalism and democratisation.

Conditionality Versus Democracy: A Summary

The doubtful benefits of external pressures on democratic consolidation in CEE confirm what the literature on political conditionality uncovered already some time ago: aid conditionality is likely to be effective only if a recipient country undertakes a policy change it would not have undertaken by itself without the pressure from the donors (Sørensen 1993: 74). In the case of CEE, the post-communist countries of the first wave of democratisation (Poland, Hungary, the Czech Republic and Slovenia)[55] were already well in the grip of their democratic change and constitutional moments that preceded an active involvement of external actors. Scholars described the early democratic reforms and improvements in human rights protection as 'anticipatory adaptation' (Schimmelfenning 2007: 133): in anticipation of, obviously, the integration with the West. Or rather, of the West's acceptance of its poor, uncivilised periphery.

Though undoubtedly correct, this is only part of the picture, but one that denies the possibility of domestic capacity for democratic change in a drive to make the transition countries a better places to live, regardless of the prospects of Western integration. Such accounts miss the development of the significant native constitutionalism and rights culture that took root in Poland from the 1970s.

An alternative to the prevailing ways of understanding the dynamics of external conditionality must at least consider the impact of the carrot of conditionality on the already well-developed indigenous democratisation and constitutionalism. For instance, one possible way of interpreting responses to conditionality was that the race for the carrot might have diverted the political momentum away from the domestic constitutional moments towards complying with the terms set by the external actors, rather than deepening the process of democratic change already under way. Ideally, the two processes should have overlapped. But, as argued above, the criteria of conditionality not always corresponded to the local needs, nor were they best suited to a particular political culture. Since not meeting the conditionality terms was simply not contemplated by the candidate states, as this would mean turning away from 'the road to civilisation and modernity', an option unacceptable from the point of domestic politics[56] – the potential for better adjustment and design of the EU policies was lost in the power asymmetry which stifled the chance for dialogue between the EU and the CEE countries. This logic might explain why strategies such as 'please the donor' and 'taking neo-liberal money to run in non-neoliberal directions' have been developed by the CEE countries receiving Western aid and assistance. Such strategies were successful in creating an appearance of consolidated democracy in the sense of putting in place institutions and procedures, but they left largely untouched the processes and culture on which those institutions' functioning depended.

---

55   There are some crucial differences between those countries and the Balkan countries or Bulgaria and Romania. Schimmelfenning (2007: 134) uses the term 'countries with liberal constellation, mixed and antiliberal constellation'.

56   The Polish PM at the time, Suchocka, stated that not being accepted into the EU would bring about a total catastrophe which would have led to 'the collapse of Polish civilisation' (1995).

The selectiveness of Western donors in assisting only groups of acceptable political orientation; the deals made with the existing business elites; the perpetuation of the patronage structures on which the old system was based – all these were matched by the EU's use of clientelist networks and allocation of funding based on political criteria rather than merit. As already argued, partly to blame was the technocratic nature of the pre-accession conditionality which design and implementation was led by the Commission (Grabbe 2006: 29 and 196). This strengthened the executive in candidate states and weakened the incentives to put in place a system of checks and controls over the process. Such a mode of functioning demonstrated by the Commission might have led the candidate states to believe that they can get away with excluding their societies from active participation in the process of fundamental re-building of their own states.

According to the 'social learning' model of the agency-centred version of sociological institutionalism, the more resonance there is at the domestic level with European [...] practices the more likely it is that they will be incorporated into existing domestic practices (Olsen 1996: 272). From this perspective, the failings of the EU political conditionality identified above can be reasonably matched with some of the most problematic features of reformed transition states. At the root of those was the collusion of elitist and technocratic tendencies on both sides – the CEE countries, where these were embedded in communist cultures; and the EU, where the main mode of policy making continues to be largely elitist and technocratic. It is likely, then, that the undemocratic practices of EU conditionality perpetuated further the gulf between the governing and the governed, bolstered the elitism inherent in the political systems of the CEE countries and legitimised the old networks of 'clientelism' and patronage, to the detriment of democratic constitutionalism.

Conclusions

It seems that both the international aid and assistance of the early 1990s and the EU politics of accession and pre-accession conditionality failed to set a good practice of democratic constitutionalism. Sajó opined that the constitutional process of accession was:

> objectively and subjectively, a process of submission – one that may well have been in the best interest of the new member states, but a submission nonetheless. (Sajó 2005: 252)

This was echoed by Grabbe, who concluded

> This technocratic approach to integration implies a democratic deficit in the whole eastern accession process. Accountability was lacking on the EU side [...], but there was little democratic participation on the CEE side. (2006: 196)

These two quotes capture some of the pervasive problems with the accession and pre-accession politics and conditionality that have long-lasting implications for the relations between the EU and candidate countries; for the potential success of the conditionality in terms of specific outcomes; and for the effectiveness of democratic learning and cultural entrenchment of the values that conditionality has been promoting.

The CEE countries' perception of the West and the EU as the epitome of stability, prosperity and civilising influence placed both in a strong position of potential influence of 'leading by example'. Yet, as far as democratisation and constitutionalism are concerned, the clearly non-democratic practices of delivery of aid and assistance, and the EU conditionality, not only challenge this perception, but also suggest that the CEE countries' understanding of what democratic process should look like might have been undermined. Moreover, some of the pathologies of the old system (Podgórecki 1994) – clientelism, favouritism, lack of transparency and accountability- were likely to have been reinforced. As a result, the limited constitutionalism and democratisation that was developing in the CEE, and in Poland since 1970s, have been diverted away from evolving into more consolidated systems in order to accommodate the EU conditionality and the Western donors pressures. Yet, those external influences proved badly aligned with the domestic context and poorly executed, hence, also for these reasons, cannot be considered as setting effective precedents of democratic and constitutional behaviour.

Chapter 4

Constitutional Tribunals in Central and Eastern Europe: Guardians of Democratic Constitutionalism?

Introduction

Modern constitutional theory places Constitutional Tribunals at the centre of constitutional democracy. Among many tasks that these Courts perform, guarding the constitution against the tyranny of a parliamentary majority and defining – by interpreting – and enforcing individual rights are some of the most fundamental. These two broad powers link the uneasy nexus of the constitutional imperative to limit political power with the democratic one, which gives a voice to citizens and protects their constitutional rights. Striking a balance between the two has been considered as fundamental in preventing constitutionalism from stifling the corrective force of democratic politics that should, in principle, underlie it (Mandel 1998; Tully 2002; Hirschl 2004; Colón-Ríos 2010). Tipping the scales towards majoritarian democracy, on the other hand, poses the threat of undermining the stability of constitutional order as suggested by Tully in his postulate for an equilibrium between *constitutional* democracy and *democratic* constitutionalism (2002: 206).

In this chapter, I analyse the contribution of the Polish Constitutional Tribunal (CT) to achieving the constitutionalism-democracy balance. Although I provide an account of the CT activities within the broad context of Polish politics, I limit my inquiry to just one aspect of the CT jurisdiction: the constitutional rights of individuals related to moral values – abortion and freedom of religion in context of religious education. These rights denote an aspect of constitutionalism that matters more for individuals whose life-styles or ethical choices put them in positions of minorities within certain cultural settings. Limiting the focus to these two type of cases is dictated by the controversial nature of the CT's judgements on abortion across the CEE region and by the fact that decisions of the Polish CT in religious freedom cases are clear examples of individual rights being sacrificed for the sake of promoting a particular value-agenda that goes against the spirit and also the letter of the 1997 Constitution. My analytical perspective uses sources that described the Polish CT's judgements in cases on abortion and freedom of religion as politically expedient (Klich 1996; Brzeziński 2000; Schwartz 2000; Sadurski 2010). I examine the possibility that the system of judicial appointments to the CT, and the influence of the organised religion might partially explain the politicisation of judgements in those cases.[1]

In the second part of this chapter I evaluate the effectiveness of the Polish CT in its role as a guardian of individual rights and freedoms and promoter of democratic constitutionalism by discussing individual constitutional complaint and by assessing the CT's influence over other courts.

Constitutional Tribunals and Democratic Constitutionalism

The role of CTs, as conceived by liberal democratic constitutional theory, illustrates one of the most acute systemic tensions, or paradoxes, of constitutional democracy, that is, between the constitutional imperative to limit political power of the legislature and executive, and the democratic principle, amounting to self-government. Being self-governed denotes the requirement of citizens' participation in shaping the fundamental laws by which they are governed, but also allows for democratic transformations of the already enacted constitutional texts (Colón-Ríos 2010: 29). To keep this process of constitutional revision in check and to prevent it from turning into the 'tyranny of the majority', the judges of (usually constitutional) tribunals wield the power of judicial review over this process and the legal acts that result from it. The judicial review power of CTs is complemented by the enforcement of constitutional rights, which is widely perceived as the most effective core mechanism of protection of rights generally, and specifically those of the minorities. Minorities which warrant constitutional protection include individual dissidents 'whether the dissidence is understood in political, moral, religious or personal lifestyle terms' (Sadurski 2005: 107).

These mechanisms of judicial guardianship over constitution amount to core aspects of a conception of constitutional democracy closely associated with liberal democratic theory which, in turn, rests on a number of assumptions. The most fundamental of these are the political independence of the judiciary and representative parliaments, elected in freely contested elections by a democratic franchise aligned with political parties whose political programmes tally with the electorate's interests. The political systems which manage most fully to realise these pre-conditions in practice will also be closest to balancing the imperatives of democratic constitutionalism against that of constitutional democracy, provided that other peripheral conditions are satisfied. These are far too numerous to list and discuss, but should include, for instance, an effective electoral system, election-

---

1   The focus of appointments of the judges to CT stays broadly in line with Sadurski's list of institutional variables 'which define a dominant model among the CEE states and which have a significant impact upon the democratic potential of those courts'. The full list of those variables is as follows: '(1) the modes of appointment and the tenure of judges; (2) who can initiate the review; (3) the type of review (ex ante or ex post, abstract or concrete); and (4) the finality of the review (2010: 99).

campaigns contested on political programmes and viable levels of political activism including civil society organisations.[2]

Most of the post-communist countries of CEE such as Poland, Hungary and the Czech Republic used the liberal democratic matrix to reform their political systems and re-draft their constitutions. This poses a number of comparative questions related not just to the effectiveness of such transplants, which have been dealt with elsewhere,[3] but, more crucially, from the perspective of this book it raises the issue of the validity of the assumptions that the liberal democratic constitutional theory rests on in context of the CEE countries. Consequently, there is a need to establish whether, and to what degree, the CTs in transition countries of CEE are politically independent, neutral and aiming to ensure that public interest is represented in judicial decisions (Raz 1977) . The need to ask such questions at the start of this inquiry relates to Alexander's (2001) suggestion that institutions in new democracies are less stable and less capable of providing a predictable framework since they tend be vulnerable to changes of rules and practices. Hence, there is a need to look beyond the appearances into the actual practices that lead to establishment of CTs in CEE, and which influence their functioning.[4]

Constitutional Tribunals in Central and Eastern Europe

CTs across CEE have been widely praised and credited with playing a central role in transitions to democracy (Brzeziński 2000; Schwartz 2000; Sadurski 2001; Epstein et al., 2001; Sadurski 2005, 2009, 2010). Sadurski described CTs in CEE as becoming 'an independent, active player[s] in the law-and policy-making processes' (Sadurski 2005: xvii). Schwartz echoed this:

> Almost all the courts in Eastern Europe have been remarkably independent – astonishingly so in some cases – and quite ready to challenge and overturn important statutes, bills and regulations. And most seem to have gotten away with it. (2000: xi)

Particia Wald proclaimed these courts as 'the flagships of the rule of law and constitutional faith in the emergent Eastern European democracies' (Schwartz 2000: x). The remarkable judgements of the Hungarian, Slovak and Polish CTs were particularly well received by academic opinion (Schwartz 2000, Sadurski 2005). Hungarian CT abolished the death penalty against the tide of public opinion on that matter; the Polish court, the pioneer among the transition states, overturned the statute on veterans pensions that excluded the employees of

---

2   Sources on democracy that list those and many other conditions are far too numerous to list here.

3   See for instance: Watson (1974), Wälde and Gunderson (1999).

4   This point, obviously, applies also to constitutional courts in more established democracies, if perhaps in a different measure.

Communist Ministry of Interior from certain pension rights; the Slovak CT has been particularly effective in reigning in Merciar's government authoritarianism. Examples of such commendable behaviour of the CTs are many, most well-known and discussed. Even though such praise is richly deserved, it should not, however, detract from those aspects of the CTs decisions which 'sacrificed judicial consistency at the altar of politics' (Klich 1996: 57). The majority of such cases relate either directly to individual rights where there is a link to moral values, or where individual's position is affected indirectly by the CT promoting a particular moral vision of state and society that is neither reflected in the Constitution, nor shared by the electorate.

These tensions, which became most acute in Poland, bear heavily on the position of individuals as they closely relate to the 'definition of a polity, and [...] construction of the status of an individual vis-à-vis the state' (Sadurski 2005: xvii). This logic, aligned with liberal constitutional theory, places constitutional rights at the centre of democratic constitutionalism (Ludwikowski 2001: 77). What makes these issues weightier in the context of the post-communist states of CEE is the combination of the weak influence of citizens on the shape of individual constitutional rights related to moral values (as argued in Chapter 2) and the problematic record of some CTs in defending them. Later sections will outline and evaluate this record through two case studies: on abortion rights and on the freedom of religion in context of teaching of religion in public schools in Poland.

To make the picture more complete, other relevant contextual issues will be covered as well:

- the system of appointment of the judges;
- the Church's influence on the CT jurisdiction;
- the success of individual actions in the CT;
- the impact of the judgements of the CT on the jurisdiction of lower courts.

The Polish Constitutional Tribunal: Guardian of the Constitution or a Player in Everyday Politics?

The Polish CT was established in 1982 by constitutional amendment of 26 March 1982, and the statute of 29 April 1985, which finally settled its legal position. It was the second tribunal of this type in CEE, after the Yugoslav one: 'a unique creation in the Soviet bloc and a radical departure from the orthodox communist constitutional practice' (Brzeziński 2000: 130). Brzeziński's observation, undoubtedly correct, does not, however, fully reflect the impact of political compromises – a necessary ingredient of the quasi-constitutionalism in Poland in the early 1980s – on the jurisdiction and powers of the Polish CT. The main limitation of the CT's jurisdiction was to subject the rulings of the CT on the unconstitutionality of the statutes to the decision of the Sejm. Despite the earlier expansion of the CT competences in 1989 and in 1992, this particular limitation was not removed until the Constitution of 1997 and the new statute of 1 August 1997. The clear lack of political will to change the weak position of the CT vis-à-vis the Sejm for the eight years that passed since the RTT agreement is a telling sign: the possibility of influencing the decisions of CT (which are normally not susceptible to appeals) was too attractive for the first democratically elected Sejm to relinquish.[5] Leaving the power of judicial appointments in the Sejm's hands further increased the power of the Sejm over the CT.

Appointment of the Judges

While the appointment of judges to Constitutional Tribunals and Supreme Courts is usually described as 'almost inevitably a political affair', in the transition countries it was denounced as 'thoroughly political' by Sadurski (2005: 15). In a broader comparative perspective Poland was mentioned alongside Hungary and Croatia as appointing the CT judges in a way that is 'more political than most' (Łętowska 1997b: 86; Garlicki 2008: 356; Safjan 2009: 16). Such an assessment refers not only to the Sejm's nearly exclusive competence in this process, but also to the unsettled political scene, where the political parties' competition for power was more disconnected from the electoral base than elsewhere, arguably facilitating the parties self-serving approach to judicial appointments.

The candidates are suggested by the Sejm's Presidium or a group of 50 MPs, and elected by the majority of the MPs out of at least half present. The governing parties do not consult professional legal organisations: there is no provision to verify the candidates' credentials, nor is there any debate. Opinions on individual candidates are sought in secret (Siedlecka 2010d). As observed by Garlicki, such an arrangement means that indirectly, decisions are taken by whichever party holds the current majority in the Sejm. In Garlicki's words, 'it would be naïve to think that the political majority of the day will rise above its own political preferences in selecting the CT's judges' [*Takie ujęcie procedury wyboru oznacza, że decyzje będzie w praktyce podejmowała aktualna większość Sejmowa, i naiwnością byłoby sądzić, że nie będzie ona brała pod uwagę swoich politycznych preferencji*] (2008: 356). Safjan makes a similar point (2009: 16). The unclear competence of the President in judicial appointments complicates this matter further: in September 2008, the President refused to nominate a candidate suggested by the National Juridical Council [*Krajowa Rada Sądownicza*], despite his lack of competence to do so. The majority of academics commented that this arbitrary intervention was contrary to the doctrine of separation of powers and the democratic rule of law (Piotrowski 2009: 43).

Should such strong influence of the Sejm over the CT appointments be seen as problematic? After all, the Sejm is, at least in principle, the democratic representative of the Polish people, hence, its involvement in judicial appointments

---

5 See for instance Scheppele (2005: 1758), who suggested that the CTs in CEE were 'squashed' by ambitious political leaders who wanted to govern without judicial constraint.

might be seen as strengthening the democratic legitimacy of the CTs. Sadurski's argument follows this line of thinking: 'a system of appointments which gives parliaments a decisive say might partially alleviate the perennial conundrum of constitutional democratic theory which questions the power of non-elected judges to strike down laws enacted by democratically elected parliaments' (2005: 37). Such manner of appointments has an additional democratic benefit, and that is the potential that judges selected by parliament will be more sensitive to the prevailing views of the general population and to the 'range of views within the community as to the meaning of broad constitutional provisions' (2005: 37). The knowledge of the judges' political sympathies and constitutional leanings, which would have directed the preferences of the MPs in the selection process, would also render the judges fairly accurate representatives of society at large. In addition, factors such as relatively short tenures (in contrast to life tenures of the US Supreme Court's judges), 'immunisation from direct societal pressures and from temptation connected with seeking re-election [...], and a degree of electoral pedigree' (appointments by democratically elected bodies), 'may provide the ideal combination of a good democratic mandate' (2005: 37). Sadurski concluded that the 'politicisation' should not be seen as aberration, but rather as a healthy dose of representativeness rendering the CT a 'democratic (or near-democratic) chamber of reflection' (2005: 37).

Undoubtedly convincing, this logic is based on a number of assumptions that require separate evaluations. This is particularly so given the weak consolidation of the CEE countries' political systems. One of the aspects of this weakness, most relevant to the present argument, is the undermining of the level of representativeness of parliaments by the self-referential political parties, whose main raison d'être is to protect their power and influence, regardless of the electorate's preferences and interests (Chruściak and Osiatyński 2001: 151). This might also explain, at least in part, the poor performance of most CEE parliaments, described by Sadurski as 'an unwholesome display of demagoguery, intellectual incompetence and corruption' (2005: 291). Public-opinion polls confirm the lack of popular trust in Sejm. Seventy-seven per cent of Poles think that the Sejm has been protecting the interests of political parties and politicians and not the country as a whole (CBOS 2007a), and that too much time was spent on discussing matters of little importance to the electorate (60 per cent). Earlier and later opinion polls are consistent with these results within a margin of 5 to 6 per cent (CBOS 2009a, 2010a, 2010b). All this means that the party, and not the public interests are likely to be decisive in determining the composition of the CT, in concord with Garlicki (2008: 356).

The round of judicial appointments to the Polish CT completed on 26 November 2010 confirms this thesis. On this occasion, for the first time in the twenty-five-years' history of the CT, the candidates were suggested by academic and professional bodies of the highest standing: the Senate of the Polish Academy of Sciences, National Judicial Council and the Law Society. The rationale for this initiative was to assist the Sejm in selecting the best candidates on merit and experience. The Sejm's reaction was hostile. In rejecting this initiative, the MPs accused the above institutions of attempting to limit the Sejm's authority and of doubting its competence to choose the right candidates. The parties represented in the Sejm proceeded to nominate their own candidates, in secret. Candidates were recommended by private individuals, allied to the main political parties (Brunetko 2010), on criteria that were not disclosed to the Sejm. Those were the last-minute nominations – which meant that little time was left to debate and form opinions about the candidates (PAP 2010). In the end, the six new judges were voted in en bloc by the Sejm. As rightly observed by Siedlecka (2010a, 2010c), such a manner of voting means that the professional and other meritorious qualifications of individual candidates were not the main criteria for appointment. Which makes it clear that this round of CT appointments – no different from the previous one – was the result of party politics of this particular formation of the Sejm.

Polish CT and the Church

The other weakness in the Polish CT performance relates to the powerful influence of the Church on the law and policy, including the CT's judgements, especially in relation to the individual rights that overlap with Church's views on morality. '[The Church's] prominence in Polish life [...] [is] demonstrated in the jurisprudence of the CT' (Fijałkowski 2010: 145). The clash between public opinion on these issues and the position of both the Sejm[6] and the CT means that there is not much of the 'overlapping consensus' between the electorate views and these two institutions'. On the other hand, the high degree of consensus between the Church, the Sejm and the CT testifies to the alienation and powerlessness of society in influencing the law and policy in this area. Opinion polls consistently show strong liberal views of Polish society on abortion and in vitro fertilisation (CBOS 2002a, 2006, 2007b, 2010d). The clash between the concurrent views of the CT, the Sejm, and the Church,[7] with that of the public makes problematic the claim to democratic legitimacy of the Polish CT based on its sensitivity to the prevailing views of the population. It also undermines the image of the CT as a 'democratic chamber of reflection', and renews doubts over democratic soundness of judicial appointments to the CT by the Sejm, neither truly representative nor trusted by the electorate, and influenced by the Church.

---

6   I am far from suggesting that the Sejm is entirely united on these issues. The SLD's position is close to that of the public. However, the legislation that was passed by the Sejm confirms that the majority of MPs support the Church's stand on abortion and religious education.

7   This sounds like a unsubstantiated generalisation. I acknowledge a certain degree of divergence of the MPs views with the changing composition of the Sejm, particularly between the SLD, on the one hand, and the PiS and the Civic Platform on the other. This divergence, however, did not lead to a change of the very restrictive abortion law, nor to the end of teaching of religion in public schools.

The two sections below discuss the Polish CT judgement on abortion and religious education in public schools, to test the suggestion that both the Polish Parliament and the CT engage in pursuit of policies that go against public interest and fail to protect the rights of minorities in these two areas of fundamental rights: right to abortion and freedom of religion. CT's decisions in these two type of cases suggest a return to the old-style politics, isolated from the society and its values, and authoritarian, in trying to impose on society rules and values that often conflict with the Constitution but which are promoted by the political and religious elites.

Abortion in the Polish CT

The CT's rulings on abortion in Poland, and also in Hungary, have been discussed by a number of scholars (Klich 1996; Brzeziński 2000; Schwartz 2000; Sadurski 2005). Comments on these rulings are invariably critical, with the Polish CT singled out for the harshest critique in CEE. The Polish CT's activism in abortion rulings reached its zenith with the judgement of 28 May 1997 (K. 26/96). At the beginning of the judgement the CT recalled a statement from the petition of the Polish Senators on which this case was based, reminding the legislature of existing limits to its power. Those limits, according to the statement, which are defined by 'the values and the inalienable and indivisible human and family rights' [*Zdaniem Wnioskodawcy ustawodawca nie ma całkowitej swobody kształtowania prawa, powinien uwzględniać wartości oraz nienaruszalne i przyrodzone człowiekowi i rodzinie praw. [...] Grupa Senatorów uważa, że przepisy te znoszą całkowicie, zawartą w przepisach prawa karnego bezpośrednią ochronę dziecka poczętego, a więc ustawodawca naruszył minimum ochrony praw ludzkiej osoby*]. (K. 26/96),[8] were infringed by the statute of 30 Aug. 1996 (Sejm 1996a), (art. 1 s. 2 and 4, subsection 4 band c; s. 5 and art. 4a, s. 1, subsection 4; art. 4, s. 1 and 2; art. 3, s. 1, 2 and 4). This statute changed the law on family planning by allowing abortion on financial and personal grounds. The basis of the CT judgement striking down this statute – in line with the Senators' petition – was the democratic rule of law, and that was because the statute 'removed any protection of the unborn'This removal of protection of the foetus was synonymous with 'discrimination against the foetus' right to life and protection of life in all stages of development' and amounted to 'infringement of the constitutional principle of protection of life' [*Przepisy ustawy wprowadziły też, szczególne kryterium dyskryminujące dziecko poczęte w jego prawie do życia i ochrony jego życia w fazie prenatalnej, co naruszyło konstytucyjną zasadę sprawiedliwości społecznej (art. 1 przepisów konstytucyjnych)*]. This principle has been extended to the foetus, despite an absence of such provision in the Constitution.[9] One of the most curious parts of the judgement revoked art. 2, s. 2 of the 1996 statute, which removes the right of the child to sue the mother for the damage suffered before it was born (Art. 4461 of the Polish Civil Code), on

---

8   All quotes in this section from CT judgement 26/96 in author's translation.
9   Compare with art. 38 of the 1997 Constitution.

the grounds that such bar 'limits the rights of the foetus, hence, it goes against the democratic rule of law and the principle of equality' [*Art. 2 pkt 2 ustawy z dnia 30 sierpnia 1996 r. o zmianie ustawy o planowaniu rodziny, ochronie płodu ludzkiego i warunkach dopuszczalności przerywania ciąży oraz zmianie niektórych innych ustaw (Dz.U. Nr 139, poz. 646)* (Sejm 1996b) *jest niezgodny z art. 1 oraz z art. 67 ust. 2 przepisów konstytucyjnych pozostawionych w mocy na podstawie art. 77 Ustawy Konstytucyjnej z dnia 17 października 1992 r. o wzajemnych stosunkach między władzą ustawodawczą i wykonawczą Rzeczypospolitej Polskiej oraz o samorządzie terytorialnym (Dz.U. Nr 84, poz. 426; zm.: z 1995 r. Nr 38, poz. 184 i Nr 150, poz. 729 oraz z 1996 r. Nr 106, poz. 488) przez to, że pozbawiając dziecko możliwości dochodzenia swych roszczeń majątkowych wobec matki, ograniczył jego prawa w sposób sprzeczny z zasadą demokratycznego państwa prawnego i z zasadą równości*].

The clearly flawed logic of this judgement attracted the following comment by Sadurski:

> [this is] probably the most outrageous case, of all constitutional courts [cases] in CEE, of judicial usurpation of the law-making power. Contrary to the explicit will of the legislative majority at the time, with basically no textual constitutional basis (there was no 'right to life' in the constitution in force at the time of the decision), and with clear indication from the constitution-makers that life "from the moment of conception was not the recognised constitutional understanding of the 'right to life' in the new constitution (already adopted but not yet in force), the Tribunal handed down a decision of great social significance that invalidated nearly all categories of abortion. (Sadurski 2005: 135)

The statute under revision in the above judgement has been enacted by the coalition government headed by the SLD, the only major party in Poland which opposes the unconstitutional influence of the Church on Polish politics[10] (SLD 2010a, 2010b; Wiadomości24.pl). In siding with this particular understanding of the inalienable and indivisible human [right to life] and family rights (K. 26/96), CT not only demonstrated its pro-Church bias, but it also positioned itself, and not for the first time, as a participant in everyday politics on the opposite side of both society and the SLD, which, on this particular issue, aligned its stance with views of the public. Sadurski quotes a comment made frequently by the critics of the CT's judgement: 'it seems no accident that the decision was made a few days before the Pope's tenth visit to Poland' (2005: 135). Clearly then, as was previously the case with the 'constitution for the Pope',[11] this judgement amounts to yet another

---

10　This influence does not mean direct pressure. Sadurski described it as 'rather a more general social and political influence exerted by the Church to have its views legally recognised and supported by the force of law' (2005: 139).

11　See Chapter 2.

instance where the protection of rights rooted in moral values was compromised to appease the Church and to celebrate the Pope.

The current debate on in vitro fertilisation in Poland, which entered its third year, illustrates particularly sharply the dynamics behind those aspects of constitutional politics that are related to moral values, both in substance and in the manner in which it is conducted. The debate is public only in the sense of being widely reported by the media, otherwise it is limited to the political and Church' elites. The views of society have been settled and remained consistent over many years (never lower than 60 per cent in support, recently raising to 77 per cent (CBOS 2009f), yet those preferences are almost completely ignored by the Church and politicians alike.[12] This debates demonstrates with particular clarity the mechanism behind the successful strategy of the Church in gaining political concessions in this and similar areas of constitutional law-making. Part of this strategy is the pressure put on MPs by instructing them how to vote. In this instance, the Church for the first time used statements which amount to the threat of excommunication, and it did so publicly: 'MPs who consciously support the in vitro method will find themselves outside the Church community' (TOK FM.PL: 2010). So far, and in line with previous cases when rights of this nature were considered, this instance of religious bullying of the MPs by the Church is proving remarkably effective.

Teaching of Religion and Freedom of Religion in the Polish CT's Jurisdiction

The current church–state relations in post-communist countries are a more straight-forward reflection of the historic role played by organised religions in those countries than was the case under the old system, which often distorted such relations by oppressive actions against Churches. Interestingly, despite the diversity of historic experiences across CEE, some form of separation of church and state was almost uniformly introduced after 1989, regardless also of whether the state-church relations caused constitutional controversy.[13] In Poland, the relation between the state and the Catholic Church are probably more complex than elsewhere, both in terms of constitutional and everyday politics. The historically powerful position of the Church has became more visible after 1989: Church officials took active part in shaping policy at the constitutional moments of Poland's recent history such as the RTT and the drafting of the 1997 Constitution. Apart from involvement in constitutional law-making, the Church has been forcing its views on abortion, in vitro fertilisation and sex education in

---

12   This is an example of the political elites devoting many hours of parliamentary time to discuss an issue that is neither socially controversial, nor that important in comparison with other truly pressing economic and political matters. In previous years debates on abortion took a disproportionate number of Sejm's hours.

13   For an overview, see for instance Garlicki (2001), Sadurski (2005: 137), Uitz (2006).

public schools, and also directing its flock to vote for Church-supported politicians under the threat of mortal sin and eternal damnation. All this fits awkwardly with the constitutional formula of the state-church relation described as 'cooperation' and 'impartiality' (Poland 1997).[14] Still more troubling is the evidence that the Polish CT supports the Church's position in its judgements, even if that goes against a clear rule of the constitutional text (Sadurski 2005: 139; Klich 1996) and the prevailing views of the Poles.

In the catalogue of cases in which the Polish CT clearly prioritised the Church-backed policy on teaching of religion in public schools over the right of freedom of religious beliefs, probably the most questionable is the case which raised the issue of the declaration of religious belief in the context of the decision to put grades for religious classes on the school report cards. This case was a culmination of a clear direction of CT jurisdiction on religious issues which was described by Sadurski as 'an unmitigated disaster in terms of the principle of neutrality of the state towards religion' (2005:140). The pro-church bias of the CT surfaced first in the earlier judgement (CT 1990, K 11/90)[15] dealing with a claim submitted by the Ombudsman against the Ministerial Instruction that introduced the teaching of religion in public school, where the issue of grades for religious classes appeared for the first time. The instruction was challenged on two grounds: procedural – asking whether such a ministerial instruction was constitutionally valid, since the introduction and organisation of religious education should be regulated by statute, not by subordinate legislation; and substantive, where the Ombudsman questioned the principle of teaching religion in public schools as potentially contrary to the principle of secularity of public education, which was further violated by putting grades for religious classes on the school report cards. The right to hang crosses in classrooms was also questioned as potentially offending religious feelings of non-Catholics and non-believers. None of these challenges were successful.

On the main issue – the freedom of religion and the right not to reveal one's religious beliefs – the CT declared that such right will not be compromised when children's intention to participate in religious classes is declared by their parents.[16] The court argued that such a declaration is a right and not a duty, hence it requires a positive, active stance, which is optional. The fact that a negative declaration was not required, meant that the right to remain silent on this issue was respected. By employing this logic, the CT failed to consider that the absence of a positive declaration amounts to a negative one, which equals the duty to announce one's lack of religious beliefs. Such a negative statement, inferred from the absence of

---

14   See Sadurski for a discussion of the principle of separation and freedom of religion (2005: 136–7) and Garlicki on neutrality, freedom of religion, separation and cooperation between the state and the church (2001: 475–9).

15   Judgement of 30 January 1991.

16   For pupils who did not wish to attend religious classes, lessons in ethics were going to be offered.

positive one, in turn compromises the protection of the right to remain silent on this issue.

Shortly after the first 'religious' judgement of the CT, the Sejm enacted the 1991 Education Act (Sejm 1991), followed by the Ordinance of the Minister of Education of 14 April 1992 (Poland 1992). In August 1992 the Ombudsman challenged paragraph 9 of the Ordinance, which regulated the placing of the grade for religion classes on the school reports, alleging the risk of intolerance that this was likely to create. A further challenge raised a potential breach of the principle of neutrality of the state, since schools reports are official documents issued by the state, and teaching religion is the prerogative of the Church. The negative declaration imposed on parents was also contested. The Ombudsman argued that in light of the constitutional principle of the state' religious neutrality no public authority could require citizens to make such declarations.

In its judgement (CT 1992, U 12/92), the CT struck down the paragraph referring to 'negative declaration', but upheld for the most part the Ordinance constitutionality and legality. This included the insertion of the mark for religious instruction. The CT held that since the mark on a school report can refer equally to religion and ethics, jointly or separately, the mark will not indicate any specific religion. This, in the CT's opinion, constituted a double safeguard against revealing religious beliefs, or their absence, of any pupil. In other parts of the judgement, the CT upheld the provision allowing the display of religious symbols in schools, and school-organised prayers. Sadurski summed up the CT position as 'establish[ing] standards of religious freedom that pay lip service to the principle of neutrality of the state towards religion but, in all practical respects, deny the spirit of such neutrality' (2005: 141).

The next relevant judgement followed on 2 December 2009 (CT 2007, U 10/07). This time the CT was tasked with examining the constitutional validity of the Ordinance of the Minister of Education of 13 July 2007 (Poland 2007) on the marking of pupils' work, which introduced the rule that marks for religious instruction or ethics would be counted towards the average final mark in a given school year. The CT held that the challenged provision of the Ordinance were compatible with articles 25, 32, 48 § 1 and 53 § 3 of the 1997 Constitution. The court repeated in part the earlier judgement of 14 April 1993: 'the counting of mark for religion towards the average annual mark and the final average mark is [...] a consequence of the recording of marks for religion on school reports in state schools.' (CT 2007, U 10/07) This rigid stance was somewhat softened by the a degree of the CT's appreciation of the social reality beyond the law:

> The Constitutional Court is aware of the fact that in specific cases, given the dominant position of the Roman Catholic faith in the religious make-up of Polish society, the choice of an additional subject (religion or ethics) by parents and pupils may not be entirely free, but may be taken under pressure from the 'local' public opinion. [...] In specific cases in which external pressure – impinging on the free choice – was exerted it would have been the result of a low level of

democratic culture. This important issue, while it is noted by the Constitutional Court, lies outside its jurisdiction … . (quoted in Strasbourg 2010: § 48)

This acknowledgement of the realities of the Polish social environment is rare in the CT's judgements, and compares positively with its narrow jurisdiction, limited to checking the validity of legal acts against the Constitution (art. 188) – an approached that is not conducive to making such observations. However, this judgement raises further questions – if the CT recognised that the existing low democratic culture might turn the provision of the Ordinance into compulsion to join religious classes, this would mean that the Ordinance, indirectly, but clearly, clashes with art. 9 and 14 of the European Convention on Human Rights (ECHR). If we factor in another circumstance – not mentioned by the CT – the disparity between the availability of classes in religious education and ethics – religious instruction is available in 85.57 per cent of schools, whereas ethics is taught only in 1.03 per cent (Strasbourg 2010: § 77), the threat to rights under art. 9 and 14 of ECHR becomes even more acute. The inevitable conclusion is that the provisions of the Ministry of Education Ordinances (of 1992 and 2007) may lead to discrimination of pupils who could not, despite their wishes, attend the course in ethics. The European Court of Human Rights (ECtHR) observed:

> Such pupils would either find it difficult to increase the average mark as they could not follow the desired optional subject or might feel pressurised – against their conscience – to attend a religion class in order to improve the average. (Strasbourg 2010: § 96)

The judgement of the European Court of Human Rights in Grzelak might be taken as a confirmation that CT's not always acts as a neutral arbiter, and an impartial authority on constitutional matters related to freedom of religion.

The Case of Grzelak Versus Poland

In the first judgment of this type,[17] the Tribunal in Strasbourg considered the claim against Poland that the rights of the applicant under art. 9 and 14 of the ECHR have been breached by the failure to organise classes in ethics, which resulted in the absence of mark in the applicant's schools reports in the space reserved for religion/ethics. The submission of Polish government largely followed the argumentation used by Polish CT in the earlier cases on the teaching of religion. Additional details were provided by the Helsinki Foundation for Human Rights

---

17 Compare with the declaration of the European Commission in the case of Saniewski (dec. no. 40319/98, 26 June 2001), where the Court had found that the applicant had not substantiated his claim that the absence of a mark for 'religion/ethics' on his school report might prejudice his future educational or employment prospects, and rejected the application as manifestly ill-founded.

(HFHR), in support of the petition. The HFHR argued that the right to choose between attending religious classes and ethics was only a theoretical possibility for the vast majority of Polish pupils, due to 'the lack of clear provisions and guidelines concerning the teaching of ethics' (Strasbourg 2010: § 78). Hence, the provisions of the Ordinance 'were illusory and ineffective' (§ 79), and the absence of a mark for religion/ethics amounted to indirect disclosure of the person's convictions (§ 82). The HFHR added that discrimination in Polish schools on the basis of beliefs 'was not merely a fringe phenomenon' (§ 82).

The Court delivered a nuanced consideration of the problem, distinguishing Poland as a country where not having a mark for 'religion/ethics' acquires a particular significance due to the majority of the population owing 'allegiance to one particular religion' (§ 95). The Court also acknowledged that the situation of pupils who do not attend religious classes will become even more problematic due to entry into force of the new Ordinance of the Minister of Education of 13 July 2007 (Poland 2007) which introduced a rule that marks obtained for religious education class or ethics would be included in the calculation of the 'average mark' obtained by a pupil in a given school year and at the end of a given level of schooling (§ 96). For these reasons, the Court concluded that school certificates where the mark for religion/ethics is replaced by a straight line and the word 'ethics' is crossed out is 'unambiguous and anything but neutral' (§ 97). These findings confirm that the earlier CTs judgemens upholding the legality of the Ordinances challenged by the Ombudsman not only go against the Polish Constitution, but also against the well-established jurisdiction of the ECtHR that defines 'the state's role as the neutral and impartial organiser of the exercise of various religions, faiths and beliefs, and [sees] this role [as] conducive to public order, religious harmony and tolerance in democratic society' (§ 86).

The ECtHR judgement against Poland was received defiantly by the Polish Ministry of Foreign Affairs. In a statement issued shortly after its announcement, the Ministry spokesman stressed that the ECtHR did not question the system of teaching religion in Polish schools, nor the inclusion of the marks for religion/ ethics into the average mark, nor the 'assessment of the pupil's progress in those subjects' [*Trybunał uznał skargę za dopuszczalną w odniesieniu do powyższego zarzutu jedynie wobec skarżącego Mateusza Grzelaka. [...] Trybunał w przedmiotowym orzeczeniu nie zakwestionował systemu organizacji nauki religii i etyki w polskich szkołach ani możliwości oceniania postępów w nauce z przedmiotów religia i etyka, jak również możliwości wliczania do średniej ocen stopni z tych przedmiotów. Stwierdzone naruszenie ma zatem swoje przyczyny w złej praktyce placówek oświatowych, w których naukę pobierał skarżący, a nie w regulacjach prawnych dotyczących nauczania religii i etyki w polskich szkołach.*] (Poland 2010). This statement of Ministry attracted critical comments that pointed out concurrence of views of the Ministry with the earlier judgements of the Polish CT (Siedlecka 2010b), in which the CT also stressed the constitutional validity of the law regulating the teaching of religion, but which failed to pay attention to the specific social conditions in which this law is implemented and to the practical consequences of such implementation.

Axiology and Legal Reasoning of the CT

The formal/positivist assessment and interpretation of the challenged Ordinances by the CT (supported by the Ministry of Foreign Affairs) stands in stark contrast to that of the ECtHR. In some instances, the CT ignored the text of the Constitution, enforcing its own concept of rights inspired by the teaching of the Catholic Church. Not just this particular case, but most of the CT jurisdiction in the area of individual rights exposes the Polish CT as hardly a champion of religious neutrality and tolerance: invalidating the relatively liberal abortion law; upholding the introduction, by ministerial decree, of religious teaching in public schools (and the Ordinances introducing the record of marks for religious/ethics classes on school cards); upholding the ban on expressions offensive to Christian values in public media – all these amount to discrimination against other religions and non-believers, and establish a privileged position for the Roman Catholic faith (Sadurski 2005: 62).

Particularly problematic in the context of the two types of cases discussed above has been the unwillingness of the CT to go beyond the textual remit in reaching its decisions (Klich 1996; Łętowska 1997b; Sadurski 2001, 2005), which can be classed as procedural problem. The substantive fault in the CTs reasoning, on the other hand, was exposed in judgements that cannot be reconciled with the explicit meaning of clear constitutional provisions. The latter, substantive issue links to the CT's political, or rather religious expediency, and the former (procedural) relates to judicial training and the dominant among the Polish judiciary type of legal reasoning – positivistic and textocentric (Łętowska 1997a). Łętowska, writing about the Polish judiciary under the 1997 Polish Constitution, argued: 'an important problem may be the lack of sufficient skills, and, more importantly, the lack of political will to exercise the judiciary's new-found power to the maximum extent possible' (1997: 89). Łętowska was alluding to the type of legal interpretation that the CT judges follow, which, in turn, determines the practical meaning of legal norms and principles. Łętowska equated the narrow, literal interpretations that the judges use with the unwritten principle *in dubio contra actionem* – when in doubt do nothing. These practices of the CT judges diminish much of the potentially beneficial function of the constitutional jurisdiction in relation to rights claimed via the individual constitutional complaint. Also undermined is the wider objective of influencing social practices that are likely to threaten individual rights, and constitutional culture, which needs active support from authoritative sources such as the CT.

Effectiveness of the Constitutional Tribunals in Promoting Democratic Constitutionalism

Among the most vital functions of constitutional courts is the facilitation and sustaining of the democratic and constitutional culture, particularly in the sense of creating models of interpretation and understandings of fundamental rights and freedoms. That means that CTs are expected not only to protect individual rights and freedoms in specific judgements, but also that the specific line of the CTs jurisdiction should influence and be followed by lower courts and other actors taking part in the operation of the legal system. The more powerful the influence of CTs over lower courts and political decision-makers will be, the more likely the CT would be to achieve an effective protection of individual rights, freedoms and security of a democratic foundation of the legal system (Stawecki et al. 2008: 8). In this sense, the CTs might be seen as guardians of social spheres of freedoms, and, in effect, creators of the constitution, by 'developing constitutional doctrine' (Schwartz 2000: 26), and not just as watchmen over the constitutional system of checks and balances, and 'mediators' between politics and law (Stawecki et al., 2008: 8). The CTs success in achieving those objectives should be measured by the CTs effectiveness in protecting individual rights, and by the willingness of the lower courts and law-makers to follow the CTs interpretation of constitutional principles. Failure to meet those expectations might result in judgements that will have no capacity to correct injustice, or which would be seen as exceptions rather than amount to a consistent line of jurisprudence.[18] Such judgements would also not change the position of the citizens and will remain 'abstract juridical constructs' (Stawecki et al., 2008: 8), a development that will, in effect, perpetuate social practices that are behind the erosion of protection of rights, hence are likely to lead to more legal challenges of this type. To evaluate the effectiveness of the Polish CT in the above aspects, I discuss, below, two issues: the availability and effectiveness of individual complaint and the influence of the CT over lower courts and the law-makers.

Individual Constitutional Complaint

The grounds for submitting individual constitutional complaint are defined very restrictively in Polish law: the complaint is allowed only against the legal grounds for the decision that is, against the law that forms the basis of a particular rights-affecting decision, rather than the actual application of the law in court (Sejm 1997b: art. 46). Consequently, complaints against specific outcomes of a court case per se are not admissible; nor are complaints that relate to the interpretation and application of the law that lead to such outcomes. Lętowska suggested that the reason for this arrangement was to prevent the CT from morphing into a 'fourth-instance appellate court' (1997b: 81). It seems that this strategy has been very

---

18   Similarly, Jowell asserted in relation to the common law that 'the content of the rule of law is defined in the course of its practical application' (2004: 246).

effective: there is little danger of the CT performing an appellate function given its current record – the number of successful complaints is very low. Out of 4,969 applications received between 1997 and 2006 only ten led to the revision of court decisions, and of these only eight were successful – that is less than 1 per cent of all submitted complaints during this period (Stawecki et al. 2008: 33–5). These data validate Łętowska's argument in which she noted the very weak impact of the CT in cases resulting from individual complaints. She blamed this on the poor understanding of the constitutional complaint and its extremely narrow parameters.[19] Łętowska further argued that these failings threaten to emaciate the CT and deprive it of the capacity to perform the protective, constitutional function in the administration of justice, and, more importantly, to influence social, judicial and legislative practices (2002).

As shown in the cases discussed above, the CT pursues an 'abstract'[20] type of constitutional interpretation. Such approach, in combination with the narrow, textual interpretation of the law, and the lack of attention to the specific circumstances of the case (which nevertheless influence the position of the claimant in an important way) produces mainly 'abstract' judgements. Such judgements are effective neither in correcting the injustice of religious discrimination, nor in improving the position of an individual who suffered as a result of the application of the law which was formally correct, but which substance and the social context in which it was applied might have led to injustice. Hence, the CT's approach in *Grzelak* and previous religious cases that ignored specific social and political context might be seen as the CT's contribution to the perpetuation of religious intolerance and undemocratic culture[21] – the very threats, as observed by the CT itself (Strasbourg 2010: § 48), that the challenged Ordinances pose. The ECtHR decision in *Grzelak*,

---

19   The case (CT 2001, SK 10/01) is an example of even more extreme narrowing of the parameters of constitutional complaint: CT rejected a discrimination claim against a statute for infringing art. 32 of the 1997 Constitution (the right to equal treatment by public bodies). This case considered compensation for people subjected to forced labour during World War II, which the statute made contingent on the place where the claimants lived before being deported, and on the place where they were employed as forced labourers. The CT, which acknowledged the discriminatory nature of the statute (Sejm 1996a), refused to act, claiming that the discriminatory provision of this act did not infringe the right guaranteed by the constitution.

20   'Abstract' in the sense of checking the lack of conflict between the challenged legal measure and the constitution, and not in the sense of interpreting the law when no case has been made to challenge it. The latter is defined as 'abstract review' of constitutional provisions. See for instance (Shvetsova, Epstein and Knight 2001: 121, Schwartz 2000: chapter 2; Garlicki 2008: 357–63).

21   The highest organs of the state perpetuate the undemocratic, intolerant culture: Donald Tusk publicly stated that paedophiles should not be seen as fully human, and that terrorists that were tortured in Polish prisons, as part of the US programme of extraordinary rendition 'do not deserve any pity, since they have many human lives on their conscience' – quoted in Piotrowski (2009: 35). These comments, clearly going against the letter and the

which clearly pointed out that the Polish CT approach is not the correct one, might be taken as evidence in support of this claim.[22]

The inevitable conclusion is that the CT clearly failed to utilise individual constitutional complaints to support protection of individual rights in the areas of religious freedom and abortion. Consequently, the CT missed an important opportunity to shape 'social, judicial and legislative practices' (Łętowska 2002) in a way which would advance constitutional and democratic culture.

Polish CT and Ordinary Courts

Yet another important role of Constitutional Tribunals is to develop an authoritative interpretation of constitutional provisions, which would amount to a consistent doctrine based on CT jurisdiction, and which would serve as a guiding paradigm for ordinary courts. This kind of interpretation does not relate to specific cases, but focuses on checking compliance of legal acts with the constitution,[23] and it is undertaken by the CT out of a general duty to maintain a high standard of the legal system and observance of the Rule of Law.[24] Only a defined class of subjects, such as the constitutional organs of the state, the Ombudsman, and the Judicial Council, can submit a request for such an action.[25] The CT's role under abstract review contrasts with another CT function, which serves a similar purpose, namely the power to strike down legal provisions found to be unconstitutional, often described as a power of a 'negative legislator' (Garlicki 2008: 355; Stawecki et al., 2008: 8). Abstract review and the power to weed out unconstitutional legal acts is complemented by the CT's 'soft influence' through authoritative judgements which, potentially, should define general directions of constitutional policy (this central role of CT must not be confused with the CT potentially acting as an appellate court), and which should be followed by the lower courts.

The effective influence of the CT over ordinary courts is, potentially, of crucial importance in any legal system, as it affects the coherence and predictability of legal norms and the way these are interpreted and applied. These core objectives are even more important in the legal systems of transition countries whose very foundations have been undergoing a dramatic reconstruction. Protection of individual rights, especially from political interference, is one of the areas most neglected under these countries' previous regimes and that is where the effective guidance of the CT acquires additional significance. Reclaiming and safeguarding individual rights could also be a way of shedding the pathologies of the old

---

spirit of the Constitution and the ECHR, did not attract any reaction from the CT or other institutions.

   22   Jowell's distinction between 'legalism' and 'legality' (2004: 251) seems to capture the difference between the judgements of the Polish CT and the ECtHR in the Grzelak case.

   23   Art. 190 § 4 of the Polish Constitution 1997. Compare also with n. 19, above.

   24   Compare with, for instance, Raz (1977).

   25   For a full list see art. 191 of Polish Constitution of 1997.

system: clientelism, patronage and political expediency. Hence, the willingness of ordinary courts to follow the line of the CT on fundamental rights should be seen as crucial, if the transformation to a rule of law is to be accomplished.

Two obstacles are likely to make this difficult, at least in Poland: the doubtful quality of the CT's judgements in the area of individual rights based on moral values, as argued above, and the weak influence of the CT's judgements on the lower courts and legislation in this area – as suggested in a persuasive study of Stawecki et al. (2008). Neither the procedural approach of the CT and the substantive decisions on abortion and religious-freedom cases suggest that judgements of the CT will make a practical difference to the position of the petitioner, nor will those judgements have the capacity to develop a line of jurisdiction which would prevent injustice occurring in these categories of cases.[26] In reference to the second point Stawecki et al. (2008) convincingly proved that the influence of the CT on lower courts and on the legislative choices is negligible. The way in which the Polish courts function was described by the authors as fragmented and independent from other courts/judicial bodies (2008: 76), which means that there is an absence of a central authority capable of securing a degree of consistency in the courts' approaches to rights protection. Stawecki et al. call the situation bad pluralism,[27] which contributes to the ineffectiveness of the protection of rights.

The abortion and religious freedom cases also expose the Polish Catholic Church visible sway over the CT, despite its lack of any formal power over the Tribunal (Sadurski 2005: 139; Fijałkowski 2010: 145). The strong concurrence of the Sejm's and the Church's agendas on abortion and religious freedom – so accurately reflected in the jurisdiction of the CT – confirms those entities as the masters of the Constitution in these matters. Neither the letter of the Constitution, nor the views of the majority of the electorate have been fully respected by the CT. This also suggests that the constitutional values related to abortion and religion became bargaining chips in the everyday political struggle for votes. In line with this argument, Piotrowski (2009); Wołek (2004) suggested that the CT in Poland might have become more of a forum for a political power struggle between the parties, the organs of government and the Church, rather than a guardian of constitutional democracy and public interest (Garlicki 2008: 353–7).

Consequently, the lack of influence of the CT over the lower courts is best seen as a mixed blessing. The desirable position is one in which the CT leads by example and creates consistency in interpretation and application of constitutional provisions. However, given the CT's doubtful record in abortion and religious freedom cases and its political expediency, its weak leadership might turn to be more beneficial for protection of individual rights in those class of cases,

---

26　See also the case of Tysiąc versus Poland, application nr. 5410/03, Strasbourg 20 March 2007.

27　This stays in line with Staśkiewicz's argument describing Polish law as a patchwork and a collection of norms and regulation which cannot be described as a system (2009).

particularly if the lower courts will be inclined to take a more constitutionally viable stance than the CT itself.

Constitutional Tribunals as Guardians of Individual Rights and Freedoms?

The emerging picture of juridical practice of the CTs, particularly in the area of protection of rights based on moral values challenges the earlier perception of the CTs in CEE as bastions of rule of law and staunch defenders of democratic values. The recent literature evaluating the functioning of the CTs in CEE is also moving beyond this earlier, often unduly optimistic assessments (Koslosky 2009).[28] The overall picture remains mixed. The Polish CT's judgements on abortion and religious freedoms[29] confirms that democracy and individual rights are secondary in its priorities. The Hungarian CT avoided confronting the issue of abortion altogether. However, those judgements, severely criticised by many scholars, contrast with a string of progressive decisions, where the CEE CTs decisively upheld many constitutional fundamentals such as the separation of powers, prohibition of retroactivity, and due process. Identifying the reasons for such discrepancy and analysing them are tasks that exceed the scope of this book: but I would like to suggest just one potential line for such inquiry.

Since the priority for the transition countries was to prove their credentials as stable rule-of-law states, the CT's decisions dealing with the issues which are central to such a perception, that is, the constitutional check and balances, separation of powers, and the rule of law (prohibition of retrospectivity, legitimate expectations, and so on) were, on the whole, dynamic and progressive.[30] The two class of cases discussed here – on abortion and freedom of religion – do not fall into this category. From the perspective of fundamental rights in European/International law, those are the areas where the doctrine of the 'margins of appreciation' might apply and where the International/European organisations will be more reluctant to raise objections.[31] The inquiry might therefore try to establish to what extent the

---

28   See also the overview of critical scholarship in Koslosky's article, particularly on p. 205.

29   Two other well-known examples of similarly controversial judgements are the June 1994 one, which upheld the clause in the 1992 law on public broadcasting requiring radio programs to 'respect viewer's religious feelings and Christian values'; the U 8/90 judgement which upheld the Ministry of Health regulation allowing doctors to refuse to perform abortions on grounds of personal convictions.

30   See also the Polish CT's recently published collection of its pronouncements testifying to the contribution of the CT to the development of the legal system and core constitutional principles (Trybunał Konstytucyjny 2010). In this comprehensive document, spanning the CT's jurisdiction from 1986 to March 2010, none of the cases discussed in this chapter appear.

31   Art. 4 (2) of the Treaty of European Union (as amended by Lisbon Treaty) reads: 'The Union shall respect [...] their [Member States] national identities, inherent in their

behaviour of the Polish CT (and other CTs across CEE) can be explained by the need to create a perception of the CTs as guardians of constitutions and the rule of law externally, and, on the other hand, to what extent the low external visibility of individual rights related to moral values turns those rights into objects of domestic power politics played out in the CTs.

Have We Changed Everything So Everything Would Remain the Same?

Mandel argued that the increasing power of the CTs and other courts enforcing Bills of Rights and exercising judicial review can be seen the legalisation of politics or 'as a antidote of democracy' (1998: 300), which is turning the courts into 'locus of political activity' (1998: 251). Hirschl's *juristocracy* thesis (2004)[32] is based on essentially the same idea: the empowerment of the judiciary threatens the capacity of democratic politics to challenge the social and political status quo and correct injustice that results from it. Both thesis fit the Polish scene relatively well but both need to be qualified. In Poland, the CT's power does not so much threaten democratic majority in the Sejm as it is aimed at keeping the democratic constituent power, which is poorly represented in the Sejm, at arm's length from having an influence over constitutional regulation (cases related to moral values such as abortion and religious freedom discussed in this chapter are probably most visible examples of a wider phenomenon) – both in the sense of having a say over the shape of these regulations and in trying to enforce them in the CT and other courts. This alienation of the electorate is achieved by the Sejm and the CT concurring in promotion of, essentially the Church agenda in those areas of constitutional provision, against the express wishes of the people. Even though the close ties between the Sejm and the CT correspond to Mandel's 'partnership' between the CTs and the Parliaments, in Poland that works differently – the CT cooperates amicably with the Sejm, or rather, it serves the Sejm's political interests, at least in this narrow class of cases discussed here. The outcome, though, is similar to the one suggested by Mandel – the preservation of status quo by keeping the democratic force of the people at bay,[33] and to that put forward by Hirschl who argued that the 'judicial empowerment through constitutionalisation [is] a form of self-interested *hegemonic preservation*' (2004: 11).

These two theses resonate with the constitutional politics in post-transition which is, in some respects, strongly reminiscent of the early Polish quasi-constitutionalism of the August 1980 agreements, RTT, the first year of systemic reforms, and the later period of constitution-making where the views of the democratic majority have been neither sought nor considered. The elitism of those watershed events demonstrated that it was the constituent power that was kept in

fundamental structures, political and constitutional.'

32   See also Tate and Vallinder (1995).
33   Mandel focuses of property, but his general argument still applies.

check, and not the majority in the Sejm which is largely disconnected from the electorate. The siding of the CT with the Sejm and the Church in its judgements on abortion and religious freedom suggests that things are bound to remain the same for some time. And this might mean that the political and legal masters of the constitution might succeed in preventing the constitutionalism to move 'toward a terrain in which citizens, not untouchable principles, rule' (Colón-Ríos 2010: 44).

Conclusions

The record of the Polish CT in protecting constitutional and democratic settlement can be only weakly related to the two first principles of constitutional theory: first, the defence of the constitution – since the Constitution of 1997 is product of the political and Church elite and not a popular projects; and second, the containment of the democratic majority – since the MPs represent mainly political interests of their parties and not their constituencies.[34] Hence, the true realisation of the liberal idea of defending the constitution against the tyranny of the parliamentary majority by the CT might be applicable to Poland, but mainly in the sense of guarding it against the powerful interests of the Church and the sectarian interests of political parties. This is unlikely to occur, given the concurrence of the CTs judgements in abortion and religious freedom cases with the Church's and the partisan agenda. This places the CT firmly within the network of interests pursued by the Church and the parties, and confirms its alienation from the citizens. These findings are likely to apply, at least in some considerable measure, to other countries in CEE.

The politicised system of the CT judicial appointments across CEE, with Poland singled out as a particularly extreme case, casts further doubts on the claim of judicial independence and the ability of the CT to perform its functions in a manner that is independent, neutral and supportive of public interests. The Polish abortion and religious freedom cases show that the agenda of the most powerful and influential, but unconstitutional political formation – the Catholic Church has been given priority over the fundamental rights related to moral values. The acquiescence of the CT in fully supporting the Church's agenda against that of the constituent power of the people and against the letter and the spirit of the 1997 Constitution undermines the CT democratic and constitutional authority. Furthermore, as Polish and Slovak experiences confirm, CTs might have become forums into which ordinary politics and the everyday power struggles characteristic of certain type of unstable political system spill over from the legislatures.

The negligible awareness of the CT role in society – only 31 per cent of Poles have a vague idea what the CT is – (CBOS 2004) and the very low number of

---

34   It is clear that most political systems struggle with similar problems to some degree. However, the scale and the sharpness of these occurring in Poland and elsewhere in CEE sets these countries apart from the more stable constitutional democracies supported by a long experience and continuity of democratic and constitutional rule.

successful individual claims indicates this institution's negligible role in upholding the democratic element of the process of constitutionalisation. The narrow, abstract quality of the CT jurisdiction, which deals only with the law that forms the basis of a particular decision that affects rights, rather the actual application of the law in court, coupled with the positivistic and textocentric interpretation of law leads to judgements of abstract quality, that are unlikely to address the injustice resulting from the application of law in specific social conditions. This further weakens the relevance of constitutional rights through which political power can be limited and reinforces the Polish tradition, reaching back to 1791, of perceiving the constitution as a symbol rather than as a legal document and a source of enforceable rights. Finally, the negligible impact of the CT's jurisdiction on other courts adds to the picture of an institution which, despite many progressive, laudable judgements, appears conflicted in its loyalties and its constitutional role.

Chapter 5
Conclusions

The main aim of this book was to consider if the weakness of democratic politics in systemic and constitutional restructuring of post-communist CEE transition countries was detrimental to these countries' democratic and constitutional development. I concluded that the legitimisation of constitutional arrangements which lacked democratic foundations may have limited the dynamics of democratic growth and led to solidifying of the democratic and constitutional underdevelopment of those countries. I further argued that this was more likely to occur when constitutional restructuring of states' order was undertaken under external pressure, such as that of the European Union and other international organisations, which also validated and legitimised the outcomes of these processes.

In carrying out this analysis I used the concept of democratic constitutionalism developed by Loewenstein and Tully, which links the uneasy nexus of the constitutional imperative to limit political power with the democratic one, which gives a voice to citizens and protects their constitutional rights. In particular, I considered if the democratic process was observed at constitutional moments of constitutional law-making and the drafting of new constitutions in CEE. To make such a discussion possible, I clarified and adopted the concept of constituent power and constitutional moments, in line with Ackerman, which I then applied to the specific developments that occurred in CEE after 1989. My main focus was on Poland, and less on other countries such as Czech Republic, Slovakia and Hungary, but my findings, with obvious modifications, are likely to apply across CEE and possibly beyond, particularly those aspects that deal with the general interpretation and application of liberal democratic constitutional theory.

One of the main points of my analysis related to Tully's argument that the political legitimacy of a constitutional system depends on the balance between democracy – in the Rawlsian sense of the sovereign people 'imposing' the constitutional system on themselves – and constitutionalism, understood as the agreed rules that limit such democratic authority. Such a balance is crucial for prospective stability, predictability and the rule of law on the one hand, and fundamental if thus conceived constitutionalism is to be prevented from stifling the corrective force of democratic politics that should, in principle, underlie it – on the other hand. Realising in practice Tully's imperative is neither entirely possible nor strictly verifiable. This, however, should not diminish its importance as one of the fundamental principles of modern constitutional theory which exposes the core tension in constitutionalism – between law and politics – and warns of the potential consequences of the lack of a democracy/constitutionalism equilibrium.

Even though the tension between constitutionalism and democracy is likely to remain unresolved in constitutional theory and practice, its foundational nature has been, yet again, made acutely apparent in the context of post-communist systemic transitions. The democratic mass movements that precipitated the fall of communism failed to convert into political and civil engagement of the people in CEE with their reconstituted systems of governance. I suggested that this may be due to the political legitimacy of the CEE constitutions and decisions of constitutional significance being largely decoupled from the question of authorship and the related question of democratic participation in constitutional moments of the CEE countries recent history: the RTTs, the redrafting of their constitutions and their accession to the EU. This, in turn, led me to argue that the success of constitutionalism in transition countries that occurred at the expense of democratic politics might be seen as a limitation on democratic development since it put a seal of legitimacy on not fully democratic systems and locked them in the dynamics of weak democratisation and constitutionalism.

The legitimating authority that allowed for such a possibility derives from liberal democratic constitutional theory and its reliance on a number of myths that have developed during the more than two hundred years of modern constitutionalism. The powerful symbolic appeal of such myths, that link constitutional texts with the core matters of sovereignty and national identity, are crucial for forging constitutional patriotisms and loyalty. However, those myths often shield the actual constitutional practices and constitutional politics from democratic scrutiny. When that happens, the popular legitimacy of the constitution is likely to be the Weberian charismatic type rather than civic republican that requires political activity and civic engagement. Consequently, it seems that the use of the myth of democratic participation at constitutional moments might be particularly controversial, as it can divert attention from poor democratic practices, and in that way allow those practices to be legitimised.

My analysis confirmed that most of the CEE regimes were constitutionalised in the absence of public debate and deliberation and that they suffer from a state of unconsolidated democracy and weaknesses in constitutional culture. This argument was developed using Poland as case-study, but, the general findings are likely to apply to other countries of CEE. More detailed findings can be summarised as follows:

- the new political and economic status quo that emerged after the 1989 mass protests was a result of the RTTs agreements between the incumbent party-state representatives and the political opposition. These settlements, later enshrined in new constitutions, legitimised the transfer of economic and political power to new elites: a class of *entrepreneurchiks* was created from the ranks of the party nomenklatura and the prominent members of the political opposition were elevated to the ranks of the governing elite;
- the masses were excluded from active participation in shaping the new constitutional order of their states at such constitutional moments as the

RTTs, but also at the drafting of the new constitutions: popular involvement was reduced to a vote in constitutional referenda. This exclusion amounted to a failure to harness the force of democratic social mobilisation that occurs at constitutional moments and turn it into a positive momentum of democratic and constitutional development. The RTT settlements and the new constitutions, seen as symbols of national unity, attracted a charismatic type of popular legitimacy that is not likely to turn the people of CEE into politically engaged and active citizens;

- the drafting of new constitutions in the National Assemblies turned into a competition for votes and power play between political party interests, influenced by the Catholic Church in Poland.

- the contribution of the CTs in CEE to the development of democratic constitutionalism present a mixed picture. Despite many progressive, laudable judgements, the Polish CT – used as a case study – appeared conflicted in its loyalties and its constitutional role. The close alignment of CT priorities with those of political parties and the Church in areas of individual rights such as abortion and religious freedom in the context of religious education, go against the popular preferences of constituent power of the people and also against the letter and the spirit of the 1997 Constitution. That undermines the CTs democratic and constitutional authority. Furthermore, as Polish and Slovak experiences confirm, CTs might have become fora into which ordinary politics and the everyday power struggles characteristic of certain types of unstable political system spill over from the legislatures. These findings, with obvious modifications, are likely to be applicable to the CTs of other CEE countries.

- the international aid and assistance of the early 1990s and the EU politics of accession and pre-accession conditionality failed to set an example of a good practice of democratic constitutionalism. The non-democratic practices of delivery of aid and assistance and the EU conditionality undermined the social learning of democracy and constitutionalism, and most likely contributed to the reinforcement of some of the pathologies already present in the old system such as clientelism, favouritism, lack of transparency and accountability. More crucially, the limited constitutionalism and democratisation that was developing in CEE, and in Poland since the 1970s, were diverted away from evolving into potentially more consolidated systems in order to accommodate the EU conditionality and the Western donors pressures. Yet, those external influences proved badly aligned with the domestic context and poorly executed, hence, also for these reasons, cannot be considered as setting effective precedents of democratic and constitutional behaviour.

The idea of rule by the people is widely supported and lies at the heart of constitutional theory. Yet, the 'We, the people' moment that brought down the party-state regimes of CEE did not outlast 1989 in any other than the formal sense.

The shift of power towards the people of CEE simply did not occur. Instead, the stability of hastily constructed institutional order was prioritised and awarded constitutional protection, without proper verification or legitimisation of this order by democratic politics. As a result, what emerged and solidified in CEE countries is 'a strange mixture of nation-state sovereignty-centred constitutional politics and reliance on democratic myth' (Sajó 2005: 247).

Bibliography

Ackerman. 1988. Neo-federalism? in *Constitutionalism and Democracy*, edited by J. Elster and R. Slagstad. Cambridge: Cambridge University Press, 153–93.

Ackerman, B. 1983. Storrs Lectures: discovering the constitution, *Yale Law Journal* 93, 1013–72.

Ackerman, B. 1991. *We the People.* Vol. 1: *Foundations.* Cambridge, Mass./ London: The Belknap Press of Harvard University Press.

Ackerman, B. 1992. *The Future of Liberal Revolution.* New Haven: Yale University Press.

Ackerman, B. 1993. *We, the People.* New Haven: Yale University Press.

Ágh, A. 2003. *Anticipatory and Adaptive Europeanization in Hungary.* Budapest: Hungarian Centre for Democratic Studies.

Albi, A. 2005. *EU Enlargement and the Constitutions of Central and Eastern Europe.* Cambridge: Cambridge University Press.

Albi, A. 2009. Publication review: EU enlargement and the failure of conditionality by D. Kochenov. *E.L. Rev.* 34(6), 986–9.

Alexander, G. 2001. Institutions, path-dependence and democratic consolidation. *Journal of Theoretical Politics*, 13(3), 249–69.

Alla, T. 1993. *Law, Liberty and Justice: the legal foundations of British Constitutionalism.* Oxford: Clarendon Press.

Anderson G. W. 2005. *Constitutional Rights After Globalization.* Oxford: Hart.

Arato, A. 1992. Dilemmas arising from the power to create constitutions in Eastern Europe. *Cardozo Law Review*, 14, 661–90.

Arnull, A. 2003. From charter to constitution and beyond: fundamental rights in the new European Union. *Public Law*, 774–93.

Ash, T. G. 1990. *We the People: The Revolution of '89 Witnessed in Warsaw, Budapest, Berlin and Prague.* Cambridge: Granta/Penguin.

Baczko, A. and Ogrocka, A. 2008. Wolontariat, Filantropia i 1%. Raport z badań. Warszawa: Stowarzyszenie Klon/Jawor. Available at: www.badania.ngo.pl.

Bartoszewski, W. 2010. Demontaż, który zaczął się w Warszawie *Gazeta Wyborcza* 26.10.2010. Available at: http://wyborcza.pl/1,75515,8570451,Demontaz_ktory_zaczal_sie_w_Warszawie.html.

Bauman, Z. 1993. Dismantling a patronage state, in *From a One-Party State to Democracy: Transitions in Eastern Europe*, edited by J. Frenzel-Zagórska, Amsterdam: Rodopi, 139–54.

Bellamy, R. 2007. *Political Constitutionalism: A Republican Defence of the Constitutionality of Democracy.* Cambridge: Cambridge University Press.

Bellamy, R. and Castiglione, D. (eds.) 1996. Constitutionalism in transformation: European and theoretical perspectives. *Political Studies* 44(3) (special issue) Oxford: Blackwell.

Berglund, S., Aarebot, F., Vogt, H. and Karasimeonovor, G. 2001. *Challenges to Democracy*. Cheltenham: Edward Elgar.

Bielasiak, J. 1992. The dilemma of political interests in the postcommunist transition, in *Escape from Socialism*, edited by W. Connor and P. Płoszajski. Warsaw: IFiS Publishers, 199–217.

Bojar, H. 2002. O źrodłach slabości etosu demokratycznego w Polsce [The roots of the democratic ethos weaknesses in Poland] in *Utracona Dynamika? O niedojrzałości Polskiej demokracji'*, edited by E. Mokrzycki, A. Rychard and A. Zybertowicz. Warsaw: IFiS, 99–109.

Bożyk, P. (1997) 'Szokowa a ewolucyjna strategia transformacji polskiej gospodarki – spojrzenie retrospektywne i porównawcze' [Shock versus evoluationary strategy of transformation of Polish economy], in *Transformacja Gospodarki*, edited by W. Jakóbik. Warsaw: Friedrich Ebert Stiftung, 49–65.

Brunetko, K. 2010. *Bój o trybunał* [Fight over the tribunal]. *Polityka*, 26 November. Available at: http://www.polityka.pl/kraj/opinie/1510936,1,wybory-sedziow-sadu-konstytucyjnego.read.

Brzeziński, M. 2000. *The Struggle for Constitutionalism in Poland.* Houndmills: Macmillan.

Burnetko, K. 2008. Państwo konfesyjne? *Polityka*, 29 March, 16–18.

CBOS. 1994a. *The Prestige of Constitution in the Perception of Poles. Komunikat z badań*, BS/43/38/94.

CBOS. 1994b. *What Do the Poles Know About the Constitution. Komunikat z badań*, BS/25/21/94.

CBOS. 1997a. *Sprawa referendum konstytucyjnego. Komunikat z badań, BS/42/42/97.*

CBOS. 1997b. *Polacy o konstytucji i referendum zatwierdzającym. Komunikat z badań*, BS/34/34/97.

CBOS. 1998. *Stosunek do aborcji po zaostrzeniu przepisów antyaborcyjnych. Komunikat z badań*, BS/20/20/98.

CBOS. 1999. *Polityk dekady. Wydarzenie dekady. Komunikat z badań*, BS/113/99.

CBOS. 2002a. *Opinie o prawie do aborcji. Komunikat z Badań*, BS/191/2002.

CBOS. 2002b. *Polacy o konstytucji i likwidacji senatu. Komunikat z badań*, BS/69/2002.

CBOS. 2004. *Polacy o działalności trybunału konstytucyjnego. Komunikat z Badań*, BS/122/2004.

CBOS. 2005. *Opinie o funkcjonowaniu UE* [Opinions about the Functioning of the EU], BS/155/2005.

CBOS. 2006. *Postawy wobec aborcji. Komunikat z Badań*, BS/173/2006.

CBOS. 2007a. *Opinion About the Work of the Sejm's Fifth Term and Expectations from the Newly Elected MPs. Komunikat z Badań*, BS/178/2007.

CBOS. 2007b. *Opinie na temat aborcji. Komunikat z Badań*, BS/152/2007.

CBOS. 2007. *Poczucie reprezentatywności partii politycznych. Komunikat z badań*, 3S/34/2007.

CBOS. 20C8. *A Look at the Past Century of Polish History. Public Opinion Poll.* ISSN 1233–7250.

CBOS. 2009a. *Opinions About Parliament, President, National Bank of Poland and Institute of National Remembrance. Komunikat z Badań*, BS/37/2009.

CBOS. 2009b. *Opinions About the Past Twenty Years. Komunikat z badań*, BS/26/2009.

CBOS. 2009c. *The Functioning of Democracy in Poland. Komunikat z badań*, BS/20/2009.

CBOS. 2009d. *EU Institutions in Public Perception. Komunikat z badań*, BS/54/2009.

CBOS. 2009e. *The 20th Anniversary of the Round Table Agreement. Komunikat z badań*, BS/17/2009.

CBOS. 2009f. *Acceptance of In-Vitro Fertilisation. Komunikat z Badań*, BS/37/2009.

CBOS. 2C09g. *Pierwsza pielgrzymka Jana Pawła II do ojczyzny – rocznicowe refleksje*, BS/83/2009.

CBOS. 2010a. *Opinons About Parliament and Local Authorities. Komunikat z Badań*, BS/112/2010.

CBOS. 2010b.*Opinions About President, Parliament, ZUS, OFE and NFZ. Komunikat z Badań*, BS/96/2010.

CBOS. 2010b. *Six Years of Poland's Membership in the EU. Komunikat z badań*, BS/56/201.

CBOS. 2010. *Ethical Issues of In-Vitro Fertilisation. Komunikat z Badań*, BS/96/2010.

CBOS. 2010. *Oceny instytucji publicznych. Komunikat z badań*, BS/54/2010.

Cepl, V. 1995. Transformations of hearts and minds of Eastern Europe, unpublished paper, quoted in I. Pogany. 1996. Constitution Making or Constitutional Transformation in Post-Communist Societies? *Political Studies*, XLIV, 568–91.

Chruściak, R. and Osiatyński, W. 2001. *Tworzenie konstytucji w Polsce w latach 1989–1997*. Warsaw: Instytut Spraw Publicznych.

Cole, D. 1999. From renaissance Poland to Poland's renaissance. *Michigan Law Review*, 97(6), 2062–2102.

Colón-Ríos, J. 2010. The end of the constitutionalism-democracy debate. *Windsor Review of Legal and Social Issues*, 28, 25–55.

Cremona, M. 2005. EU enlargement: solidarity and conditionality. *European Law Review*, 30(1), pp. 3–22.

CT. 1991. Judgement K 11/90, 30 January 1991.

CT. 1993. Judgement U 12/92, 14 July 1993.

CT. 2001. Judgement SK 10/01, 24 October 2001

Davis, N. 1981. *God's Playground: A History of Poland*. Oxford: Clarendon Press.

Davis, N. 2001. *Heart of Europe*. 3rd ed. New York: Oxford University Press.

Davy, R. 1992. (ed.) *European Détente: A Reappraisal*. London: Sage.

Dembour, M.-B. and Krzyżanowska-Mierzewska, M. 2004. Ten years on: the popularity of the convention in Poland. *European Human Rights Law Review*, 4, 400–23.

Derleth, J. 2000. *The Transition in Central and Eastern European Politics*. New Jersey: Prentice Hall.

Dobson. L. 2007. *Supranational Citizenship*. Manchester: Manchester University Press.

Dyzenhaus, D. 2007. The politics of the question of constituent power, in *The Paradoxes of Constitutionalism*, edited by M. Loughlin and N. Walker. Oxford: Oxford University Press, 129–47.

Dziadul, M. 2003. Inwazja świń [Invasion of the pigs]. *Polityka*, 1 March. Available at: http://archiwum.polityka.pl/art/inwazja-swin,377866.html [accessed: 1 January 2011].

Eberts, M. 1998. The Roman Catholic Church and democracy in Poland. *Europe-Asia Studies*, 50(5), 817–42.

Editorial, 1990. Doświadczani Balcerowiczem, *Gazeta Wyborcza,* 30 January, 2.

Elcock, H. 1996. The Polish Ombudsman and the transition to democracy. *International and Comparative Law Quarterly*, 45(3), 684–90.

Elgie, R. and Zielonka, J. 2001. Constitutions and constitution-building: a comparative perspective, in *Democratic Consolidation in Eastern Europe*, edited by J. Zielonka. Oxford: Oxford University Press, 25–48.

Elster, J. 1993. Constitution-making in Eastern Europe: Rebuilding the boat in the open sea. *Public Administration*, 71, 169–217.

Elster, J. 1995. Forces and mechanisms in the constitution-making process. *Duke Law Journal*, 45, 364–95.

Elster, J. 1996. (ed.) *Round Table Talks and the Breakdown of Communism*. Chicago: University of Chicago Press.

Elster, J. 1998. (ed.) *Deliberative Democracy*. Cambridge: Cambridge University Press.

Epstein, L., Knight, J. and Shvetsova. O. 2001. The role of constitutional courts in the establishment and maintenance of democratic systems of government. *Law and Society Review*, 35 (1), 117–64.

Featherstone, K. and Radaelli, C. M. 2003. *The Politics of Europeanisation*. Oxford: Oxford University Press.

Fijałkowski, A. 2010. *From Old Times to New Europe: The Polish Struggle for Democracy and Constitutionalism*. Farnham: Ashgate.

Finkel, E. 1994. *Defending Rights, Promoting Democracy: The Institution of Ombudsman in Poland, Russia and Bulgaria*. Available at: http://www.ef.huji.ac.il/publications/finkel.pdf.

Flash News. 2009. EU agrees on Czech opt-out from EU Charter of rights Slovak Spectator 30 October 2009. Available at: http://spectator.sme.sk/articles/view/36966/10/eu_agrees_on_czech_opt_out_from_eu_charter_of_rights.html

Friis, L. and Jarosz, A. 2000. When the going gets tough: the EU enlargement negotiations with Poland. *Journal of European Integration*, 23(1), 29–61.

Ganev, V. I. 2005. The 'triumph of neoliberalism' reconsidered: critical remarks on ideas-centred analysis of political and economic change in post-communism. *East European Politics and Societies*, 19, 343.

Gardawski, J. 1996. *Przyzwolenie ograniczone: robotnicy wobec rynku i demokracji*. Warsaw: PWN.

Gardawski, J. 2001. *Związki zawodowe na rozdrożu* [Trade unions at a crossroads]. Warsaw: Friedrich Ebert Stiftung.

Gardawski, J., Gąciaż, B, Mokrzyszewski, A. and Pańków, W. 1999. *Upadek bastionu? Związki zawodowe w gospodarce sprywatyzowanej*. Warsaw: Instytut Spraw Publicznych.

Garlicki, L. 2001. Perspectives on freedom of conscience and religion in the jurisprudence of constitutional courts. *Brigham Young University Law Review*, 2, 467–510.

Garlicki, L. 2008. *Polskie prawo konstytucyjne* [Polish Constitutional Law]. Warsaw: Liber.

Gavison, R. 2002. What Belongs in a Constitution? *Constitutional Political Economy* 13, 89–105.

Gazeta. 2010. Koniec z religią w szkołach? SLD pracuje nad dokumentem ws. Rozdziału Kościoła od państwa. PAP, 5 August. Available at: http://wiadcmosci.gazeta.pl/Wiadomosci/1,80708,8215891,Koniec_z_religia_w_szkolach_SLD_pracuje_nad_dokumentem.html.

Gebethner, S. 1992. Political institutions in the process of transition to a postsocialist formation: Polish and comparative perspectives, in *Escape from Socialism*, edited by W. Connor and P. Płoszajski. Warsaw: IFiS Publishers, 231–55.

Geremek, B. 1996. Paper for the conference *Ideas and Reality in Transformation in Poland*. Stanford University, 1–2 November 1996.

Gliński, P., Lewenstein, B. and Siciński, A. (eds.) 2002. *Samoorganizacja Spoleczeństwa Polskiego: Trzeci Sektor*. [Self organisation of Polish Society: the Third Sector]. Warsaw: IFiS PAN.

Godzic, W. 2009. Sytuacja Polskich mediów audiowizualnych w latach 1989–2008. Raport opracowany na zlecenie Ministerstwa Kultury i Dziedzictwa Narodowego, jako jeden z Raportów o Stanie Kultury. Warsaw: Ministerstwo Kultury i Dziedzictwa Narodowego.

Goetz, K. 2005. The new member states and the EU: responding to Europe, in *The Member States of the European Union*, edited by S. Bulmer and Ch. Lequesne. Oxford: Oxford University Press, 254–80.

Gołębiowski, J. 1995. *Political, Social and Cultural Factors of Systemic Transformation in ECE. World Economy Research Institute Working Papers*.

Gomulka, S. and Polonsky, A. (eds.) 1990. *Polish Paradoxes* London: Routledge.

Gonenc, L. 2002. *Prospects for Constitutionalism in Post-Communist Countries*. Leiden: Brill.

Gowin, J. 1995. *Kościół po Komuniźmie* [Church after Communism]. Kraków: Społeczny Instytut Wydawniczy Znak.

Grabbe, H. 2006. *The EU's Transformative Power*. Houndmills: Palgrave Macmillan.

Gralczyk, R. 1997. *Konstytucja dla Polski: Tradycje, Doświadczenia, Spory*. Kraków: Znak.

Gray, J. 1993. From post-communism to civil society: the reemergence of history and the decline of the western model. *Social Philosophy and Policy*, 10(2), 26–50.

Grey, T. 1984. The constitution as scripture. *Stanford Law Review*, 37(1), 1–25.

Grimm, D. 2010. The achievement of constitutionalism and its prospects in a changed world, in *The Twilight of Constitutionalism?*, edited by P. Dobner and M. Loughlin. Oxford: Oxford University Press, 3–23.

Grudzińska-Gross, I. 1997. When Polish constitutionalism began. *East European Constitutional Review*, 6(2–3), 64–76.

Grugel, J. 1991. Transitions from authoritarian rule: lessons from Latin America. *Political Studies*, 39, 363–8.

Grugel, J. (ed.) 1999. *Democratization Without Borders: Transnationalisation and Conditionality in New Democracies*. Florence, KY: Routledge.

Grzymała-Busse, A. and Innes, A. 2003. Great expectations: the EU and domestic political competition in East Central Europe. *East European Politics & Societies*, 17, 64–73.

Gwiazda, A. 2008. Party patronage in Poland, democratic left-alliance and law and justice compared. *East European Politics & Society*, 22, 802–27.

Habermas, J. 1995. Reconciliation through the public use of reason: remarks on John Rawls's political liberalism. *Journal of Philosophy*, 92(3), 109–31. Repr. in *The Inclusion of the Other: Studies in Political Theory*, edited by C. Cronin and P. de Greiff. Cambridge, MA: MIT Press.

Habermas, J. 1996. *Between Facts and Norms*. Cambridge: Polity Press.

Hamilton, A., Madison, J, and Jay, J. 1992. *The Federalist*. Dent: London.

Harper, M. 2000. Economic voting in postcommunist Eastern Europe. *Comparative Political Studies*, 33(9), 1191–1227.

Hausner, J. 1992. *Populist Threat in Transformation of Socialist Society*. Warsaw: Friedrich-Ebert-Foundation.

Hausner, J. 2003. Akt oskarżenia [Indictment]. *Polityka*, 19 June, no. 25.

Hausner, J. and Marody, M. 2000. *The Quality of Governance: Poland Closer to the Europen Union?* Kraków: Friedrich-Ebert Stiftung.

Hayden, J. 2006. *The Collapse of Communist Power in Poland*. London: Routledge.

Heller, A. 2000. Between past and future, in *Between Past and Future: The Revolutions of 1989 and their Aftermath*, edited by S. Antohi and V. Tismaneanu. Budapest: Central European University Press, 3–13.

Herman, E. and Chomsky, N. 2002. *Manufacturing Consent*. New York: Pantheon Books.

Hillion, Ch. 2004. The European Union is dead: long live the European Union. A commentary on the Treaty of Accession 2003. *European Law Review*, 29(5), 583–612.

Hirschl, R. 2004. *Towards Juristocracy: the Origins and Consequences of the New Constitutionalism*. Cambridge, MA: Harvard University Press.

Hirschl, R. 2005. Preserving hegemony? Assessing the political origins of the EU Constitution. *International Journal of Constitutional Law*, 3(2–3), 269–91.

Holmes, S. 1993. Back to the drawing board. *East European Constitutional Review*, 2(1), 21–5.

Holmes, S. and Sunsteinm, C. 1995. The politics of constitutional revision in Eastern Europe, in *Responding to Imperfection*, edited by S. Levinson. Princeton: Princeton University Press, 275–306.

Hughes, J., Sasse, G. and Gordon, C. 2004. *Europeanization and Regionalization in the EU's Enlargement to Central and Eastern Europe: The Myth of Conditionality*. Palgrave: Basingstoke.

Innes, A. 2002. Party competition in post-communist Europe. *Comparative Politics*, 35(1), 85–104.

Janicki. M. and Władyka, W. 2009. Politycy w zakrystii [Politicians in presbytery]. *Polityka*, 39, 26 September, 16–18.

Jarosz. M. 2007. *Transformacja. Elity. Społeczeństwo*. Warsaw: ISP.

Jasiewicz, K. 1992. Polish Elections, 1989–1991: Beyond the 'pospolite ruszenie', in *Escape from Socialism*, edited by W. Connor and P. Płoszajski. Warsaw: IFiS Publishers, 181–99.

Jowell, J. 2004. The Rule of Law's long arm: uncommunicated decisions. *Public Law*, Summer, 246–51.

Kaldor, M. and Vejvoda, I. 1999. *Democratisation in Central and Eastern Europe*. London: Pinter.

Kallas, M. 2992. *Projekty Konstytucyjne 1989–1991*. Warsaw: Wydawnictwo Sejmowe.

Karnowska, D. 2008. Religia i polityka. O mariażu sacrum i profanum na przykładzie Polski, in *Demokracja w Polsce*, edited by D. Karnowska. Toruń: Adam Marszałek, 237–43.

Karpowicz, E. and Osiecka, J. 2001. *Społeczny wizerunek Sejmu* [Sejm in social perception]. *Raport Nr. 198*. Warsaw: Kancelaria Sejmu, Biuro Studiów i Ekspertyz. Available at: http://biurose.sejm.gov.pl/

Katka, K. 2005. Podpisanie Porozumień Sierpniowych. *Gazeta Wyborcza*. 20 June [Online]. Available at: http://wyborcza.pl/1,93886,2777535.html [accessed: 15 June 2010].

Kideckel, D. 1994. Us and the concepts of East and West in the east European transition, in *Cultural Dilemmas of Post-communist Societies*, edited by A. Jawłowska and M. Kempny. Warsaw: IFiS.

Kiss. E. 1996. Do parties distort democracy? *East European Constitutional Review*, 5(1), 73–7.

Klich, A. 1996. Human rights in Poland: the role of the constitutional tribunal and the commissioner for citizens' rights. *St. Louis-Warsaw Transatlantic Law Journal*, 33–64.

Klingemann, H. Fuchs, D. and J. Zielonka (eds). 2006. *Democracy and Political Culture in Eastern Europe*. London: Routledge.

Kochanowski, J. 2003. Trzy powody czy też symptomy kryzysu prawa [Three symptoms or reasons for the crises of law], in *Nadużycie Prawa* [The Abuse of Law], edited by A. Stelmachowski, J. Kochanowski, W. Staśkiewicz, H. Izdebski and A. Stepkowski. Warsaw: Liber.

Kochenov, D. 2007. *EU Enlargement and the Failure of Conditionality: Pre-accession Conditionality in the Fields of Democracy and the Rule of Law*. Austin, TX: Wolters Kluwer.

Koczanowicz, L. 2004. Mity Solidarności i co z nich wynikło, in *Demokracja Spektaklu*, edited by P. Żuk. Warsaw: Wydawnictwo Naukowe Scholar.

Kolarska-Bobińska, L. 1993. The role of the state: contradictions in the transition to democracy, in *Constitutionalism and Democracy*, edited by D. Greeberg et al., New York: Oxford University Press, 300–11.

Kolarska Bobińska, L. and J. Kucharczyk (eds) 2009. *Demokracja w Polsce 2007–2009*. Warsaw: Instytut Spraw Publicznych.

Kolarska Bobińska, L. (ed.) 2008. *Co warto, co należy zmienić? Poprawa Jakości demokracji w Polsce*. Warsaw: Instytut Spraw Publicznych.

Koslosky, D. 2009. Toward an interpretative model of judicial independence: a case study of Eastern Europe. *University of Pennsylvania Journal of International Law*, 31(1), 203–55.

Kowalik, T. 1994. Za dużo czy za mało państwa [Too much or too little state] in, *Społeczne konsewkwencje transformacji ustrojowej*, edited by M. Grabowska, K. Pankowski, and E. Wnuk-Lipinski. Warsaw: ISP PAN, 71–5.

Kowalik, T. 2004. Oligarchiczny kapitalizm drogą do oligarchicznej demokracji in *Demokracja Spektaklu?*, edited by P. Żuk. Warsaw: Scholar, 14–33.

Kozarzewski, P. 2007. Społeczeństwo i elity o transformacji in *Transformacja, Elity, Społeczeństwo*, edited by M. Jarosz. Warsaw: Instytut Studiów Politycznych PAN, 23–65.

Krzemiński, I. and Śpiewak, P. 2001. *Druga rewolucja w małym mieście* [The second revolution in a small town]. Warsaw: Oficyna Naukowa.

Kurczewski, J. 1993. *The Resurrection of Rights in Poland*. Oxford: Clarendon Press.

Kurczewski, J. 2003. Parliament and political class in the constitutional reconstruction of Poland: two constitutions in one. *International Sociology*, 18, 162–80.

Kursa, M. 2010. Niekonstytucyjność działań Komisji będzie dużo kosztowała [Unconstitutional conduct of the Comission will costs a lot]. *Gazeta Wyborcza*, 23 September 2010. Available at: http://wyborcza.pl/1,75478,8413765,Niekon stytucyjnosc_dzialan_komisji_bedzie_duzo_kosztowac.html.

Kursa, M., M. Pietraszewski and M. Skowrońska 2010. Łapówki za ziemię? Pośredrik Kościoła aresztowany. [Bribes for land? Church's middleman arrested]. *Gazeta Wyborcza*, 22 September. Available at: http://wyborcza. pl/1,75478,8408973,Lapowki_za_ziemie__Posrednik_Kosciola_aresztowany. html.

Kursa, M., W. Czuchnowski, and M. Pietraszewsk 2010. Niecne mienie Kościoła [The Church's ignominious estates]. *Gazeta Wyborcza*, 23 September. Available at: http //wyborcza.pl/1,75478,8414075,Niecne_mienie_Kosciola.html.

Kurz, M. Barnes, A. 2002. The political foundations of post-communist regimes: market.zation, agrarian legacies, or international influences. *Comparative Political Studies*, 35: 524–53.

Kymlicka, W. 2001. *Contemporary Political Philosophy: An Introduction*. Oxford: Oxford University Press.

K. 26/96. *Judgement of the Polish Constitutional Tribunal of 27 May 1997*, available at: http://www.trybunal.gov.pl/index2.htm [accessed: 17 October 2010].

Landes, W. and Posner, R. 2009. Rational judicial behaviour: statistical study. *The Journal of Legal Analysis*, 1(2), 775–831. Available as *Online Working Paper* No. 404 at http://papers.ssrn.com/sol3/papers.cfm?abstract_id=1126403.

Łętowska, E. 1992. *Jak zaczynal Rzecznik Praw Obywatelskich* [The early days of the Ombudsman]. Łódź: Agencja Master.

Łętowska, E. 1997a. The Barriers of Legal Thinking in the Perspective of European Intergration. *Yearbook of Polish European Studies*, 1, 55–73.

Łętowska, E. 1997b. Courts and tribunals under the constitution of Poland. *St. Louis-Warsaw Transatlantic Law Journal*, 69–89.

Łętowska, E. 2002. O mizerii skargi Konstytucyjnej. Czy warto było jeść tą żabę? *Rzeczpospolita,* 2 March. Available at: http://new-arch.rp.pl/artykul/376057_ Czy_warto_bylo_jesc_te_zabe.html.

Lewis, P. 2007. Political parties, in *Developments in Central and East European Politics*, vol. 4, edited by S. White, J. Batt and P. Lewis. Basingstoke: Palgrave, 174–93.

Lipset, S. M. 1960. *Political Man*. London: Heinman.

Loewenstein, K. 1965. *Political Power and the Governmental Process*, 2nd ed. Chicago: University of Chicago Press.

Łoś, M. and Zybertowicz, A. 2000. *Privatizing Police-State*. Basingstoke: Macmillan Palgrave.

Loughlin, M. and Walker, N. 2007. *The Paradox of Constitutionalism*. Oxford: Oxford University Press.

Ludwikcwski, R. 2001. Constitutional culture of the new east-central European democracies, in *Constitutional Cultures*, edited by M. Wyrzykowski. Warsaw: Institute of Public Affairs, 55–83.

Łukowski, J. 1991. *Liberty's Folly*. London: Routledge.

Mączak, A. 1984. Vicissitudes of feudalism in modern Poland, in *The Power of the Past*, edited by P. Thane and G. Crossick. Cambridge: Cambridge University Press, 283–99.

Madeley, J. and Enyedi, Z. (eds) 2003. *Church and State in Contemporary Europe*. London: Frank Cass.

Mandel, M. 1998. A brief history of the new constitutionalism, or 'how we changed everything so that everything would remain the same'. *Israel Law Review*, 32(2), 250–300.

Manin, B. 1987. On legitimacy and political deliberation. *Political Theory*, 15, 338–68.

Markowski, R. 2010. Wkurzeni na proboszczów. *Gazeta Wyborcza*, 23 July. Available at: http://wyborcza.pl/Polityka/1,103835,8172209,Wkurzeni_na_ proboszczow.html.

Marody, M. and Wilkin, J. 2004. *On Course? Poland on the Eve of EU Accession. EU-monitoring* VII. Kraków: Friedrich Ebert Foundation.

Mason, D. 1992. Public opinion in Poland's transition to market democracy, in *Escape from Socialism: The Polish Route*, edited by W. Connor and P. Płoszajski. Warsaw: IFiS Publishers, 147–67.

Mazurkiewicz, P. (ed.) 2003. *Kościół katolicki w przededniu wejścia Polski do Unii Europejskiej* [The Catholic church before Poland's accession to the EU]. Warsaw: Instytut Spraw Publicznych.

McMann K. 2006. *Economic Autonomy and Democracy*. Cambridge: Cambridge University Press.

Michnik, A. 1984. *Polska wojna a szanse polskiej demokracji*. London: Aneks.

Miller, W. L., White, S. and Heywood, P. M. 1998. *Values and Political Change in Postcommunist Europe*. Basingstoke: Palgrave.

Mokrzycki, E., Rychard, A., and Zybertowicz, A. (eds.) 2002. *Utracona dynamika? O niedojrzałości Polskiej demokracji*. Warsaw: IFiS PAN.

Monaghan, H. 1981. Our perfect constitution. *New York University Law Review*, 358–60.

Morawski, L. 1993. Instrumentalizacja prawa [Instrumentalisation of law]. *Państwo & Prawo*, 6, 16–28.

Murkens, J. E. K. 2009. The quest for constitutionalism in UK public law discourse. *Oxford Journal of Legal Studies*, 29(3), 427–55.

Nowicka, W. 2010. NGO-sy od wewnątrz. Społeczeństwo nie chce się organizować [NGOs from the inside. Society refused to get organized]. *Gazeta Wyborcza*, 11 January. Available at www.wyborcza.pl/.

O'Dwyer, C. 2004. Runaway state building: how political parties shape states in postcommunist Eastern Europe. *World Politics*, 56(4), 520–53.

Olsen, J. 1996. Europeanization and nation-state dynamics, in *The Future of Nation-State*, edited by S. Gustavsson and L. Lewin. London: Routledge, 245–85.

Orenstein, M. 2009. Out-liberalizing the EU: pension privatization in Central and Eastern Europe, in *International Influence Beyond Conditionality*, edited by R. Epstein and U. Sedelmeier. London: Routledge, 104–23.

Orenstein, M. 2009. What happen in East European (political) economies? A balance sheet for neoliberal reforms. *East European Politics and Societies*, 23(4), 479–90.

Osiatyński, W. 1991. The constitution-making process in Poland, *Law and Policy*, 13, 125–33.

Osiatyński, W. 1993. Perspectives on the current constitutional situation in Poland, in *Constitutionalism and Democracy: Transitions in the Contemporary World*, edited by D. Greenberg et al. *The American Council of Learned Societies Comparative Constitutionalism Papers*. New York: Oxford University Press, 312–20.

Osiatyński, W. 1996. The Round Table talks in Poland, in *The Round Table Talks and the Breakdown of Communism*, edited by J. Elster. Chicago: University of Chicago Press, 21–69.

Osiatyński, W. 2000. Constitutionalism, democracy, constitutional culture, in *Constitutional Cultures*, edited by M. Wyrzykowski. Warsaw: Institute of Public Affairs, 151–9.

Osiatyński, W. 2003. Paradoxes of constitutional borrowing. *International Journal of Constitutional Law*, 1(2), 244–68.

Ostrowski, P. 2009. *Powstawanie związków zawodowych w sektorze prywatnym w Polsce* [The establishment of trade unions in private sector in Poland]. Warsaw: Beck.

Ost, D. 2002. Imagining and creating the enemy: trade unions in the new Polish democracy, in *Utracona Dynamika? O niedojrzalosci Polskiej demokracji*, edited by E. Mokrzycki, A. Rychard and A. Zybertowicz. Warsaw: IFiS PAN, 113–29.

Ost, D. 2005. *The Defeat of Solidarity: Anger and Politics in Postcommunist Europe*. Ithaca: Cornell University Press.

Paczyńska, A. 2005. Inequality, political participation, and democratic deepening in Poland. *East European Politics & Societies*, 19, 573–613.

PAP. 2010. Organizacje pozarządowe ostro krytykują wybory do Trybunału Konstytucyjnego [NGOs harshly criticise appointments to Constitutional Tribunal], *Gazeta Prawnicza*, 15 November. Available at: http://www.gazetaprawna.pl/drukowanie/465248.

Pentor. 2007. Polacy o Konstytucji RP. *Wprost*, 20 June. Available at: http://www.pentor.pl/49959.xml [accessed: 4 August 2010].

Petrażycki, L. 1955. *Law and Morality*, transl. by H. W. Babb. Cambridge, MA: Harvard University Press.

Pijl, van der, K. 2006. A Lockean Europe. *New Left Review*, 37, 9–37.

Pinder, J. 1994. The European Community and democracy in CEE, in *Building Democracy? The International Dimension of Democratisation in Eastern*

Europe, edited by G. Pridham, E. Herring, and G. Sanford. Leicester: Leicester University Press, 119–44.

Piotrowski, R. 2009. Spory o konstytucję Rzeczpospolitej Polskiej [Disputes about the Polish constitution], in *Demokracja w Polsce*, edited by L. Kolarska-Bobińska and J. Kucharczyk. Warsaw: Instytut Spraw Publicznych, 15–55.

Podgórecki, A. 1994. *Polish Society*. Wesport, CT: Praeger.

Pogany, I. 1993. Constitutional reform in Central and Eastern Europe: Hungary's transition to democracy, *International and Comparative Law Quarterly*, 42, 332–55.

Poland. 1992. Rozporządzenie w sprawie warunków i sposobu organizowania nauki religii w szkołach publicznych z dnia 24 kwietnia 1992. *Dziennik Ustaw*, 36, poz. 155.

Poland. 1997. The Constitution of the Republic of Poland of 2 April 1997. *Dziennik Ustaw*, 78, poz. 483.

Poland. 2007. Rozporządzenie Ministra Edukacji Narodowej z dnia 13 lipca 2007. w sprawie warunków I sposobu oceniania, klasyfikowania I promowania uczniów i słuchaczy orza przeprowadzania sprawdzianów i egzaminów w szkołach publicznych. *Dziennik Ustaw*, 83, poz. 562.

Poland. 2010. Statement on the Judgement of the ECtHR of 15 June 2010. *Ministry of Foreign Affairs*. Available at: http://www.msz.gov.pl/Wyrok,,Eu ropejskiego,Trybunalu,Praw,Czlowieka,z,dnia,15,czerwca,2010,r.,w,sprawie, Grzelak,p.,Polsce,36511.html.

Popławska, E. 2008. Constitution-making in Poland: some reflections on popular involvement. *Zbornik radova Pravnog fakulteta w Splitu*, 45(2), 279–86.

Poznański, K. 1999. Recounting Transitions. *East European Politics and Societies*, 13(2), 328–44.

Pravda, A. and Zielonka, J. (eds) 2001. *Democratic Consolidation in Eastern Europe*. Vol. 2: *International and Transnational Factors*. Oxford: Oxford University Press.

Preuss, U. 2007. The exercise of constituent power in CEE, in *The Paradox of Constitutionalism*, edited by M. Loughlin and N. Walker. Oxford: Oxford University Press, 211–29.

Přibáň, J. 2002. *Dissidents of Law: On the 1989 Velvet Revolutions, Legitimations, Fictions of Legality and Contemporary Version of the Social Contract*. Dartmouth: Ashgate.

Přibáň, J. 2007. *Legal Symbolism: On Law, Time and European Identity*. Aldershot: Ashgate.

Přibáň, J. 2010. Constituting the heterarchy of European constitutionalism in the EU's new member states, in *Central and Eastern Europe after Transition: Towards New Socio-Legal Semantics*, edited by A. Febbrajo and W. Sadurski. Farnham: Ashgate, 13–35.

Pridham, G. 2002. EU-enlargement and consolidating democracy in post-communist states – formality and reality. *Journal of Common Market Studies*, 40(5), 953–73.

Pridham, G. and Vanhanen, T. 1994. *Democratization in Eastern Europe: Domestic and international perspectives*. London: Rutledge.

Pridham, G., Herring, E. and Sanford, G. (eds) 1994. *Building Democracy? The International Dimension of Democratisation in Eastern Europe*. London: Leicester University Press.

Przeworski, A. 1986. Some problems in the study of transition to democracy, in *Transition from Authoritarian Rule: Comparative Perspectives*, edited by G. O'Donell, P. Schmitter and L. Whitehead. Baltimore: Johns Hopkins University Press, 47–63.

Przeworski, A. 1991. *Democracy and the Market: Political and Economic reforms in Eastern Europe and Latin America*. Cambridge: Cambridge University Press.

Raadt, J. de 2009. Contested constitutions: legitimacy of constitution-making and constitutional conflict in central Europe. *East European Politics & Societies*, 23(3), 315–38.

Radaelli, C. 2003. The europeanization of public policy, in *The Politics of Europeanization*, edited by K. Featherstone and C. Radaelli. Oxford: Oxford University Press, 27–56.

Raz, J. 1977. The rule of law and its virtue, *Law Quarterly Review*, 93, 195–201.

Regulska, J. 1998. Local government reform, in *Transition to Democracy in Poland*, edited by R. F. Staar. New York: St Martin's Press, 113–32.

Reykowski, J. 1992. Psychological dimension of a socio-political change: the Polish case, in *Escape from Socialism*, edited by W. Connor and P. Płoszajski. Warsaw: IFiS Publishers, 217–13.

Rose-Ackerman, S. 2007. From elections to democracy in central Europe: public participation and the role of civil society. *East European Politics & Societies*, 21: 31–47.

Rose, R., Mishler, W. and Haerper, Ch. 1998. *Democracy and Its Alternatives*. Oxford: Blackwell.

Sadurski, W. 2001. *Postcommunist Constitutional Courts in Search of Political Legitimacy. EUI Working papers*. Florence: European University Institute.

Sadurski, W. 2002. Charter and enlargement. *European Law Journal*, 3(8), 340–62.

Sadurski, W. 2003. Accession's democracy dividend: the impact of the EU Enlargement upon democracy in the new member states of Central and Eastern Europe. *Yearbook of Polish European Studies*, 7. Available at: http://www.ce.uw.edu.pl/program_wydawniczy/rocznik.html?id_periodyk=67#roczniki.

Sadurski, W. 2005. *Rights Before Courts a Study of Constitutional Courts in the Postcommunist States of CEE*. Dodrecht: Springer.

Sadurski, W. 2006. *Political Rights under Stress in 21st Century Europe*. Oxford: Oxford University Press.

Sadurski, W. 2008. Kwestie konstytucyjne [Constitutional matters], in *Co warto, co należy zmienić? Poprawa jakości demokracji w Polsce* [What can be changed what should be changed? The improvement of democracy in Poland], edited by L. Kolarska-Bobińska. Warsaw: Instytut Spraw Publicznych, 17–33.

Sadurski, W. 2009. Twenty years after the transition: constitutional review in Central and Eastern Europe. *Legal Studies Research Paper* No. 09/69. Available from the Social Science Research Network Electronic Library at: http://ssrn.com/abstract=1437843.

Sadurski, W. 2010. Constitutional courts and constitutional culture in central and eastern Europe, in *Central and Eastern Europe After Transition: Towards New Socio-legal Semantics* edited by A. Febbrajo and W. Sadurski. Farnham: Ashgate, 99–119.

Safjan, M. 2009. Politics – and constitutional courts (Judge's personal perspective). *Polish Sociological Review*, 1(165), 3–25.

Sajó, A. 2005. Constitution without the constitutional moment: a view from new member states. *International Journal of Constitutional Law*, 3(2–3), 243–61.

Sajó, A. and Losonci, V. 1993. Rule by law in East Central Europe, in *Constitutionalism and Democracy: Transitions in the Contemporary World*, edited by Douglas Greenberg et al. Oxford: Oxford University Press, 321–34.

Sanford, G. 1994. Communism's weakest link – democratic capitalism's greatest challenge: Poland, in *Building Democracy: The International Dimension of Democratisation in Eastern Europe*, edited by G. Pridham, E. Herring and G. Sanford. London: Leicester University Press.

Sanford, G. 2002. *Democratic Government in Poland: Constitutional Politics since 1989*. Gordonsville, VA: Palgrave Macmillan.

Scheppele, K. 2005. A comparative view of the Chief Justice's role. Guardians of the constitution: constitutional court presidents and the struggle for the rule of law in post-Soviet Europe. *University of Pennsylvania Law Review*, 154, 1757–1845.

Schimmelfenning, F. 2007. European regional organizations, political conditionality, and democratic transformation in Eastern Europe. *East European Politics & Societies*, 21(1), 126–41.

Schimmelfenning, F. and Sedelmeier, U. 2004. Governance by conditionality: EU rule transfer to candidate countries in Central and Eastern Europe. *Journal of European Public Policy*, 11(4), 661–79.

Schimmelfenning, F. and Sedelmeier, U. 2005a. Introduction: Conceptualizing the Europeanization of Central and Eastern Europe, in *The Europeanization of Central and Eastern Europe*, edited by F. Schimmelfenning and U. Sedelmeier. Ithaca: Cornell University Press, 1–28

Schimmelfenning, F. and Sedelmeier, U. (eds) 2005b. *The Europeanization of Central and Eastern Europe*. Ithaca and London: Cornell University Press.

Schmitter, P. 1993. *Dangers, Dilemmas and Prospects for the Consolidation of Democracy*. Manuscript, Stanford.

Schmitter, P. 1996. The influence of the international context upon choices of national institutions and policies in neo-democracies, in *The International*

Dimensions of Democratization, edited by L. Whitehead. Oxford: Oxford University Press, 26–55.

Schmitter, P. 2001. *Contrasting Approaches to Political Engineering: Constitutionalisation and Democratisation. EUI Working papers.* Florence: European University Institute.

Schonlau, J. 2005. *Drafting the EU Charter: Rights, Legitimacy and Process.* Basingstoke: Palgrave.

Schöpflin, G. 1992. The problem of nationalism in the postcommunist order, in *Bound to change: Consolidating Democracy in East Central Europe*, edited by P. Volten. New York: Institute for East-West Studies, 27–41.

Schöpflin, G. 1993. *Politics in Eastern Europe.* Oxford: Blackwell.

Schöpflin, G. 1994. Postcommunism: the problems of democratic construction. *Daedalus*, 123(3), 127–43.

Schwartz, H. 2000. *The Struggle for Constitutional Justice in Post-Communist Europe.* Chicago: University of Chicago Press.

Sedelmeier, U. 2009. After conditionality: post-accession compliance with the EU law in East Central Europe, in *International Influence Beyond Conditionality* edited by R. Epstein and U. Sedelmeier. London: Routledge, 11–30.

Sejm. 1989a. *Ustawa o zmianie niektórych przepisów prawa karnego. Dziennik Ustaw*, 29 May, 34, poz. 154.

Sejm. 1989b. *Rozporządzenie rady Ministrów w sprawie zwolnienia osób prawnych kościołów i innych związkó wyznaniowych od podatku obrotowego i dochodowego. Dziennik Ustaw*, 12 October, 57, poz. 340.

Sejm. 1989c. *Ustawa z dnia 17 maja 1989. r. o stosunku Państwa do Kościoła Katolickiego w Rzeczypospolitej Polskiej. Dziennik Ustaw*, 29, poz. 154.

Sejm. 1989d. *Ustawa o zmianie konstytucji Polski Rzeczpospolitej Ludowej. Dziennik Ustaw*, 29 December, 75, poz. 444.

Sejm. 1991. *Ustawa o systemie oświaty z 7 września 1991. Dziennik Ustaw*, 95, poz. 425.

Sejm. 1992. *Ustawa o trybie przygotowania i uchwalenia konstytucji Rzeczypospolitej Polskiej. Dziennik Ustaw*, 23 April, 67, poz. 336, 337.

Sejm. 1994a. *R. Bugaj MP. Pierwsze czytanie projektów konstytucji Rzeczypospolitej Polskiej. National Assembly*, 22 September.

Sejm. 1994b. Pierwsze czytanie ustawy konstytucyjnej o zmianie ustawy konstytucyjnej o trybie przygotowania i uchwalenia Konstytucji Rzeczypospolitej Polskiej (druk nr. 252). *National Assembly*, 17 February.

Sejm. 1994c. *Ustawa Konstytucyjna o zmianie ustawy konstytucyjnej i trybie przygotowania i uchwalenia Konstytucji Rzeczypospolitej Polskiej, Dziennik Ustaw*, 22 April, 61, poz. 251, 252.

Sejm. 1994d. Uchwała zgromadzenia narodowego dla uchwalenia konstytucji Rzeczypospolitej Polskiej. *Monitor Polski*, 22 September, 54, poz. 453.

Sejm. 1994e. MPs Jaskiernia, Gwiżdż, Falandysz, 10th and 12th sittings of the National Assembly. *Stenographic reports.* Available at: www.sejm.gov.pl.

Sejm. 1994f. M. Krzaklewski. *National Assembly* 22 September. *Stenographic reports*. Available at: www.sejm.gov.pl.

Sejm. 1996a. *Ustawa z dnia 31 maja 1996. r. o świadczeniu pieniężnym przysługującym osobom deportowanym do pracy przymusowej oraz osadzonym w obozach pracy przez III Rzeszę i Związek Radziecki.*

Sejm. 1996b. *Ustawa o zmianie ustawy o planowaniu rodziny, ochronie płodu ludzkiego i warunkach dopuszczalności przerywania ciąży z 30.08.1996, Dziennik Ustaw*, 30 August, 139, poz. 646.

Sejm. 1997a. *Konstytucja przeczpospolitej Polskiej. Dziennik Ustaw*, 2 April, 78, poz. 483.

Sejm. 1997b. *Ustawa o Trybunale Konstytucyjnym z dnia 1 sierpnia 1997. roku. Dziennik Ustaw*, 1 August, 102, poz. 643.

Sen, A. 2009. *The Idea of Justice*. London: Allan Lane.

Shuibhne, N. 2009. The reality of rights: from rhetoric to opt-out. *European Law Review*, 34(6), 815–16.

Shvetsova, O., Epstein, L. and Knight, J. 2001. The role of constitutional courts in the establishment and maintenance of democratic systems of government. *Law and Society Review*, 35(1), 117–64.

Siedlecka, E. 2010a. Wyścigi po łupy [Race after loot]. Gazeta Wyborcza, 30 November. Available at: http://wyborcza.pl/1,75515,8741448,Wyscigi_po_lupy.html.

Siedlecka, E. 2010b. Wstydzę się za polskie państwo [I am ashamed of the Polish state]. *Gazeta Wyborcza*, 16 June. Available at: http://wyborcza.pl/1,76842,8019425,Wstydze_sie_za_polskie_panstwo.html.

Siedlecka, E. 2010c. Partie nad Trybunałem. [Parties above the tribunal] *Gazeta Wyborcza*, 27 November. Available at: http://wyborcza.pl/1,75248,8727347,Partie_nad_Trybunalem.html.

Siedlecka, E. 2010d. Do Trybunału znowu wybiorą bez pytania? *Gazeta Wyborcza*, 20 September. Available at: http://wyborcza.pl/1,75478,8403589,Do_Trybunalu_znowu_wybiora_bez_pytania_.html [accessed: 20 September 2010].

Siedlecka, E. 2010e. Żyjemy w państwie wyznaniowym. Interview with Paweł Borecki. *Gazeta Wyborcza*, 5 August. Available at: http://wyborcza.pl/1,75478,8220057,Zyjemy_w_panstwie_wyznaniowym.html [accessed: 9 August 2010].

Skąpska, G. 1999. Paradigm lost? The constitutional process in Poland and the hope of a 'grass root constitutionalism', in *The Rule of Law after Communism*, edited by M. Krygier and A. Czarnota. Brookfield: Aldershot, 149–175.

Skąpska, G. 2009. Economic transformation and corruption after the fall of the Berlin Wall. *Hague Journal on the Rule of Law*, 1, 284–306.

Skórzyński, J. 2006. *Rewolucja okrągłego stołu* [The Round Table Revolution]. Kraków: Znak.

SLD. 2010a. Podpisanie apelu w obronie Konstytucji, 10 August. Available at: http://www.sld.org.pl/aktualnosci/p-r-m-a-5433/aktualnosci.htm.

SLD. 2010b. Religia zagraża neutralności państwa, 11 August. Available at: http://www.sld.org.pl/aktualnosci/p-r-m-à-5444/aktualnosci.htm.

Smith, K. 2001. Western actors and the promotion of democracy, in *Democratic Consolidation in Eastern Europe*, Vol. 2: *International and Transnational Factors*, edited by A. Pravda and J. Zielonka. Oxford: Oxford University Press, 31–57.

Sokolewicz, W. 1990. Democracy, rule of law and constitutionality in post-communist society of Eastern Europe. *Polish Contemporary Law*, 2(86), 3–23.

Sørensen, G. ed. 1993. *Political Conditionality*. London: Frank Cass.

Staniszkis, J. 1991. Political capitalism in Poland, *East European Politics and Societies*, 5(1), 127–41.

Staniszkis, J. 1991. Political capitalism in Poland, *East European Politics and Societies*, 5(1), 127–41.

Staśkiewicz, W. 2009. Stanowienie prawa w pierwszym okresie rządów PO-PSL [Law-making in the first period of the Civic Platform-Polish People's Party coalition government], in *Demokracja w Polsce 2007–2009*, edited by L. Kolarska-Bobińska and J. Kucharczyk. Warsaw: Institut Spraw Publicznych, 55–89.

Stawecki, T., Staśkiewicz, W.,Winczorek, J. 2008. *Między policentrycznością a fragmentaryzacją. Wpływ Trybunału Konstytucyjnego na polski porządek prawny* [Between polycentricism and fragmentation. The influence of the Polish CT on Polish legal order]. Warsaw: Ernst & Young. Available at: http://webapp01.ey.com.pl/EYP/WEB/eycom_download.nsf/resources/prezentacja_TK.pdf/$FILE/prezentacja_TK.pdf [accessed 9 January 2011].

Stepan. A.. 2005. Religion, democracy and the 'twin tolerations', in *World Religions and Democracy*, edited by L. Diamond, M. F. Plattner and P. J. Costopoulos. Baltimore: The John Hopkins University Press, 3–27.

Strasbourg. 2010. ECtHR Judgement in the case of Grzelak v. Poland. *Application no. 7710/02*.

Suchocka, H. 1995. *Sprawozdanie Sejmowe*, 25 May. Available at: http://www.sbc.org.pl/Content/12171 [accessed 9 January 2011].

Sunstein, C. 2001. *Designing Democracy: What Constitutions Do*. Oxford: Oxford University Press.

Szacki, J. 1994. *Liberalizm po komuniźmie*. Warsaw: Znak.

Szahaj, A. 2004. Niesprawiedliwość a demoralizacja [Unjustice versus demoralisation], in *Demokracja Spektaklu?* edited by P. Żuk. Warsaw: Scholar, 33–47.

Szostkiewicz, A. 2010. Wybory Kościoła. *Polityka*, 27 July . Available at: http://www.polityka.pl/kraj/analizy/1507444,1,polski-kosciol-mocno-zaangazowany-politycznie.read [accessed: 9 August 2010].

Tate, C. and Vallinder, T. (eds) 1995. *The Global Expansion of Judicial Power*. New York: New York University Press.

Tazbir, J. 2007. Interview in *Gazeta Wyborcza*, 3 February. [available at: http://www.gazeta.pl].

TOK FM. PL. 2010. *Milczenie przez 20 lat, teraz groźby. Debata w TOK FM o in vitro* [Silence over the past 20 years and not threats. Debate in TOK FM on in-vitro. Available at: http://www.tokfm.pl/Tokfm/1,103454,8551544,_Milczenie_przez_20_lat__teraz_grozby___Debata_w_TOK.html [accessed: 1 January 2011].

Traynor, I. 2007. *Poles apart. The Guardian*, 22 June.

Traynor, I. and P. Wintour. 2007. Poland evokes war dead as EU talks get tough. *The Guardian*, 22 June. Available at: http://www.guardian.co.uk/politics/2007/jun/22/eu.politics.

Trybunał Konstytucyjny. 2010. Proces prawotwórczy w świetle orzecznictwa Trybunału Konstytucyjnego: Wypowiedzi Trybunału Konstytucyjnego dotyczące zagadnień związanych z procesem legislacyjnym [Law-making process in light of the Constitutiona Tribunal Jurisdiction: the CT pronouncements related to the law-making process]. Warsaw: Wydawnictwa Trybunału Konstytucyjnego. Available at: http://www.trybunal.gov.pl/index2.htm.

Tully, J. 1995. *Strange multiplicity. Constitutionalism in the age of diversity.* Cambridge: Cambridge University Press.

Tully, J. 2002. The unfreedom of the moderns in comparison to their ideals of constitutional democracy *The Modern Law Review*, 65(2), 204–28.

Tully, J. 2007. The imperialism of modern constitutional democracy, in *The Paradox of Constitutionalism*, edited by M. Loughlin and N. Walker. Oxford: Oxford University Press, 315–39.

Uitz, R. 2006. Aiming for state neutrality in matters of religion: the Hungarian record *University of Detroit Mercy Law Review*, 83(5), 761–88.

Urbański, A. 1994. O szansach systemu partyjnego w Polsce, in *Społeczne konsewkwencje transformacji ustrojowej*, edited by M. Grabowska, K. Pankowski, and E. Wnuk-Lipinski. Warsaw: ISP PAN, 125–31.

Vahudova, M. 2005. *Europe Undivided: Democracy, Leverage and Integration after Communism.* Oxford: Oxford University Press.

Volten, P. 1992. Introduction and assessment, in *Bound to Change: Consolidating Democracy in East Central Europe*, edited by P. Volten, New York: Institute for East-West Studies, 1–27.

Wagner, W. 1970. *Polish Law Throughout Ages.* Stanford: Hoover Institute Press.

Wälde, T. and Gunderson, J. 1994. Legislative reform in transition economies. *International and Comparative Law Quarterly*, 43, 347–79.

Wälde, T. and Gunderson, J. 1999. Legislative reform in transition economies: western transplants: a short-cut to social market economy status?, in *Making Development Work: Legislative Reform for Institutional Transformation and Good Governance* edited by A. Seidman, R. Seidman and T. Wälde. The Hague: Kluwer International, 67–95.

Walicki, A. 1990. The three traditions in Polish patriotism, in *Polish Paradoxes*, edited by S. Gomulka and A. Polonsky. London: Routledge, 30–35.

Walker, N. 2003. Postnational constitutionalism and the problem of translation, in *European Constitutionalism Beyond the State*, edited by J. H. H. Weiler and M. Wind. Cambridge: Cambridge University Press, 27–54.

Watson, A. 1974. *Legal Transplants*. Charlotteville: University Press of Virginia.

Wedel, J, 1990. The ties that bind in Polish society, in *Polish Paradoxes*, edited by S. Gomulka and A. Polonsky. London: Routledge, 237–60.

Wedel, J. 1998. *Collision and Collusion*. New York: St. Martin Press.

Weiler, J. H. H. and Wind, M. 2003. Introduction: European Constitutionalism beyond the state, in *European Constitutionalism beyond the state*, edited by J. H. H. Weiler and M. Wind. Cambridge: Cambridge University Press, 1–7.

Weiß, W. 2005. Eastern enlargement and European constitutionalisation. *Queen's Papers on Europeanisation* no. 1. Belfast: Queen's University.

Whitehead, L. 1994. East-Central Europe in comparative perspective, in *Building Democracy? The International Dimension of Democratisation in Eastern Europe*, edited by G. Pridham, E. Herring and G. Sanford. London: Leicester University Press, 32–59.

Whitehead, L. 1996b Democracy and decolonization: East-Central Europe, in *The International Dimensions of Democratization*, edited by L. Whitehead. Oxford: Oxford University Press, 356–92.

Whitehead, L. (ed.) 1996a *The International Dimensions of Democratization*. Oxford: Oxford University Press.

Wiadomości24.pl. 2010. *Wiec SLD w obronie konstytucji i świeckości państwa*, 10 August. Available at: http://www.wiadomosci24.pl/artykul/wiec_sld_w_obronie_konstytucji_i_swieckosci_panstwa_153815.html.

Winczorek, P. 2000. The influence of constitution-making procedures on the development of constitutional culture, in *Constitutional Cultures*, edited by M. Wyrzykowski. Warsaw, Institute of Public Affairs, 15–36.

Wiśniewski, O. 2010. Rozbity Kościół, święte frazesy [Shattered Church and holy platitudes], *Gazeta Wyborcza*, 14 December. Available at: http://wyborcza.pl/1,75515,8813484,Rozbity_Kosciol__swiete_frazesy.html [accessed: 1 January 2011].

Wołek, A. 2004. *Demokracja Nieformalna*. Warsaw: PAN, ISP.

Zahorski, A. 1991. *Konstytucja Majowa*. Warsaw: Państwowe Wydawnictwo Naukowe.

Zarycki, T. 1997. The attitudes towards the West and the East as the main component of the Central European identity, in *The Identity of Central Europe*, edited by G. Gorzelak and B. Jalowiecki. Warsaw: Europejski Instytut Rozwoju Regionalnego, 97–106.

Zielonka, J. 2008. Europe as a global actor: empire by example. *International Affairs* 84(3), 471–84.

Zirk-Sadowski, M. 2006. Transformation and integration of legal cultures and discourses: Poland, in *Spreading Democracy and the Rule of Law? The Impact of EU Enlargement on the Rule of Law, Democracy and Constitutionalism in*

Post-Communist Legal Orders, edited by W. Sadurski, A. Czarnota and M. Krygier. Dordrecht: Springer, 299–311.

Żuk, P. 2004. Demokracja symulacji, czyli mcdonaldyzacja życia publicznego w III RP [Democracy of simulation, or Macdonaldisation of public life], in *Demokracja Spektaklu?*[Democracy of Spectacle], edited by P. Żuk. Warsaw: Scholar, 47–65.

Zuzowski, R. 1998. *Political Change in Eastern Europe: Prospects for Liberal Democracy and Market Economies*. Westport, CT: Greenwood.

Zybertowicz, A. 2002. Demokracja jako fasada: przypadek III RP [Democracy as a façade: the case of Third Polish Republic], in *Utracona Dynamika? O niedojrzalosci Polskiej demokracji* [Lost momentum? The immaturity of Polish democracy], edited by E. Mokrzycki, A. Rychard and A. Zybertowicz. Warsaw: IFiS PAN, 173–214.

Index